Rhetoric and Religion in the Twenty-First Century

Rhetoric and Religion in the Twenty-First Century

Pluralism in a Postsecular Age

EDITED BY MICHAEL-JOHN DEPALMA,
PAUL LYNCH, AND JEFF RINGER

Southern Illinois University Press
Carbondale

Southern Illinois University Press
www.siupress.com

Printed in the United States of America

26 25 24 23 4 3 2 1

Support for the publication of this book was provided by Baylor University, Saint Louis University, and the University of Tennessee, Knoxville

Library of Congress Cataloging-in-Publication Data

Names: DePalma, Michael-John, 1977– editor. | Lynch, Paul, 1971– editor. | Ringer, Jeffrey M., 1976– editor.
Title: Rhetoric and religion in the twenty-first century : pluralism in a postsecular age / edited by Michael-John DePalma, Paul Lynch, and Jeff Ringer.
Identifiers: LCCN 2023014760 (print) | LCCN 2023014761 (ebook) | ISBN 9780809339167 (paperback) | ISBN 9780809339174 (ebook)
Subjects: LCSH: United States—Religion. | Pluralism—United States.
Classification: LCC BR513 .R45 2023 (print) | LCC BR513 (ebook) | DDC 200.973—dc23/eng/20230818
LC record available at https://lccn.loc.gov/2023014760
LC ebook record available at https://lccn.loc.gov/2023014761

Printed on recycled paper ♲

SIU
Southern Illinois University System

Contents

Foreword

For people who pride themselves on understanding the constructed nature of human reality, academics can be awfully self-assured, dogmatic even, when it comes to their condescension toward religion. I remember a comment I received when I was giving a mock job talk at the institution where I earned my doctorate. My talk involved as an illustration an analysis of a biblical debate over women's preaching. During the public feedback period after the talk, a prominent faculty member warned me that analyzing biblical arguments would be detrimental to my chances of securing a job since most academics are atheist or agnostic and bristle at religion. Thankfully, one of my mentors took me aside after the talk to assure me that the work I was doing counted as a worthy academic pursuit and that I did not need to rewrite my job talk, which I was scheduled to deliver two days later. Still, I was shaken.

I was then and am still now a Christian, and I understand that Christianity holds a privileged status in the United States. I am also Black, a product of the African Methodist Episcopal Church, one of the most historically important institutions in Black America and hardly a hegemonic force in society. As a person of color, I am statistically more likely to be religious than my White counterparts. Implicit in the disapproving faculty member's warning was the accusation that I was religious since I needed to be reminded of the general a-religiosity of academe. The faculty member, a White woman, evidently did not consider that she was shaming one of the few Black people in the predominantly White room. Her main concern, it seemed, was to reinforce the division between the academy and religion, the rational and the irrational, the scientific and the superstitious.

This incident was neither the first nor the last time I have run into an aversion to studying religion, or an aversion to religious people, in the closely allied fields of English, rhetoric, and writing. This attitude that religion and academe are mutually exclusive is strikingly similar to an equally pernicious dichotomy I heard growing up as a closeted gay teen: you can't be gay and Christian. When I hear academics disparage religion, they usually have one archetype in mind: White conservative Christianity. This reductionism is opposite to the kind of nuanced and complex thinking we employ in our scholarship and teach to our students, yet I have witnessed this flattening in academic spaces again and again. I usually feel my own religious identity as a Black Protestant demeaned and erased when I hear these one-dimensional disparagements, almost always offered with an air of self-evidence. And I imagine that faculty and students of other faiths feel even more marginalized in these moments.

Despite the predictions (or wishes) of some, religion remains a ubiquitous and substantial force. On the basis of this fact and the premise that "religious diversity is a fact of human life in the twenty-first century," the editors offer the present volume. But this volume is not merely a set of field-shaping and -defining essays on the subject of religious rhetorics, a worthy feat in its own right. The editors and contributors set their sights on an even more ambitious goal of working toward the achievement of pluralism. Pluralism, a societal state in which people of various religious or nonreligious inclinations can constructively engage one another and flourish together, is "a thoroughly rhetorical project," the editors explain. While it may seem logical to silo pluralism in the part of the field devoted to religious rhetorics, the editors wisely resist this temptation. They issue their call to pluralism to the whole field, writing in the introduction that pluralism "should be a central focus of rhetorical studies. Rather than a niche concern, religious rhetorics matter for all scholars and students of rhetoric." Most rhetoricians would agree that we want a pluralistic society where people with a range of religious beliefs and practices, or none to speak of, can live out their convictions and learn from those who differ from them. But every time we devalue rhetorical analysis of religion, ignore religious resources for argument, or disparage religious rhetors, we work against this goal. Certainly, there are many nonacademic forces working to homogenize our society, stamping out or restricting other ways of living meaningful lives. But it is too easy for us as academics to point to people outside the ivory tower, including often our students, as the main source of our society's struggles with pluralism. Our own house is not in order, and we as scholars of rhetoric need this book. Its call to pluralism is a call to us.

What does it look like to strive for pluralism in an academic context? This collection of essays, birthed from seminars and keynotes at the 2018 "Rhetoric and Religion in the 21st Century" conference, embodies one viable and attractive answer. Moving beyond the field's myopic focus on White evangelical Christianity, its chapters span Buddhist, Christian, Indigenous, Islamic, and Jewish rhetorics and discuss religion's intersections with feminist historiography, queer rhetorics, and race. The chapters are not organized by religious tradition but by their primary orientation toward religious rhetorics in service of pluralism, whether critically examining scholarly conceptions, conventions, and orientations toward religious rhetorics (section 1) or forging new ways of studying, investigating, and thinking about religious rhetorics (section 2).

The chapters convincingly demonstrate that it is impossible to disentangle religion from rhetorical theory, activity, or analysis. Religion is a not a domain of meaning making that is categorically separate from all others. Many of our major, epideictically hailed rhetors were religious. A number of our rhetorical concepts have religious origins or inflections. Rhetorical pedagogy has been influenced by religious ideals and spiritual practices. And religion participates in the rhetorical construction of race, gender, and sexual orientation. By teasing out religion's permeating influences and probing its multifaceted depths, these chapters stretch, enrich, and complicate our views of rhetoric in a broad sense, proving that comments like the one I received after my mock job talk are ridiculous and academically impoverishing. Rhetorical scholars cannot escape religion, and it is not clear that they should want to.

In a brilliantly innovative structural move, the editors have included between the chapters shorter "Interludes." Written by pioneering scholars of religious rhetorics, these interludes vividly detail these scholars' attraction to religion as an area of study; the impact that religion has had on their research, pedagogy, and even their personal lives; and historical turning points concerning religion in rhetorical scholarship. By interposing these short reflections, the editors increase the plurality of perspectives without unduly increasing the length of the book. This generic mixing strongly suggests that for rhetorical studies to support the project of pluralism, we need to diversify the forms that "proper" scholarly work can take in order to invite and incorporate knowledges that the standard academic essay may exclude. The first-person perspective of the interludes productively disrupts the normal scholarly-essay-to-scholarly-essay march of an edited collection, illustrating that the personal and the professional cannot be completely prized apart—a recognition that several of the chapter authors also evidence by meshing these two modes in their own contributions. Several of the interludes and chapters thus model the kind of honest and critical introspection that is a necessary step for rhetorical studies to be a field that fosters pluralism.

This collection also points the way forward for a more pluralistic field by addressing pedagogy. Each of the chapters ends with reflections and advice on how to teach religious rhetorics to our students, and some of the interludes contain such discussion as well. The contributors recommend a variety of pedagogical strategies and approaches for productive engagements with religious rhetorics in the classroom: centering questions, deconstructing the canon, confounding stereotypes of religions and their believers, incorporating reflection, connecting academic study to action, reading comparatively, teaching historiography, returning to the original sources, and resisting tokenization, among others. A few of the contributions also address questions about teaching religious students who explicitly ground their academic work in their faith. These contributors reject the disdain, demonization, or dismissiveness sometimes directed at religious students, especially those of a conservative bent, that I have witnessed from colleagues in the field. They suggest instead that teachers work to move beyond a conflictual or charity-based orientation to a posture of compassion, respect, and hospitality in which we account for our students' religious identities as we craft our courses, creating spaces for deliberation and being careful not to treat religion and academic inquiry as antithetical. I was one of those students who grounded my work in my faith, and I am grateful for the professors who initiated me into modern academic conventions without forcing me to make a false choice between a life of the mind and a life of faith.

As I continued my academic journey after college, I thankfully found mentors and colleagues who encouraged me to study religious rhetoric, who demonstrated what rigorous academic inquiry into religion looked like, who modeled how faith can motivate scholarship without veering into missionary work, and who taught me that secular and believing faculty can fruitfully plumb the depths of religious rhetoric together. While this volume is written for the field of rhetorical studies at large, it is a special gift for those of us who study religious rhetorics, particularly those of us who aspire to rigorous analysis without a desire to either pillory religion as false or champion it as true in our scholarship. Caught between these too-often-expressed, opposing expectations, I have at times in my career felt academically homeless. This book paints a picture of the disciplinary home I have long yearned for. The contributors to this volume are the colleagues that I want to have conferences with, I want to break bread with, I want to collaborate with; and thankfully, I have had that opportunity with several of them.

This collection exemplifies what the subdiscipline of religious rhetorics can and should be: a big tent where people of all faiths and of no faith can engage in the exciting, surprising, challenging, and meaningful work of studying this broad constellation of human phenomena we call religion. If rhetoricians want to substantively contribute to building a more inclusive, just, and peaceful world, we must pay attention to religion in careful, considered, and complex ways. Let us heed this book's call to work toward pluralism and follow its example in engaging the religious and rhetorical.

Martin Camper

Acknowledgments

It is only fitting to begin by expressing our gratitude to the writers, scholars, and teachers who share their expertise, insights, and wisdom in the pages that follow. As editors of this project, we have had the privilege to learn much about the variety, depth, and richness of religious rhetorics from the eighteen contributors to *Rhetoric and Religion in the Twenty-First Century.* We have been challenged, reoriented, and energized through our engagement with the range of perspectives offered by these luminaries in the field.

The conversations that animate this book emerged during the "Rhetoric and Religion in the 21st Century" conference (RR21C) at the University of Tennessee–Knoxville in the fall of 2018. RR21C offered a means of exploring the various relationships among religious rhetorics in our pluralistic context; an opportunity for scholars to engage with the diverse approaches available for studying, teaching, and inventing religious rhetorics in our present moment; and an occasion to consider how scholarly work on religion and rhetoric can speak to emerging trends in our current culture. The collaborative keynote presentations and seminars at RR21C served as vital occasions for engaging generative lines of inquiry into research, teaching, and public engagement related to religion and rhetoric. Many of the insights that took shape during those discussions served as starting points for the chapters in this book. We are grateful for the more than 140 scholars who attended the conference and participated in these conversations, and we are thankful for the many seminar leaders, scholars, and volunteers who made RR21C possible.

We also owe a debt of gratitude to the organizers of the 2005 conference "Inquiries into Rhetoric and Christian Tradition" at DePaul University in Chicago: Elizabeth Vander Lei, Beth Daniell, Tom Amorose, Anne Ruggles Gere, and David Joliffe. That gathering not only provided space for scholars of rhetoric and writing to engage exigent lines of inquiry at intersections of rhetoric, composition, and Christianity, but it also in many ways legitimized scholarly inquiry into rhetoric and religion and led to the formation of a subfield that is now burgeoning in rhetoric and writing studies. In the years following the 2005 conference, there has been an explosion of scholarly inquiry into religious rhetorics. We are therefore thankful that so many scholars and practitioners set this work in motion and continue to contribute to its growth in significant ways.

This book was made possible by generous financial support from several entities at Baylor University, the University of Tennessee–Knoxville, and Saint

Louis University. Many thanks to Dean Lee Nordt and Dean Kim Kellison in the College of Arts & Sciences at Baylor; Kevin Gardner, chair of English at Baylor; and Darin Davis, director of the Institute for Faith & Learning at Baylor, for the funding to support RR21C and the writing of this book. We also want to thank Allen Dunn, the former department head of English at the University of Tennessee, and the trustees of the Hodges Better English Fund for their generous financial support of RR21C and our book project. We'd also like to express our gratitude to the College of Arts and Sciences of the University of Tennessee for the grant we received from the Mildred Haines and William Elijah Morris Lecture Endowment, a fund that supports campus visits of lecturers and scholars in all disciplines of the College of Arts and Sciences. We are also deeply appreciative of the support we received from Saint Louis University, including from the Department of English, the Georgia K. Johnston fund, the College of Arts and Sciences, and the Scholarship Opportunity Fund.

We are immensely thankful to Kristine Priddy, who offered crucial encouragement and guidance at the earliest stages of the project. We also wish to thank Sylvia Frank Rodrigue, who has continued to support and guide the project throughout its completion. Their editorial wisdom and commitment—particularly through the middle of a pandemic—have been invaluable. Likewise, the outstanding work of several other collaborators at Southern Illinois University Press is deserving of recognition. Thanks to Amy Etcheson, Sarah Jilek, Judy Verdich, Mandi Jourdan, Linda Jorgensen Buhman, Khara Lukancic, Chelsey Harris, and Jerry Richardson. We are equally appreciative of the anonymous reviewers' thoughtful engagement with our book. Their insightful feedback and recommendations over multiple rounds of review really helped to strengthen the project.

Each of us individually would also like to thank the family members, friends, and colleagues who encouraged and supported us as we worked on this book project.

From Mike. I am grateful for my colleagues and friends at Baylor University for sharing insights, resources, and guidance that shaped the contours of this book. I have been fortunate to have remarkable mentors during every stage of my academic and professional life. The best of this book bears marks of their care, influence, and friendship. Working alongside Jeff and Paul has been transformational, life-giving, and a ton of fun. I am thankful for the time we have spent together taking up important questions and forging friendships that will long outlast our collaboration on this project. I also owe a debt of gratitude to my San Diego family, especially Lynn and Donald, the Dull family, and my New York family for being ever-present sources of kindness and support in my life. It is a rare gift to discover companions for the journey. August Cardona,

Karl Sacco, Johnny Barr, Dan Paik, Jimmy Severino, Chris Ray, Andrew Kotlow, Jason Dube, Justin King, Mike Apple, Brad Trottier, Brett Bashaw, and the Cousins are mine. Huge thanks for keeping me grounded in what matters most. Charmaine, Jackson, and Ashley, I am thankful we are family. Judah and Shiloh, I am proud to be your uncle and grateful for every minute we are together. Tom, there is no one who makes me laugh harder or knows me better. I cannot be persuaded that there's a better brother on the planet. Mom and Dad, no amount of thanks will ever do justice to the countless ways that I have been formed by your love, affection, and encouragement. No matter the geographical distance between us or the amount of time that passes, you are always right here cheering me on and bringing that same light I have known from the start. Courtney, Lily, and Thomas, you are my homeland in this life and in the worlds beyond it. Courtney, no one strengthens me, renews me, or sets my heart at peace the way you do. I am grateful beyond words for you, My Love. Lily and Thomas, I adore you. I cherish you. I love you. Know this always: there is nothing I treasure more than the gift of being your dad. Finally, for this book, for the summons to write, and for the opportunity to teach writers, thanks be to God.

From Paul. First, I'd like to thank Mike and Jeff for inviting me to collaborate on the conference that led to this book. I'm also grateful to my colleagues in the Department of English at Saint Louis University, particularly my late colleague Georgia K. Johnston, whose generosity made possible the Georgia K. Johnson Professorship. I was awarded the Johnston Professorship from 2021 to 2023, a period during which I have had extra research time that was crucial for finishing this work. I'd also like to thank my colleagues in English for creating the professorship to support the research activity of associate professors. Their support of scholarship in rhetorical studies is much appreciated. Above all, my deepest gratitude for my family: Melody, Beatrice, and Josie.

From Jeff. Thanks to Mike and Paul for being such generous, patient, and capable collaborators. Thanks for helping bring this book to fruition, as well as the conference that led to it. I'm also grateful for the support I received for this project from my colleagues at the University of Tennessee. Of course, no small amount of thanks goes to Sarah, Zoe, and Ben, who provide wonderful encouragement and timely distractions, often in the same moment. But I would most like to acknowledge my father, Howard, who died while this book was in process, and my mother, Lana, who continues to remind me that the best things in life are those that require full devotion.

Michael-John DePalma, Paul Lynch, and Jeff Ringer

Rhetoric and Religion in the Twenty-First Century

Introduction: Looking for Resonances

Rhetoric and Religion in the Twenty-First Century

MICHAEL-JOHN DEPALMA, PAUL LYNCH, AND JEFF RINGER

> A Sunday morning gathering in London. The congregation sways together in unison, their hands stretched skyward. The acceleration of the drumbeat propels the rhythm of bodies. Swinging back and forth at a quickening pace, congregants add their voices to the chorus, creating new harmonies. A few in the assembly call out expressions of gratitude. Others simply cry out. Every member of this congregation is an atheist.
>
> An academic conference on religious rhetoric, where a panel of established scholars from communication and English discuss a variety of perspectives. The panelists and the attendees are mostly interested in some variety of Christian tradition. Some are Christians themselves. A question from the back: "What even is religious rhetorics? Can we define it?" After an awkward silence, one of the presenters finally offers, "That's a really good question."
>
> A Muslim boy and his father drive to watch a college football game at the Catholic university where the father is an MBA student. On the way to the game, they stop at a campus shrine to the Virgin Mary, where they light candles and stand in silence. As the boy gets older, he wonders about this ritual and asks his father why Muslims would pray at a Catholic shrine. The father tells his son, "Always look for resonances."

In each of the three scenes above, rhetoric and religion animate each other in profound ways. In the first, members gather for the Sunday Assembly, an "atheist church" founded by two British comedians who wanted to create "something that was like church but totally secular and inclusive of all—no matter what they believed" ("About Sunday Assembly"). The congregants are transported by their makeshift liturgy, a practice with a wide set of discursive and nondiscursive available means—and one that suggests, even in a so-called secular age, that religion endures in new and interesting ways. In the second scene, scholars supposedly best positioned to understand the relation of religion and rhetoric find themselves unable to define the basic terms of the inquiry. A seemingly straightforward question—what *is* religious rhetoric?—renders a room full of rhetoricians silent. Finally, Muslim interfaith scholar and activist Eboo Patel recalls standing in silence before an image of the Virgin Mary as his father pointed to candles inside a cove and urged his son to remember, "The Qur'an describes God as light upon light" (*Interfaith* 161).

Looking for resonances—listening for them, attuning ourselves to them—is also the project of this collection. In the essays presented here, the reader will find answers more robust than the one offered by our confounded panelist. But what the reader will not find is a final answer, or any answer that would purport to settle the question of religious rhetoric once and for all. The search for definitional certainty, whether in religious or rhetorical studies, has failed to settle the question satisfactorily. Both religion and rhetoric are simply too diverse, too multifarious, to be contained by any single understanding. Given these complexities, the advice offered by Patel's father seems wise, and we thus find the metaphor of resonance to be a particularly generative one for our project. A resonance implies the fundamental rhetorical act of listening and a sympathetic response: things resonate with us and ultimately within us. Resonances evoke images, recall memories, provoke emotions—all of which precede the kind of intellectual act required to define an experience or phenomenon and assign it to the categories "religious" or "rhetorical." A resonance *re-sounds*: it is a reverberation sent back to a signal that elongates the original sound.

Finally, and perhaps most importantly, listening for resonance also makes it possible to hear dissonance, nonharmonious combinations of sound that result when conflicting reverberations collide. The search for resonance should not flatten the sounds of difference and distinction. Resonance and dissonance are inherently plural phenomena, appropriate to the study of religion and rhetoric in the twenty-first century, when singular understandings of religion or rhetoric will no longer suffice. Luigi Spina rightly counsels, "one should always talk about religion in the plural and about religious phenomena in the singular, just as the rhetorical phenomenon of persuasive communication is—as such and every time—a singular event while concepts of rhetoric in diverse cultures are multiple" (214). In this volume, we propose to talk about religion and rhetoric as fundamentally diverse, meaning that we and our contributors are committed to listening for dissonances as well as for resonances.

Our commitment to listening for both dissonance and resonance begins with the recognition that religious diversity is a fact of human life in the twenty-first century. Certainly, this fact is true in the global context, but it is also increasingly true in the American context. As Robert P. Jones and Daniel Cox assert in their 2017 Public Religion Research Institute study, "The American religious landscape has undergone dramatic changes in the last decade and is more diverse today than at any time since modern sociological measurements began" (10). The question for rhetorical studies is not simply how to recognize this diversity globally and in the United States but also how to encourage hospitable, just, and inclusive engagement with that diversity. One way to conceive of accomplishing that goal is to distinguish between diversity and pluralism, a distinction made by multiple scholars in the sociology of religion and religious studies. Diana Eck makes that distinction as follows:

> Pluralism takes the reality of difference as its starting point. The challenge of pluralism is not to obliterate or erase difference, nor to smooth out differences under a universalizing canopy, but rather to discover ways of living, connecting, relating, arguing, and disagreeing in a society of differences. This is no small challenge, given the fact that some of the most contentious differences are within religious communities and even within particular sectarian or denominational movements. (745)

Interfaith organizer Eboo Patel defines pluralism using a crucial distinction: "Where diversity is a fact, pluralism is an achievement" (*Interfaith* 92). Moreover, achieving pluralism is a fundamentally rhetorical project.

Taken together, Eck and Patel articulate what we see as a challenge for rhetorical studies in the twenty-first century. If pluralism seeks to discover ways of living, connecting, relating, arguing, and disagreeing in a society of differences, then the achievement of pluralism is a thoroughly rhetorical project. Pluralism is rhetorical in that it pursues a discursive culture in which arguing and disagreeing are not simply evidence of a fall from some paradisal state of harmony. Indeed, arguing and disagreeing serve the same function as connecting and relating: they enable us to live together, both across traditions and within them. Pluralism seeks to respect difference and to engage it in ways that promote intersubjectivity—to recognize the value of the other while resisting the urge to flatten that otherness. As a fundamentally rhetorical project, pluralism requires careful listening, generous reading, cautious speaking, and precise writing. And like all rhetorical work, it requires sustained attention to the particular contexts in which we and our interlocutors find ourselves.

This collection aims to provide sustained attention toward how rhetorical studies in the twenty-first century can work to achieve the pluralism that Eck and Patel call for. Both present and future publics will continue to be shaped by an ever more diverse set of traditions, communities, and practices. Much of rhetoric's historical recovery, however, has been premised on Hellenistic traditions. As several contributors in this collection discuss, that frame limits our understanding of the full range of rhetorics and religious traditions. Additionally, while rhetorical studies has in recent decades enjoyed a surge of interest in religious rhetorics, that interest has often coalesced around narrow conceptions of religion, namely those that align with Christian traditions. We see *Rhetoric and Religion in the Twenty-First Century* as working to complicate that picture by reflecting a wider diversity of religious traditions and, equally important, by working to complicate our very conceptions of "religion" and "rhetoric," terms that, as some of our contributors suggest, bear the stamp of Western and often Christian assumptions.

Achieving pluralism in our politically and religiously fraught century will be complicated and hard won—a project that is well beyond the reach of any single book. No one volume can cover the full range of religious traditions or achieve the pluralism described above. Yet we see this collection of arguments, stories, and perspectives as doing important work toward that goal. The scholarship presented here focuses on traditions including Buddhism, Judaism, and Islām. The book also features chapters on the African American prophetic tradition and on Jesuit rhetorics, and it offers research that engages the intersections of religion and feminist historiography, religion and LGBTQ rhetorics, and religion and Indigenous rhetorics. In the remainder of this introduction, we discuss the endurance, diversification, and evolution of religion in the twenty-first century, the central exigences for the present collection. We then discuss more fully the notion of pluralism as an achievement, with a focus on how rhetoric is central to that project. Finally, we lay out the specifics of this edited collection and discuss the contributions of each chapter.

Religion Endures

Diversity of religion and religious traditions is a fact of the world. Implied in this fact, however, is an even more basic or foundational reality: religion as a force in society not only persists in the twenty-first century, but it has also expanded in substantial ways. Indeed, rapid and continuous changes to the global religious landscape are projected to alter—but not necessarily decrease—the demographics of the world's religious profile over the next several decades. According to a 2012 study of the Pew Research Center, 84 percent of the world's population identified as religiously affiliated (Pew Forum, "Global" 9). Even among the remaining unaffiliated—who, after Christians and Muslims, constitute the world's third largest "religious" identity—spiritual beliefs persist. In China, which accounts for 62 percent of the world's religiously unaffiliated (Pew Forum, "Global" 26), 7 percent of adults reported a belief in God, while 44 percent revealed that they had worshiped at a grave during the previous year (24). Meanwhile, in France, 30 percent of unaffiliated adults claimed a belief in God or a higher power (15). Whatever the declines in formal identification and participation, religion remains a powerful and influential force for a majority of people worldwide, a force for which rhetorical studies must account if it aspires to a global perspective.

While the United States has long been an outlier among developed nations for its widespread religiosity, the religious landscape in the United States is also growing increasingly complex. As Putnam and Campbell put it, "Any discussion of religion in America must begin with the incontrovertible fact that Americans are a highly religious people. One can quibble over just how religion, and religiosity, should be gauged, but, by any standard the United States (as a whole) is a religious nation" (7). This impression is confirmed by the fact that more than 75 percent of Americans continue to identify as affiliated with a religion (Pew Forum, "Religious Landscape"). Yet the nature of the nation's religiousness is changing rapidly. Christianity has seen a sharp decline in recent years. While 65 percent of American adults described themselves as Christians in a 2018–2019 phone survey, this figure marks a drop of twelve percentage points from the previous decade (Pew Forum, "In U.S., Decline" 3). In addition, the so-called nones—those who report no formal religious affiliation—are on the rise. The number of Americans who declined to express a religious affiliation rose from 17 percent in 2009 to 26 percent a decade later (Pew Forum, "In U.S., Decline" 3). Among younger Americans—including those sitting in our classrooms—the numbers are even more striking: according to a 2012 Pew study, 32 percent of those under thirty claimed no religious affiliation (Pew Forum, "Nones" 10). But these figures do not mean that the young have walked away from religion entirely. Among the "spiritual but not religious" in the United States, for example, 44 percent reported that they pray daily (Pew Forum, "Nones" 44). As Tara Isabella Burton puts it in her book *Strange Rites*, the nones "may not be traditionally religious, in the sense that either Jerry Falwell or Sam Harris may be used to. But they're not exactly *secular*, either" (17). Clearly, the religiously unaffiliated remain interested in questions and possibilities usually grouped under the heading "religion." Though traditional religious observance may be decreasing, new beliefs, practices, and congregations are rapidly replacing the losses. In a recent article, Byron R. Johnson and Jeff Levin write, "The religious landscape in the U.S. is changing but not in the ways that draw headlines. Hundreds of new denominations have quietly appeared, as have thousands of church plants (new congregations) and numerous non-Christian religious imports." It thus seems that the reports of religion's demise are greatly exaggerated.

The blurring of the religious and the secular observed by these scholars further challenges the "secularization thesis," the claim that sociological trends in the twentieth century pointed to the inexorable decline of religious influence. As sociologist Bryan Wilson put it, the secularization thesis assumes that people will "act less and less in response to religious motivation: they assess the world in empirical and rational terms, and find themselves involved in rational organizations and rationally determined roles which allow small scope for such religious predilections as they might privately entertain" (x). Wilson's particular project was to observe religious influence in Britain and the United States, but the idea of inexorable secularization reflects assumptions present within Western consciousness for two centuries: in the face of technological, medical, and economic development, the need for religion would gradually fall away. Similarly, sociologist C. Wright Mills recounts the story this way: "Once the world was filled with the sacred." But after "the forces of modernization swept across the globe," it was only a matter of time before "the sacred" disappeared from public life and was relegated to "the private realm" (qtd. in Norris and Inglehart 3). Clearly, this has not happened. One need not look far to see that religion remains a powerful force in the twenty-first century, influencing domestic politics, international relations, cultural and social movements, civic life, and education. While simplistic notions of the sacred and secular might construe religion as a private matter, religion continues to pervade the public square. Religiously motivated citizens continue to make religiously motivated arguments, despite any claim that such arguments are illegitimate in a secular society.

More subtly but no less powerfully, religion continues to shape culture even in ostensibly secular situations—the anecdote above about the Sunday Assembly is a case in point. If religion's influence has endured, it has done so by evolving and adapting itself to a changing zeitgeist. These transformations happen within a scene often described as "postsecular," a term that describes the persistence and evolution of religion in the wake of a secularization that never quite came to pass, at least not in the ways its prophets predicted. As with postmodernism and posthumanism, the discourses of the postsecular and postsecularity are "perhaps best understood not as any kind of clear position, but as a *spectrum* of concerns and possibilities" (McLennan 4). This spectrum includes the political, the epistemological, the literary, and of course the theological and the spiritual. But across this spectrum, intellectuals concerned with the postsecular are interested in the ways in which religion continues to make its presence felt long after it was supposed to have disappeared. Jürgen Habermas describes as postsecular those societies in which "religion maintains a public influence and relevance, while the secularist certainty that religion will disappear worldwide in the course of modernization is losing ground" (21). As the statistics above indicate, traditional religious observance may be losing ground, yet religious interests persist. Rosi Braidotti observes this postsecular persistence in feminist theory. Where the feminist movement, particularly in Europe, has generally been antireligious and anticlerical, many feminist thinkers draw on religious and spiritual thought to advance their intellectual and political projects (7). Braidotti notes "that some of the most pertinent critiques of advanced capitalism today, and of the structural injustices of globalization, are voiced by religiously driven social movements" (9). The absence or withdrawal of the religious is not an essential precondition of incisive social critique.

In *Formations of the Secular*, meanwhile, Talal Asad pursues a series of genealogical studies to trace the ongoing mutual constitution of the sacred and secular. To take one example: Modern scripture study sets aside the idea of the Bible as divine revelation and instead approaches it with historical and literary methodologies. Yet this shift does not erase notions like inspiration, spirituality, or even faith. Instead, these terms take on new meanings. Critics may still speak of a "spiritual" communication between poet and reader and describe its effect as an "epiphany" (41). In addition, the emergence of modern scientific discourse helps transform the idea of faith from a virtue to an epistemology, "a way of knowing supernatural objects, parallel to the knowledge of nature (the *real* world) that reason and observation provided" (Asad 38–39). Asad traces this kind of mutual formation in a variety of contexts to conclude that "'the secular' should not be thought of as the space in which *real* human life gradually emancipates itself from the controlling power of 'religion' and thus achieves the latter's relocation" (191). Instead, modernity occasions a variety of "secularisms," only some of which insist on either a descriptive or normative definition of secularization as the public evacuation of religion.

Charles Taylor also rejects the idea of what he calls a "subtraction story," a narrative that defines the secular as that which is left over once religion is somehow drained from public life. Rather, a postsecular age is one formed by the "immanent frame," a prevailing cultural assumption that the world lacks a transcendent foundation or orientation; within the immanent frame, "unbelief has become for many the major default option" (Taylor 14). Some readers may balk at this claim, especially those who live in communities where strong religious faith still dominates the scene. But Taylor's argument is that in a secular age, religious faith sits alongside a newly emergent exclusivist humanism, which claims no transcendent or supernatural reference. Put otherwise, humans can get along quite fine in contemporary society without having to concern themselves with questions related to the supernatural, the transcendent, or the divine.

Yet the seeming collapse of the transcendent does not close the question of ultimate significance. Paradoxically, it sets off an explosion of varieties of the search for such significance. "We are now living," writes Taylor, "in a spiritual super-nova" (300). In this supernova, the choice is no longer between theism and atheism but rather among a dizzying array of options, some linked to faith in the supernatural, some not. As the available religious and spiritual options increase, they also "fragilize," which is to say they become more vulnerable, more doubtful, more open to questioning. Fragilization occurs "when through increased contact, interchange, even perhaps inter-marriage, the other becomes more and more like me, in everything else but faith: same activities, professions, opinions, tastes" (Taylor 304). When one's colleague, neighbor, or even partner does not share the same transcendent assumptions, the religious may be more inclined to question their own. Certainly, some questioning of religious faith is welcome and necessary, particularly in the face of absolutist or fundamentalist religious claims. But fragilization can also cut public discourse adrift from any sense of shared meaning or commitment. As Habermas notes, the uncertainties of our postsecular age can occasion not just reactionary fundamentalisms but also what he calls a new-age "Californian syncretism" (19). If the former threatens a poisonous form of belonging, the latter may threaten a poisonous form of individualism and subservience to consumer culture.

Nor is a fragilized world necessarily the antidote to poisonous belonging. In a world delimited by the immanent frame, the loudest religious voices may be the most reactionary. As Martin E. Marty has observed, "The collision of faiths, or the collision of peoples of faith, are among the most threatening conflicts around the world in the new millennium. They grow more ominous and more lethal every season" (1). One need only think of conflicts in Northern Ireland, India, Sri Lanka, the Middle East, and Nigeria—to name but a few—in order to understand the reason why Stephen Prothero describes religion as "the most volatile constituent of culture" (5). Closer to home, the emergence of Christian nationalism in the United States in recent years reflects the extent to which religious commitments can inform perspectives that, implicitly or explicitly, enact violence on those perceived to be outside the drawn boundaries. For one recent example, we can consider the crude appeal to "Christian values" of President Trump's Bible photo op in front of St. John's Church in Washington, DC, taken during protests in response to the killing of George Floyd. Staging the photo required that protestors be driven from the square by batons, tear gas, and rubber bullets. Even more disturbing, the dominating presence of Christian messaging and imagery at the January 6, 2021, attack on the Capitol confirmed the depth to which religious identity can be exploited and therefore result in increased social fracturing, community isolation, identity-based conflicts, and outright bloodshed.

But these results are by no means inevitable. The project of pluralism is to discover new ways of living, connecting, relating, arguing, and disagreeing in a society where traditional religious diversity is increasing against a backdrop in which the existing vocabularies for "religious" and "secular" matters are no longer stable. Sorting through these complexities is a distinctly rhetorical project. If rhetoric is the purification of war, as Burke insists, then religious rhetoric might best be understood as the purification of inter- and intra-religious conflict. Rhetoric and writing studies are well positioned to be at the forefront of achieving this aspiration, as we attend to both the resonances and the dissonances that mark the varieties of religious rhetoric in the twenty-first century.

Rhetoric's Role in Achieving Pluralism

If the preceding argument is true—if our current world is one in which former vocabularies no longer reflect the phenomena they purport to name—then it follows that we need to develop terminologies that can facilitate the new "ways of living, connecting, relating, arguing, and disagreeing in a society of differences" for which Eck has called. Such a project should be a central focus of rhetorical studies. Rather than a niche concern, religious rhetorics matter for all scholars and students of rhetoric. Burke's foundational *Rhetoric of Religion* taught us to find the most powerful expressions of language in religion. As Burke wrote, "The subject of religion falls under the head of *rhetoric* in the sense that rhetoric is the art of *persuasion*, and religious cosmogonies are designed, in the last analysis, as exceptionally thoroughgoing modes of persuasion" (v). If Burke is right, then we can find powerful forms of symbolicity, practice, motivations, and moods—along with vital and perilous forms of belonging—within the diverse intersections of religion and rhetoric in a postsecular context.

But to contend with religious rhetorics productively in a religiously diverse global context, rhetorical studies needs to intensify its own awareness of two realities related to rhetorical theory, namely, (1) that our rhetorical vocabularies are infused with assumptions frequently derived from the Christian and Hellenistic traditions and (2) that the field needs to be honest about the religious influences that have long informed our purportedly secular terminologies. We address each concern below.

While rhetorical studies has in recent decades enjoyed a surge of interest in religious rhetorics, that interest has often coalesced around conceptions of religion that fall within the purview of Christian tradition. This focus is, of course, a worthy and important goal—Christian rhetorics of various sorts have been influential for millennia, and exploring them in all of their diversity by scholarly means is important for rhetorical studies to continue to do. And yet, too often "religious rhetorics" is assumed to be a kind of shorthand for "Christian rhetorics," a point reflected in Celeste Michelle Condit's observation that Burke's "*Rhetoric of Religion* is about Christianity and logology is therefore about language in a Christianized social system" (352). This assumption that religious rhetoric is synonymous with Christian rhetoric is deeply problematic because of the vast religious diversity it occludes. By featuring contributions that speak to the intersections of rhetoric and religious traditions in Islām, Buddhism, Judaism, and others, we hope that *Rhetoric and Religion in the Twenty-First Century* works to challenge our too-easy association of "religion" with "Christian."

Of course, such a conflation reflects the fact that, at least in Western contexts like the United States, varieties of Christianity have enjoyed something close to hegemonic status. While that hegemony appears to be cracking—or "fragilizing," to echo Taylor—the project of pluralism demands that rhetorical studies acknowledge the extent to which existing rhetorical terminologies too often bear the stamp of Western, Christian ideologies. Deborah Holdstein has made this argument powerfully. In her contribution to *Judaic Perspectives in Rhetoric and Composition*, she argues that the "Christian ideologies" underpinning rhetoric and writing studies are "transparently assumed and unquestioned" (14). She also notes the ways in which Christian ideologies, including anti-Judaism and anti-Semitism, shaped the Hellenistic tradition on which the contemporary recovery of rhetoric was initially founded (19). An example of how Christian assumptions shaped that recovery is evident in the work of Richard Weaver. In his canonical "Language Is Sermonic," for example, Weaver characterizes the activity of persuasion in terms that are recognizably (though not exclusively) Christian. He writes that rhetoric involves "a quasi-religious metaphysics, if you will, because it ascribes to the highest reality qualities of stasis, immutability, eternal perdurance—qualities that in Western civilization are usually expressed in the language of theism" (1355). As this passage suggests, theories of rhetoric have often been shot through with Western philosophical and theological assumptions that may run counter to the ways of knowing and being that constitute non-Western, non-Christian rhetorical traditions.

Rhetoricians therefore need to acknowledge the fact that commonly used terms and concepts from rhetorical theory have religious underpinnings. Our claim here reflects our discussion of the postsecular: various religious discourses animate rhetorical theory, and so understanding rhetoric and writing studies as a field necessitates understanding the deep currents of religious thought—sometimes centuries removed—that undergird many of our contemporary ideas about rhetoric and how it functions. We make this claim not as a statement of quality but rather as one of conjecture. Understanding even the residual connections will enrich our understanding of both rhetoric and religion.

To take just one example: In *The Rhetoric of RHETORIC*, Wayne Booth defines "rhetorology" as the deepest form of "listening rhetoric," which includes "the whole range of communicative arts for reducing misunderstanding by paying full attention to opposing views" (10). Rhetorology, Booth hopes, "teaches that learning to listen, and encouraging our opponents to listen, can *sometimes* yield moments of sheer illumination: a trustful pursuit of truth replacing what had appeared to be a hopeless battle" (172). This faith in rhetoric is well understood in our field. Less understood, however, is the extent to which Booth's Mormonism informed his understanding of rhetoric. In *My Many Selves: The Quest for a Plausible Harmony*, Booth links the formation of his thinking about rhetorology to his Mormon faith:

> Nothing we ever work at, I came to believe, is more important than the drive not just to maintain peace with rivals or enemies or misguided friends, not just to tolerate them generously, not just to condescend to them with a benign smile or hide something they would hate, but to understand them, to learn to think with them while assisting them to think with you in return. That faith abides, and it informs many of the best moments of my life. [. . .] And the role of Mormonism in that faith continues. Just as your deeper faith—whether "religious" or "atheist" or "agnostic"—penetrates all that you do, so what I sometimes call "the good side of Mormonism" penetrates my life and will be with me till I die. (133–34)

Booth's rhetorology is among his most important and lasting contributions, and his assertion that Mormonism remained an important animating force in his thinking about rhetorology prompts us to consider how our understanding of Booth's rhetorology might be deepened if we were to revisit his rhetorical thought attuned to its religious underpinnings. What might we see if we attend to the interanimation of rhetoric and Mormonism in Booth's rhetorical thought? What do we fail to see when the connections between Booth's faith and his rhetorical contributions are severed or obscured? What difference does it make that Booth's ideas of listening rhetoric were informed by his Mormon faith?

Of course, these questions should not be limited to Booth and his work, and one does not have to look far to find other examples of prominent rhetoricians whose body of work was deeply influenced by religion or spirituality. In addition to figures whose ideas about rhetoric are long understood to have been shaped by the varieties of Christian tradition (e.g., Augustine, Fell, Campbell, Grimke, etc.), there are many other scholars whose work has been animated by religion. For example, while we have already mentioned Kenneth Burke as a central figure in religious rhetorics, we think it would behoove the field to consider how his Christian Science upbringing influenced his criticism and theory (Feehan; Zamparutti). Despite Burke's purported stripping of the theological dimension from his logological approach, he still uses distinctly Christian terminology to frame his rhetorical theory. The other great founder of the New Rhetoric, Chaïm Perelman, was also influenced by his religious background. As David Frank has noted, Perelman's rhetorical theory "is founded on an essentially cosmopolitan Jewishness, expressed in a Talmudic sense of reason and argument" (78). We might also consider Paolo Freire, whose critical pedagogy was shaped by Catholic liberation theology (see Daniell; Berthoff; Stenberg; Pace and Merys). Likewise, it seems impossible to understand Walter Ong's study of rhetoric without reference to his Catholicism and status as a Jesuit (Lauer Rice). These influences raise the question of whether we might observe similar influence on the thought of other figures. For instance, how should we account for Catholic influence on Bruno Latour, whose dissertation was centered on a study of the resurrection? Or, for that matter, how might we account for the atheism of Karl Marx or Michel Foucault? Paul Ricoeur has insisted that the masters of suspicion do not simply undermine religion, but they also open the way to new possibilities of religious expression. Witness, for example, the ways that liberation theology draws on Marxism. Foucault, meanwhile, came to study writing as a technology of the self, an inquiry that, while perhaps not conventionally religious, made key contributions to the study of spiritual practices and their relation to social and political life.

We can also look beyond individual scholars to concepts themselves. For example, how should we contend with James Kinneavy's argument that *pistis* is both the Greek word for persuasion and the Christian term for belief? In *Greek Rhetorical Origins of Christian Faith*, Kinneavy invites us not only to remember that rhetorical persuasion and Christian belief share the same root word in Greek but also that rhetoric itself may be "a possible origin, source, or analogue of the Christian concept of faith" (3–4). If Kinneavy's argument is accurate, then the implications for Hellenistic rhetoric are significant. To put it in terms we unpacked at the beginning of this introduction: the fact that Christian faith and Hellenistic rhetoric share terms in common means that talking about one in terms of the other is likely to produce a high degree of resonance. Again, nothing is wrong with that reality, except for when they resonate so much that you can't hear anything else. As a result of that resonance, the perspectives that compose it—in this case, the terms and concepts that align with Hellenism and Christianity—come to function as a default perspective assumed to be universal, as opposed to one that is contingent and located. We note, for instance, that the vast majority of the examples above relate to some version of Christianity. While there certainly are exceptions—Perelman's Jewishness is one, though there are certainly others—this list appears to confirm Holdstein's observation that the ideological formations undergirding rhetoric and writing studies tend to be not only Western but also Christian, albeit "Christian" from a variety of contested perspectives—Burke's Christian Science, Booth's Mormonism, Freire's Catholicism.

The question then is how becoming aware of these resonances might help scholars in rhetorical studies avoid masking important dissonances. We argue that attuning ourselves to such undercurrents can help us understand better the ideologies subsumed under even the most common concepts in rhetorical studies. Margaret Zulick has described the rhetoric of religion as an "immense undiscovered country" that demands a plurality of scholarly interventions (125). Such interventions include not only projects that study the religious influences on particular rhetoricians but also projects that pursue Foucauldian archaeologies of the origins of terms, concepts, and legacies to understand whether and how religious motives informed the rhetorical theory that we write with, think with, and see through on a regular basis.

About the Book

Attunement to the dynamics of our religiously diverse global context compelled contributors to *Rhetoric and Religion in the Twenty-First Century* to pursue the aspiration of pluralism through two interrelated means: interrogating extant rhetorics and inventing exigent rhetorics. Contributors' interrogations of "rhetoric" and "religion" in the first section of the book are vitally important to rhetorical studies' pursuit of pluralism. In "Section I: Interrogating Rhetorics," contributors reveal the need to expand our field's conventional emphasis on Western, Hellenistic rhetorics in order to capture the diversity of religious rhetorics and reimagine the relationships among rhetorical traditions, and they demonstrate the importance of employing contextually sensitive, nuanced, and self-reflexive approaches to religion that resist either overextension or reductive representation. Contributors' invention of exigent rhetorics in "Section II: Inventing Rhetorics" likewise takes strides toward pluralism by recovering and theorizing rich rhetorical traditions that have thus far been invisible, misunderstood, or overlooked in the field of rhetorical studies. In making these rhetorics visible, they offer possibilities for ways of being, knowing, living, connecting, relating, arguing, and disagreeing as we attempt to navigate the supernova that characterizes our postsecular context.

To foster a rhetorical education that can help achieve the pluralism we call for in this collection, each chapter includes an "Entry Points" section aimed at helping rhetorical educators engage productively with the variety of religious rhetorics included in the book. Rhetorical education is a primary means through which to achieve pluralism, and a central purpose of rhetorical education is to provide students with knowledge and practices that will enable them to participate fully in various publics. This view of rhetorical education as preparation for engagement in deliberative democracy and civic life is reflected in the "Mt. Oread Manifesto," which asserts that a major aspiration of rhetorical education is that "[a]ll stakeholders in public life feel motivated and competent enough in their communication skills to advance an idea in the public sphere and engage in meaningful deliberation about ideas" (3). Recognizing religion's functions and influence in our religiously diverse global context enables us to see that preparing communicators for thoughtful public participation means fostering writers and speakers who are equipped to engage with religious diversity in productive ways.

This acknowledgment prompted us to invite contributors to draw on their experience of teaching and researching religious rhetorics to name key questions, texts, approaches, or strategies that they have found beneficial. Given the challenges associated with teaching religious rhetorics, each contributor also discusses potential pitfalls to avoid in the classroom. Teaching religious rhetorics of any sort demands a wide range of considerations about how to proceed in ways that students find accessible, and the Entry Points section in each of our chapters provides instructors with guidance. Because of the range of perspectives and traditions represented in the book, the Entry Points sections grow organically from the substance of their chapters rather than following a prescribed format. This diversity of approach reflects the book's commitment to pluralism.

The project of pluralism is also pursued through the inclusion of short, personal essays written by leading scholars in the field. In these "Interludes," luminaries Patricia Bizzell, Beth Daniell, Beverly Moss, Laurent Pernot, Patricia Roberts-Miller, Elizabeth Vander Lei, and Robert Yagelski reflect on the range of motives, experiences, and tensions that led them to pursue inquiry into religious rhetorics. The purpose of these reflective interludes is to offer narratives of possibility. As Martin Camper's opening story in the foreword to this book suggests, scholars—especially those just beginning their careers—are still sometimes steered away from engagement with religion for a host of reasons. Collectively, these interludes demonstrate that work in religious rhetorics is possible, necessary, diverse, and beneficial. Our hope is that they help authorize new work in the field that takes up and expands on this book's call to achieve pluralism. Regarding the order of the interludes, we arranged them alphabetically by author last name so as not to imply any direct link between these stand-alone interludes and the chapters that precede or follow them. Readers are encouraged, of course, to look for resonances and dissonances that might exist between the chapters and interludes.

Decisions about the arrangement of the collection as a whole were guided by our recognition that attending to resonances and dissonances is essential to the pursuit of pluralism. We attempted to be mindful of the potential to wrongly assume, impose, or create dissonance, and we were aware of the pitfall of creating neat and orderly resonances that paper over difference. Relatedly, our deliberation about arranging the contributions to the collection was undergirded by a commitment to order the collection in such a way that readers are invited to engage with both resonance and dissonance across all chapters of the book. One way to realize this goal was to resist thinking about the chapters in terms of rhetorical or religious tradition and instead consider how each one is moving rhetorical studies toward the goal of pluralism. From that vantage, the two-part structure of the book emerged. Chapters by Lisa King, Lisa Zimmerelli, T J Geiger II, and John C. Brereton and Cinthia Gannett are featured in "Section I: Interrogating Rhetorics." Contributions by Janice W. Fernheimer, Kurt Spellmeyer, Rasha Diab, and Andre E. Johnson are included in "Section II: Inventing Rhetorics."

Lisa King's chapter, "To Do Things in a Good (Decolonial) Way: Putting Indigenous Rhetorics and Rhetorics of Religion in Conversation," addresses the ways that Euro-American and Christian attitudes have and continue to shape the colonial project and inform how religion is framed, on these lands and elsewhere. King argues that Indigenous ways of knowing and being do not necessarily fit the Western/colonial notion of religion and so remain largely unrecognized or even misrepresented in discussion. She thus suggests that what we call "Indigenous rhetorics" are part of past, present, and future Indigenous ways of knowing and being and that decolonial ways of understanding one another are a beginning point for the meeting of religious rhetorics and Indigenous rhetorics. King is hopeful that if we can recognize religious discourse to be a pervasive part of discourse *and* acknowledge the existence and life of Indigenous rhetorical practices, it is possible to discover a way forward that values Indigenous rhetorical practices and seeks to de-link from the violence of the rhetorical erasure of Indigenous peoples in our field and in our classrooms.

In "Feminist Rhetorical Historiography and Religion," Lisa Zimmerelli also calls on scholars to rethink our conceptions of religion. To make her case, Zimmerelli traces discussions within feminist rhetorical scholarship on the ethical issues and methodological concerns related to historiography centered on religious communities and religious subjects. She argues that religion is not simply a trope, nor should it be relegated to the private or the unverifiable. It is rather "a primary generator of discourse" and ought to be engaged as such within feminist historiographic scholarship. In addressing the ways that work on feminist historiography and religion is significant to the discipline, Zimmerelli demonstrates how religion as a site of identity can be a fruitful, generative lens for understanding the texts, motivations, and sensibilities of the people studied by scholars of rhetoric. She supports this argument by providing a storiography of Frances Willard. By linking feminist historiographic practices with religion and resisting the reductive treatment of religion, Zimmerelli makes clear that the field has much to gain if qualities characteristic of feminist rhetorical historiography (e.g., reflexivity, inclusivity, diversity) are mobilized in future studies of religious rhetoric.

In "'Joy Anyway!' Narratives of Harm and Flourishing at the Intersections of Religious and LGBTQ+ Rhetorics," T J Geiger II responds to the problem of oft-reductive yet commonplace narratives that construct LGBTQ+ and religious rhetorics as joined only in binary opposition. Writing from a place of rhetorical empathy, Geiger strives to resist either/or thinking regarding the blended forms that sexual and spiritual identities and ideologies might take. By attending to the intersections of queer rhetorics and religious rhetorics in ways that resist oppositional framing, Geiger aims to support efforts to construct narratives that contribute to human flourishing and that acknowledge harm, and he encourages additional scholarship in the areas of researcher positionality through narrative frameworks and of archival or historical projects. Pursuing these lines of inquiry, Geiger argues, can assist scholars and teachers striving to understand potential impediments to, and opportunities for, deliberation within and among different constituencies.

John C. Brereton and Cinthia Gannett's chapter, "'We Are Not Born for Ourselves Alone': Jesuit Rhetoric for the Twenty-First Century," likewise invites us to (re)consider the relationship of Jesuit rhetorics to the field of rhetoric and writing studies. They argue that understanding Jesuit rhetorics offers insight into a vital strand of rhetoric and writing studies' tacit tradition—a legacy that continues to influence our field in generative ways to this day. By tracing the ways that key spiritual pedagogical concepts and practices from the Jesuit tradition inflected the writing and thinking of two luminaries in rhetorical studies—Edward P. J. Corbett and John Bean—Brereton and Gannett make visible the influence of Jesuit rhetorics on modern rhetorical scholarship and teaching. Through their chapter, they reveal how the Catholic imagination and religious worldview that undergird Jesuits rhetorics have played an important role in shaping the consciousness of the field as a whole.

Janice W. Fernheimer's chapter, "Creating Pathways for Ethical (Inter)Actions: New Directions for Jewish Rhetorics," proposes "to-ness" as a historiographic method that scholars of Jewish rhetorics and religious rhetorics more broadly might adopt as a means of building relationships among rhetorical traditions, across both space and time, and creating conversations that consider various traditions in relationship to one another rather than in isolation. Fernheimer argues that to-ness provides a model for enacting ethical relations and research that are not only deeply interconnected and interactive but also geared to recognize rather than write over difference and mutual influence. To-ness provides a basis for Fernheimer's claim that Jewish rhetorics ought to be taught as part of (not apart from) the rhetorical tradition and in relational conversation with other religious traditions and rhetorics for the purpose of educating students and citizens who are equipped to deal ethically with others.

In "Buddhism and Rhetoric Unchained," Kurt Spellmeyer's engagement with another tradition that has garnered too little attention in rhetorical studies also provides a means of reconceptualizing Western, Hellenistic understandings of rhetoric and rhetorical education. Spellmeyer argues that Buddhism might make common cause with posthumanist rhetoricians who hold a pluralism that attributes the multiplicity of our ways with words not to a deficit of knowledge but to the growth of our understanding. Such a perspective undergirds what Spellmeyer calls a pedagogy of the un-commonplace—an approach in which the task of the rhetorical educator is to multiply the opportunities for confusion, misunderstanding, disagreement, and misreading, while at the same time helping students exercise their ability to create a multiverse out of nothing—a feat in the West reserved for God—and then to notice, along the way, just how exciting it is to be alive without foundations.

Rasha Diab's chapter, "Engaging with Arab(ic)-Islamic Religious Rhetorics: Why It Matters to Rhetorical Studies," charts the long-standing invisibility of Arab(ic)-Islamic rhetorics in rhetorical studies. Diab shows how the tapestry of religious rhetorics is misshapen by continued disregard for the unique context of Islām and the rhetorical exigencies of Muslims around the world. In recovering two important strands of Arab(ic)-Islamic rhetorics—*khuṭbah* (oration) and *tafsīr* (exegesis)—Diab highlights the ways that employing appropriate culture-specific definitions in the study of religious rhetoric challenges assumed one-to-one correspondence between Arab(ic)-Islamic rhetorics and Western, Hellenistic rhetorics.

In "Race at the Intersection of Rhetoric and Religion," Andre E. Johnson makes visible the distinctions between African American prophetic rhetorics and Eurocentric definitions of prophetic rhetoric that have been widely adopted in our field. In doing so, Johnson illustrates that accounting for race changes how we understand prophetic rhetoric itself—an argument that has far-reaching implications not only for studies of prophetic rhetorics but for all areas of rhetorical studies.

Our hope is that, taken together, the chapters, with their Entry Points, and the interludes between them encourage scholars to engage with religious rhetorics in ways that help rhetorical studies work toward achieving pluralism.

WORKS CITED

"About Sunday Assembly." *Sunday Assembly*, sundayassembly.online/about-sunday-assembly/. Accessed 21 Sept. 2022.

Asad, Talal. *Formations of the Secular: Christianity, Islam, Modernity*. Stanford UP, 2003.

Berthoff, Ann E. "Introductory Remarks." *College Composition and Communication*, vol. 45, no. 2, 1994, pp. 237–38.

Booth, Wayne C. *My Many Selves: The Quest for a Plausible Harmony*. Utah State UP, 2006.

—. *The Rhetoric of RHETORIC: The Quest for Effective Communication*. Blackwell, 2004.

Braidotti, Rosi. "In Spite of the Times: The Postsecular Turn in Feminism." *Theory, Culture, and Society*, vol. 26, no. 6, 2008, pp. 1–24.

Burke, Kenneth. *The Rhetoric of Religion: Studies in Logology*. U of California P, 1961.

Burton, Tara Isabella. *Strange Rites: New Religions for a Godless World*. Public Affairs, 2020.

Condit, Celeste Michelle. "Post-Burke: Transcending the Substance of Dramatism," *Quarterly Journal of Speech*, vol. 78, 1992, pp. 349–55.

Daniell, Beth. "Composing (as) Power." In "Interchanges: Spiritual Sites of Composing." *College Composition and Communication*, vol. 45, no. 2, 1994, pp. 238–46.

Eck, Diana. "Prospects for Pluralism: Voice and Vision in the Study of Religion." *Journal of the American Academy for Religion*, vol. 75, no. 4, 2007, pp. 743–76.

Feehan, Michael. "Kenneth Burke and Mary Baker Eddy." *Unending Conversations: Writings by and about Kenneth Burke*, edited by Greg Henderson and David Williams, Southern Illinois UP, 2001, pp. 206–24.

Frank, David A. "The Jewish Rhetoric of the Twentieth Century: Chaïm Perelman, *Double Fidélité*, and the Pre-Holocaust Roots of the New Rhetoric Project." *Jewish Rhetorics: History, Theory, Practice*, edited by Michael Bernard-Donals and Janice W. Fernheimer, Brandeis UP, 2014, pp. 77–92.

Habermas, Jürgen. "Notes on a Post-secular Society." *New Perspectives Quarterly*, vol. 25, no. 4, 2008, pp. 17–29.

Holdstein, Deborah. "The Religious Ideology of Composition Studies." *Judaic Perspectives in Rhetoric and Composition*, edited by Deborah Holdstein and Andrea Greenbaum, Hampton Press, 2008, pp. 13–22.

Johnson, Byron, and Jeff Levin. "Religion Is Dying? Don't Believe It." *Wall Street Journal*, 28 July 2022, www.wsj.com/articles/religion-is-dying-dont-believe-it-nones-others-surveys-faith-institutions-atheists-agnostics-practice-minority-11659017037.

Jones, Robert P., and Daniel Cox. "America's Changing Religious Identity: Findings from the 2016 American Values Atlas." Public Religion Research Institute, 2017, www.prri.org/wp-content/uploads/2017/09/PRRI-Religion-Report.pdf.

Kinneavy, James L. *Greek Rhetorical Origins of Christian Faith*. Oxford UP, 1987.

Lauer Rice, Janice. "Walter Ong: A Jesuit Rhetorical and Interdisciplinary Scholar and Educator." *Traditions of Eloquence: The Jesuits and Modern Rhetorical Studies*, edited by Cinthia Gannett and John C. Brereton, Fordham UP, 2016, pp. 188–99.

Marty, Martin E. *When Faiths Collide*. Wiley-Blackwell, 2003.

McLennan, Gregor. "The Post-secular Turn." *Theory, Culture, and Society*, vol. 27, no. 4, 2010, pp. 3–20.

"The Mt. Oread Manifesto of Rhetorical Studies 2013." *Rhetoric Society Quarterly*, vol. 44, no. 1, pp. 1–5. *Taylor & Francis Online*, doi:10.1080/02773945.2014.874871.

Norris, Pippa, and Ronald Inglehart. *Sacred and Secular: Religion and Politics Worldwide*. Cambridge UP, 2012.

Pace, Thomas, and Gina M. Merys. "Paulo Freire and the Jesuit Tradition: Jesuit Rhetoric and Freirean Pedagogy." *Traditions of Eloquence: The Jesuits and Modern Rhetorical Studies*, edited by Cinthia Gannett and John C. Brereton, Fordham UP, 2016, pp. 234–47.

Patel, Eboo. *Interfaith Leadership: A Primer.* Beacon Press, 2016.

Pew Forum on Religion and Public Life. "The Global Religious Landscape: A Report on the Size and Distribution of the World's Major Religious Groups as of 2010." Pew Research Center, 2012. *Pewforum.org*, www.pewforum.org/2012/12/18/global-religious-landscape-exec/.

—. "In U.S., Decline of Christianity Continues at Rapid Pace." Pew Research Center, 2019. *Pewforum.org*, www.pewforum.org/2019/10/17/in-u-s-decline-of-christianity-continues-at-rapid-pace/.

—. "'Nones' on the Rise: One-in-Five Adults Have No Religious Affiliation." Pew Research Center, 2012. *Pewform.org*, www.pewresearch.org/wp-content/uploads/sites/7/2012/10/NonesOnTheRise-full.pdf.

—. "Religious Landscape Study." Pew Research Center, 2015. *Pewform.org*, www.pewforum.org/religious-landscape-study/.

Prothero, Stephen. *Religious Literacy: What Every American Needs to Know—and Doesn't.* HarperOne, 2007.

Putnam, Robert D., and David E. Campbell. *American Grace: How Religion Divides and Unites Us.* Simon & Schuster, 2012.

Spina, Luigi. "Fall and Rise of Religion and Rhetoric." *Rhetorica*, vol. 26, no. 3, 2008, pp. 209–20.

Stenberg, Shari J. "Liberation Theology and Liberatory Pedagogies: Renewing the Dialogue." *College English*, vol. 68, no. 3, 2006, pp. 271–90.

Taylor, Charles. *A Secular Age.* Harvard UP, 2007.

Weaver, Richard. "Language Is Sermonic." *The Rhetorical Tradition*, edited by Patricia Bizzell and Bruce Hertzberg, 2nd ed., Bedford/St. Martin's, 2001, pp. 1351–60.

Wilson, Bryan. *Religion in a Secular Society.* C. A. Watts, 1966.

Zamparutti, Louise. "Plato, Mary Baker Eddy, and Kenneth Burke: Can We Talk about Substance?" *Rhetoric Review*, vol. 37, no. 2, 2018, pp. 199–211.

Zulick, Margaret. "Rhetoric of Religion: A Map of the Territory." *The SAGE Handbook of Rhetorical Studies*, edited Andrea A. Lunsford et al., SAGE, 2008, pp. 125–38.

Section 1. Interrogating Rhetorics

1. To Do Things in a Good (Decolonial) Way

Putting Indigenous Rhetorics and Rhetorics of Religion in Conversation

LISA KING

First, a land acknowledgment: As I write, the land upon which I live and work is part of the traditional territory of the Aniyunwiya peoples (now Eastern Band of Cherokee Indians, Cherokee Nation of Oklahoma, and United Keetoowah Band of Cherokee Indians), Shawnee peoples, and Tsoyaha peoples (Yuchi, Muscogee). It is important I tell you this, remind you of this, because there is no place, no university or college in North or South America[1] that isn't built on Indigenous land. Invisibility and forgetfulness feed colonial tendencies to claim and stereotype Indigenous peoples and cultures, but returning to the history of the land and our relationship to it means we have to see and remember. It's a start.[2]

Now, a story: It's November of 2017. It's Native American Heritage Month in the United States, though the holiday of the month more likely to be observed by most folks is Thanksgiving. I am working from my campus office at the University of Tennessee–Knoxville when I get a peculiar email in my campus account from a stranger asking for a Native American person to read a prayer at a nearby ecumenical Thanksgiving service. Wary—really, ask anyone who is Native or who works in Native American/Indigenous[3] studies what a landmine such a request is—I decide I don't have the energy to give to it at the moment, and I ignore it.[4] Not an hour later, my office phone rings, with the author of the email making their request again, asking insistently for a Native American person to help with their Thanksgiving service. What particular help are you needing, I ask. "I need someone to read a prayer for us. Don't worry, you don't have to come up with anything on your own; we already have a prayer chosen. We just need a Native American to read it." Unsettled and feeling as though we are inching closer to that landmine, I ask if they can send me the text of the prayer, and I tell them I will confer with my Native colleagues on campus and get back to them. "That's fine. I wouldn't ask except the two Native American women who came last year and drummed and sang for us aren't answering my calls. I don't know why."

Dear reader, you might guess where this goes. The text of the prayer was as problematic as one might expect: a generic "Oh, Great Spirit" blessing without tribal affiliation or acknowledgment, with a kernel of truth to it but utterly decontextualized from any source or landbase and reappropriated for an ecumenical Christian celebration of a holiday that many Indigenous peoples, including the Wampanoag, whose ancestors sat at that table in 1621, consider the beginning of physical and cultural genocide. I sat with it for a while, then emailed my two Native colleagues, Julie Reed (Cherokee Nation) and Joy Harjo (Mvskoke Creek); it turns out both of them had received the same email and multiple calls and voicemails with the same request. None of us wanted to touch it, but it had to be addressed. The question was where to begin.

I tell this story to reveal how difficult these conversations can be, especially when well-intentioned non-Native people want to be inclusive of Indigenous lifeways and/or spirituality[5] but lack any context or understanding of Indigenous cultures, histories, traumas, and boundaries. But this story isn't an isolated incident. If anything, it indicates a broader problem, one that exists just as much in the field of rhetoric and composition as it does anywhere else. With this in mind, and in response to the conversations begun at the 2018 "Rhetoric and Religion in the 21st Century" conference, this chapter addresses some crucial beginning points for recognizing Indigenous rhetorical and epistemological practices as a foundational part of the rhetorical traditions of the Americas and as a critical ongoing practice. At the same time, I hope to offer some ideas for how to enact that recognition in a decolonial way that does not violate or enact further colonial violence on Indigenous individuals and communities.

One of the strongest motivations for this collection has been to ask how the study of religious rhetorics enriches the field of rhetorical studies. On this Indigenous land, such a question takes us in two directions: first, one that asks how the very rhetorical frameworks we consider canon or mainstream are themselves always already connected to or existing in conversation with historical religious traditions and epistemologies; and second, one that requires a recognition of the Indigenous epistemological and rhetorical traditions that were already here and are still, and an earnest engagement with the colonial history bound up with all other traditions that have arrived on these shores. While this chapter cannot be exhaustive in tracing these two lines, nonetheless I will provide some interlocking beginning points for discussion.

In the next section, I address the ways that Euro/American and Christian[6] attitudes have and continue to shape the colonial project and how "religion" is framed, on these lands and elsewhere. Next, I discuss how Indigenous ways of knowing and being do not necessarily fit the Western/colonial notion of religion and so remain largely unrecognized or even misrepresented in discussion. Finally, I suggest that what we call "Indigenous rhetorics" are part of past, present, and future Indigenous ways of knowing and being, and that decolonial ways of understanding one another are a beginning point for the meeting of religious rhetorics and Indigenous rhetorics. What I hope is that if we can recognize religious discourse to be a pervasive part of discourse *and* the existence and life of Indigenous rhetorical practices, then I see a way forward that values Indigenous rhetorical practices and seeks to de-link from the violence of the rhetorical erasure of Indigenous peoples in our field and in our classrooms.

Where We've Been: Telling the Hard Truths First

As someone who works from a cultural rhetorics and Indigenous rhetorics orientation, I understand "rhetoric" as meaning-making practices not limited to language, and practices that both make culture and are made by culture (Powell et al.). As such, rhetorical practices and the cultures they make/through which they manifest come to us in recursive spirals as an inheritance both given and chosen. As I frequently remind my students, this tension between what we are born into and what we choose, between what feels set and what we can shape, is a space of potential and is deeply rhetorical in nature. How shall we choose to work with what we have been given, what will we sort out of it, and what will we in turn make with it? And with whom? These choices are rarely made on a purely individual basis, and they connect us to others in a constellation of relationships with varying power dynamics, traditions, and histories.

If we are going to think about what kinds of conversations can be had with or about Indigenous rhetorics in relationship to religious rhetorics, we have to examine the canonical inheritances of our field. More pointedly, we have to understand the ways in which the texts we take for granted as canonical are grounded in cultural frameworks that include religion/spirituality, recognize the ways "religion" and "spirituality" are defined in the first place through those frameworks, and then acknowledge the ways those texts have been adapted for use or designed for use in the colonial project on this continent. Furthermore, we need to recognize the Indigenous rhetorical traditions already existing here, past and present, in order to imagine what kind of conversations could happen. In other words, we need to do the work of understanding our rhetorical, epistemological inheritances, identify our relationships with them, and accept the responsibilities of those relationships and their consequences.

Plenty has already been written on the various ways that religion has played a role in the development of the Greco-Roman/Christian/Euro-American rhetorical tradition (traditions?). A cursory look at the table of contents of and introduction to the grad-student-dubbed "rhetorical bible" of the field, *The Rhetorical Tradition* (Bizzell and Herzberg), demonstrates the ways in which the field traces itself from antiquity to the present and how frequently religious discourse is a part of that work. Laurent Pernot reminds us that the Greco-Roman rhetorical tradition was part of religious discourse at the time, and a look at Paul Lynch and Matthew Miller's published bibliography "Twenty-Five Years of Faith in Writing" demonstrates the deeply embedded nature of more recent religious discourse as rhetorical discourse inside and outside our classrooms. Arguably, even texts such as Enlightenment-era treatises and other scientific studies still bear the mark of religious forebears, in the sense that explicit or implicit definition against a religious tradition is still using it as a kind of yardstick, and so the relationship—however fraught—is still there.

I admit to painting with a broad brush, but as Lynch and Miller observe, there is an emerging pattern: because culture and religion intertwine, much if not all of the recorded rhetorical work we preserve is actually linked in some way to religious frameworks, and the vast majority of contemporary work on this intersection of rhetoric/writing and religion, especially at present, primarily deals with various iterations of Christianity. Furthermore, we can make the argument that the relationship between rhetoric and religion flows in both directions; we can say that the rhetorical tradition is inclusive of religious acts and texts, but we must also acknowledge that religious frameworks make a tremendous impact on political and secular discourses.

Indigenous peoples know this connection between European and Euro-American cultures and religion in intimate, violent, and centuries-old ways. The habits of mind supporting colonialism regularly demonized, dismissed, exploited, marginalized, and even desired to eradicate Indigenous peoples as impediments to European-style civilization. Such actions were and are supported by the narrative that Euro-American and Christian ways of knowing and being are the only legitimate ones, and therefore all other frameworks must be brought into line or eliminated. For example, from the journals of Christopher Columbus to the early documents from the Plimoth colony in Massachusetts, we see a repeated pattern of European explorers and colonists who claim that the Indigenous communities they meet have no "real" religion and as such are blank slates on which Christianity should be written or, worse, are creatures of the devil, even as those colonists exploit Indigenous peoples for land and natural resources. As Roy Harvey Pearce documents in *Savagism and Civilization: A Study of the Indian and the American Mind*, the shifting ideological framework through which Europeans and Euro-American settler colonists understood the

"Indian" was heavily influenced by religious—primarily Christian—discourses. Furthermore, Robert F. Berkhofer provides his own reading of European and Euro-American ideological framing of Indigenous peoples in *White Man's Indian: Images of the American Indian from Columbus to the Present*, observing how the rhetorical image of the "Indian" changes across time according to the need of the settler colonists, from needing a spiritual evil as a foil for Christian piety to the hopeless noble savage as a foil for the inevitable march of progress and civilization. While neither of these texts has been updated since the 1980s, they both provide crucial perspectives from the long view of history and reveal the ways in which the stereotypes that contemporary non-Native mainstream culture maintains about Indigenous peoples are not accidental and have deep roots. Much current scholarship on Indigenous representation builds on their work.

Regardless of the rhetorical intentions behind the construction and reconstruction of the "Indian" for Euro-American purposes, and the efforts of some clergy, politicians, and activists over time to counteract policy emerging from those constructions, the rhetorical effects have been devastating. The papal bulls of 1455 and 1493 enshrined European Catholic/Christian rights to capture, enslave, and vanquish all non-Christians, that is, "Saracens and pagans" ("Romanus Pontifex"), take their territories, and then furthermore Christianize them as their lands and goods were taken ("Inter Caetera"). These papal bulls also established precedent for colonization, as their intents were to address the growing rivalry between Spain and Portugal for dominance outside Europe, especially in the Caribbean and North and South America. The "Doctrine of Discovery" developed from these bulls, or the right to claim lands not occupied by Christians (and therefore *terra nullius*), became one of the driving forces of colonial policy across the Americas, including other European and British colonizers, Protestant and Catholic. Much of Indian removal policy is tied to this ideological framework.[7]

Conquering and accumulating Indigenous lands were not the only results of colonization, however. Indigenous ways of living and being were also documented, derided, and attacked as inferior or barbarous at best and Satanic or interfering with the progress of civilization at worst. The imposition of Christian belief from a variety of denominations and churches was assumed by many missionaries to be an obligation in the name of their understanding of God, with the obliteration of Indigenous belief and the reshaping of Indigenous cultures in the image of Euro-American Christian civilization as the goal.

At the Carlisle Indian Industrial School and other boarding schools, to "kill the Indian, and save the man" was the explicit goal (Pratt), accomplished by removing Indigenous children from their parents and forbidding the speaking of Indigenous languages and enactment of ceremony in order to Christianize and civilize (Child; Newland). In these schools and at other mission sites, individual Indigenous cultural protocols regarding gender roles were replaced with Euro-American Christian concepts of gender, depriving Indigenous women, Two-Spirit people, and a range of other genders of their traditional roles and authority within tribal communities (Anderson). The balance of Indigenous communities was often entirely upended, and governance and kinship networks damaged or destroyed. Linguistic documentation of Native languages by the Bureau of American Ethnology (BAE) in the late nineteenth century was used as evidence of a fundamental difference in mind and capability between Indigenous peoples and Euro-Americans, "bolster[ing] racialized theories of cultural evolution and ultimately served as a foundation for the BAE's uneven evaluation of religious myths, rituals, and healing practices" (Dees 197).[8]

The outright banning of Indigenous ceremonial and cultural practices in the United States developed from a series of laws called the "Indian Religious Crimes Code" at the Bureau of Indian Affairs in 1883, and Indigenous ceremonial practices were codified as criminal offenses in 1892 in the "Rules for Indian Courts" by Commissioner of Indian Affairs Thomas J. Morgan (Irwin 295–96). Ceremonial and sacred objects and regalia were frequently confiscated as a penalty in addition to withholding of rations and/or imprisonment should a Native person be caught, and Indian agents sometimes amassed collections of artifacts that they kept for themselves or sold to collectors. Today, federal and state governments still regulate who may have possession of items such as eagle feathers or other animal parts used in regalia or ceremony.

Even for Indigenous communities that accepted or blended Christianity as part of their way of life, no protection was guaranteed; from the Gnadenhutten Massacre—the deliberate execution of nearly a hundred men, women, and children from a Christianized Moravian Delaware community in 1782—to the removal of the Cherokee and other four Civilized Tribes of the U.S. Southeast in the 1830s, the rhetorical intention in its many guises and approaches was to eliminate the "Indian Problem" through disappearing or reshaping Indigenous belief and life into something more closely resembling U.S. Christian denominations and making Indigenous bodies disappear as visibly Indigenous (or just completely). As Lee Irwin puts it, "this strategy of accommodation proved to be primarily a one-way accommodation. . . . [W]hile Native groups struggled to adapt or accommodate invading Anglo-Europeans, this accommodation was rarely if ever reciprocated" (297).

The laws prohibiting the exercise of Indigenous belief and ceremony were not repealed until nearly a century later in 1978 with the American Indian Religious

Freedom Act (Irwin 295–96). Yet that significant change has not allowed Indigenous peoples the full ability to participate in their own cultures. For example, access to sacred sites is limited or outright prohibited when they are cordoned off behind the borders of government lands or destroyed in development projects. Vine Deloria Jr. observes across multiple court cases that state and federal governments have consistently sided with developers:

> In *Sequoyah* the Tennessee Valley Authority flooded sacred Cherokee sites, in *Badoni* the Glen Canyon Dam flooded Rainbow Bridge and made it possible to have a floating marina bar for tourists . . . thereby destroying the atmosphere necessary for conducting Navajo ceremonies. In *Fools Crow* the state of South Dakota made a tourist attraction out of Bear Butte . . . in *Inupiat* the development of off-shore oil in the Arctic has impaired the conducting of ceremonies. In *Wilson* the development of a ski resort has inhibited ceremonies performed by Navajo and Hopi religious practitioners. (*American Indian Policy* 226)

In the *Lyng v. Northwest Indian Cemetery Protective Association* (1988) decision, the Supreme Court found that "because Native petitioners were neither coerced into violating their religious beliefs nor denied benefits enjoyed by other citizens, the First Amendment need not apply, especially because '[w]hatever rights the Indians may have to the use of the area . . . do not divest the Government of its right to use what is, after all, its land'" (*Lyng* qtd. in General). Though subsequent laws, such as the Native American Graves Protection and Repatriation Act, do provide some support to Indigenous peoples to have some sacred sites and burial grounds protected, to date there is no comprehensive legal protection for Indigenous peoples equal to the First Amendment. In other words, everyone except Indigenous peoples has freedom of religion.

The 2007 "United Nations Declaration on the Rights of Indigenous Peoples" presented a worldwide outline for the protection and support of Indigenous peoples, and Article 12 presents very clear language about the protection of Indigenous spiritual and ceremonial practices: "Indigenous peoples have the right to manifest, practise [*sic*], develop and teach their spiritual and religious traditions, customs and ceremonies; the right to maintain, protect, and have access in privacy to their religious and cultural sites; the right to the use and control of their ceremonial objects; and the right to the repatriation of their human remains." Though UNDRIP is not legally binding (see "UNDRIP FAQ"), it provides a guiding framework to address the human rights violations that various governments worldwide have perpetuated and continue to perpetuate against Indigenous nations and communities in various ways. The United States and

Canada did not immediately support the declaration, and while they have come somewhat closer to doing so, the Trump administration has shown a general disregard for UNDRIP or laws protecting sacred sites. From its green-lighting of the Dakota Access Pipeline in Standing Rock over the protests of the Standing Rock Sioux Nation and more than a hundred supporting Indigenous nations and legal frameworks requiring archaeological and environmental guidelines ("Standing Rock Syllabus"; McKenna), to the attempted sale of gas and oil leases in Bears Ears National Park, a site regarded as sacred cultural ground for the Hopi Tribe, Navajo Nation (Diné), Ute Mountain Ute Tribe, Pueblo of Zuni, and Ute Indian Tribe ("Bears Ears"), current politics concerning land and Indigenous rights to the sacred follow well-established colonial patterns.

In just this short summary, we can see the intertwining of religion and culture and racial constructs, enacted through various texts and acts, in ways that extend back centuries and deeply shade the history of this continent. I know that, again, in this small space, I am sketching broadly. Every Indigenous community and nation has its own interactions and history with the ensuing physical and cultural colonization and fight for rights and culture and lands, and those details should be recognized. It is also true that sometimes for a generation a Euro-American community and Indigenous community could live in relative peace, but there are many more stories of horror and destruction. I address these difficult truths because without that recognition, there is no way forward.

Where We Need to Go: Recognize and Decolonize

The historical thumbnail in the previous pages is necessary because without context, it is far too easy to overlook Indigenous peoples' understandings of the sacred or co-opt them into the Euro-American framework of "religion." Returning to Lynch and Miller's bibliography, we see virtually nothing on the subject of Indigenous practices related to lifeways or spirituality. There are several reasons for this, and I don't pretend to list them all, but a few come immediately to mind:

1. Indigenous sacred, ceremonial, or spiritual practices do not fit the Euro-American framework of religion and thus have (as seen above) been banned or stigmatized in favor of Euro-American-sponsored religion or have not often been recognized in their own right, on their terms. Many Indigenous languages do not even have a word for "religion" as such.

2. There is such a wide variety of Indigenous sacred, ceremonial, or spiritual practices and beliefs that it is dangerous to lump them together as merely "Indian," as if all Indigenous peoples and communities in the United States or North America or worldwide are equivalent.
3. Often protocol means that certain stories, practices, or ceremonies are not for public consumption, and so no one should be writing about them at all. While historically the European and American scholarly pursuit of knowledge has claimed that nothing should be beyond its investigation, many Indigenous peoples argue otherwise. Scholars are not entitled to have access to or know all the things.
4. When Indigenous people have written about the sacred or spiritual as protocol permits (see Vine Deloria Jr., Paula Gunn Allen, Robin Wall Kimmerer, and others), because it doesn't look "religious," it is categorized as anthropological/ethnographic or creative work. Too often these tellings are relegated to *mere* "stories" (as in fairy tales or children's stories), primitive relics, or a specific creative writing genre. Or sometimes the only way to get an audience to take it seriously in any way is fitting it into those categories (trying to publish as a Native person is a whole other discussion).

We can look to some of the more recent debates in the field of religious studies to understand some of these conflicts. Religious studies has emerged from the same European and Euro-American frameworks that produced contemporary rhetorical studies. As a result, religious studies has many of the same issues. Native American and Indigenous practices have not received the same kind of attention as the so-called Big Five (Christianity, Islam, Buddhism, Hinduism, and Judaism) but instead have remained outliers in study from the conceptual point of view of "world religions." Earlier attempts to document Indigenous practices and languages fell under the purview of anthropology departments, and there is a well-established history of how these attempts at documentation were generally carried out from a Euro-American point of view and often led to exploitive relationships with Indigenous communities. Some contemporary scholars in religious studies have made the argument for broader conceptions of world religions, arguing that scholars should move past the Big Five in the name of diversity and inclusion, and for challenging labels such as "primitive" or "primal" (for example, see Cox). Others, like Tomoko Masuzawa, have challenged the notion of inclusion in existing paradigms to examine the very notion of "religion" itself as a European and Euro-American frame that, by default, cannot contain the world. Recent discussions about the impact of ethnic studies on religious studies indicate that Masuzawa's line of thinking may be finally taking root: rising scholars are challenging the idea of what "religion" is, even as they tackle the fraught intersections of colonialism, imperialism, and religion as it was and is defined from a European and Euro-American perspective. As scholar Tiffany Hale puts it, colonization has taken a great deal from Native peoples, "[b]ut the study of religion can offer an ethical approach for dealing with these complicated issues of colonization, missionization, and history—they're all tied together. What religious studies can do, when done well, is to expose that process of exploitation, tie it into the broader story of settler colonization, and push to ask different questions." (qtd. in Borja) Those different questions would undoubtedly include serious consideration of the role of colonialism, imperialism, and settler colonization as a routine part of thinking about Indigenous lifeways and all religious traditions.

In short, the field has not yet fully worked with Indigenous peoples' understandings of the world, but the frame of "religion" doesn't really fit. Some argue for inclusion, others feel that Indigenous-guided scholarship is the way forward (Irwin), and there are other perspectives that warn of the violation of sacred spaces and practices that should not welcome voyeuristic academic exploitation. The conversation must happen cautiously, and carefully, especially given the destruction done by Christianity and other complicit religions in various forms.

Another complicating factor is the sheer variety of experience. There is no one "Indian" religion. At the time of this writing, we are talking about 573 federally recognized tribes in the United States alone, plus state-recognized tribal communities, and all the variety within and across those communities and nations. We are also talking about a range of experiences with settler colonial religions, particularly Christianity, which have produced a significant assortment of individual, community, and cultural approaches to belief and practice, including the Native American Church, reservation and urban church communities with relationships to mainstream Christian denominations, and other personal and community blendings. Powwows have provided support for broad discussions and expressions of pan-Indigenous beliefs and concepts, especially as those beliefs are embodied in dances that began as tribally specific but traveled and have become rooted on the powwow circuit (Kelley). And intertribal political movements have provided the foundation for intertribal traditionalism to emerge as a unifying force across Indigenous communities and nations (Treat). All of this is to say, to speak of "Indian religion" is to do no one and nothing justice, and the complexities, continuities, and specificities of Indigenous beliefs and practices, past and present, must be recognized in their singularities and in their constellations of relationships.

Yet this is what we can say: if the study of religious rhetorics and the rhetorics of religion wants to exist in any ethically meaningful way in relationship to Indigenous peoples, then decolonization as a practice must be the very foundation of what we do.

But what is "decolonization," or its relation, "decoloniality"? The origins of "decolonization" as a concept entailed the removal of a colonizing force (the British leaving India, for example), but the implication of simply unplugging or de-bugging a system did not hold. Walter Mignolo observes that the decolonization project of the Cold War era was only partly successful,[9] because those Indigenous people with privilege who came to power simply reinforced the colonial structures, "but in the name of [Indigenous] national sovereignty" (Coughlin). This left many colonial structures and attitudes more or less intact but now with Indigenous actors supporting them to the same ends, not transformed ends (Mignolo qtd. in Coughlin). Furthermore, North and South America (as with other parts of the world) currently exist in a paracolonial situation, in which the colonizing force isn't going back to its origins. There is no way to excise it. Instead, *decoloniality* "denotes ways of thinking, knowing, being, and doing that began with, but also precede, the colonial enterprise and invasion. It implies the recognition and undoing of the hierarchical structures of race, gender, heteropatriarchy, and class that continue to control life, knowledge, spirituality, and thought" (Walsh 17). Decoloniality therefore gives us a name for the process of making Western rationality and Christian theologies visible as only one option among many, not the only option; it also points us toward "de-linking" from the logics of colonialism as they manifest today (Mignolo qtd. in Coughlin).[10] It is not simply a new theory to be picked up and placed among other ways of reading or analyzing; it is a fundamental shift in thinking. As Walsh puts it, "decoloniality seeks to make visible, open up, and advance radically distinct perspectives and positionalities that displace Western rationality as the only framework and possibility of existence, analysis, and thought" (17). That is, the work of decoloniality and decolonizing calls the entire colonial project and all its associated theories into question and requires that we sort through every theoretical frame and perspective for its complicity in the colonial enterprise and then seek a different way to be and do that does not perpetuate those hierarchies.

Therefore, *Indigenous* decolonization, as the term has been picked up and put to new use, recognizes decoloniality as the beginning point and then the process of decolonization as "an ongoing, radical resistance against colonialism that includes struggles for land redress, self-determination, healing historical trauma, cultural continuance, and reconciliation" (Driskill 69); it is a "goal but not an endpoint" (Ritskes); and for Indigenous communities and nations it means finding ways through "everyday acts of resurgence" to reconnect to land, culture, and community in the ongoing conditions and structures of colonialism as they manifest today (Corntassel 88). In academia it does not necessarily mean, Linda Tuhiwai Smith observes, "a total rejection of all theory or research or Western knowledge. Rather, it is about centring [*sic*] our [Indigenous] concerns and world views and then coming to know and understand theory and research from our own perspectives and for our own purposes" (41). Or as Shawn Wilson puts it in *Research Is Ceremony: Indigenous Research Methods*, it's about beginning from Indigenous perspectives, ontologies, epistemologies so that we approach any research work as a series of relationships from which we derive our understanding of ourselves and our world. Therefore, research is also a series of responsibilities that hold us accountable to one another so that we may act in reciprocity. Additionally, there are powerful examples specific to this collection concerning how this happens in work by scholars (frequently Indigenous themselves) in religious studies; for example, the recent edited collection titled *Native American Rhetoric* (Gross) covers multiple ways of understanding culturally specific spiritual practices *as* rhetorical practices from within Indigenous communities. In sum, decolonization work has to do with Indigenous peoples reorienting themselves to and reclaiming connections to language, culture, community, and land, sometimes in confrontation with colonizing forces and sometimes by turning inward toward their communities.[11]

For non-Indigenous peoples, decoloniality and decolonization have to do with supporting these efforts on Indigenous peoples' own terms and assisting in the radical reimagining of possibilities, but not on the terms of broader social justice movements or civil rights (though there may be relationships between them). Eve Tuck and K. Wayne Yang warn us, "decolonization is not a metaphor." It is not a trendy buzzword or the theory du jour, and Tuck and Yang point out how easy it is for decolonization to become superficially appropriated into or made equivalent with other social justice work. Instead, we must be ever aware and critical of the ways in which all of us participate in colonizing structures and take action to change that, or Indigenous concerns are again erased. "The easy absorption, adoption, and transposing of decolonization is yet another form of settler appropriation," they argue, but "solidarity is an uneasy, reserved, and unsettled matter that neither reconciles present grievances nor forecloses future conflict" (Tuck and Yang 3). It means getting comfortable with sitting in discomfort and being willing to try and fail and try again and to understand the work as a process, not a checklist. I discuss this more below.

Why This Matters: Finding Wiser Options

If we use decoloniality as a guiding principle in thinking about how rhetorics of religion and Indigenous rhetorics may meet, then it makes sense to understand them in terms of their relationship via colonial/paracolonial frameworks. This would mean understanding the participation of colonizer/settler religious rhetorics, particularly of Christian religious rhetorics, in terms of colonization and its ongoing impact on Indigenous peoples in all its shapes and nuances. Such an approach would also recognize the multiplicity of ways Indigenous individuals, communities, and nations articulate their own ways of knowing and understanding the world in terms of "religion" or "spirituality" but not limited to those frameworks or terms. Indigenous decolonization applied here would mean reorienting any discussion of religious rhetorics per se to the terms and ways of knowing a given Indigenous individual, community, or nation would use to describe themselves, and I would go so far as to suggest that means explicitly giving up the notion of religious rhetorics just as Masuzawa has argued elsewhere. Or if the term is kept, we understand it to apply to cultures that use the term "religion" and not to all cultures and communities everywhere. Furthermore, in line with Smith and Wilson's work, any research or work done with—and not "on"—Indigenous peoples would need to be reciprocal and mutually beneficial.

These principles sound good in theory and are much more difficult in practice. Academic systems, after all, are paracolonial systems, and "research" and "pedagogy" as projects have their epistemological roots in the very paradigms that decolonial work would resist, change, or overturn. Universities are notorious for using "diversity and inclusion" programming as a way to superficially treat systemic racism and colonialism without addressing the roots in terms of how research is carried out or what and how we teach our students or how administrative structures recognize some kinds of work and people and delegitimize others, or how our institutions are literally built on Indigenous lands and all the history that entails; our institutions are nearly always physical and epistemological intrusions.

This does not mean that decolonizing work cannot be done, but it does mean that when taken up, decolonizing work in the university means disrupting the ways we think, write, act, teach, and hire. It means thinking beyond the university, supporting community-based and public-facing work, and building relationships beyond the ivory tower, not for profit but for mutual support. It means facing the hard histories of who we are in relationship to one another and trying to do better, not based on what the historically privileged party thinks is "doing better," but rather on whether or not everyone's needs are being met and justice is being done.

In "Oratory on Oratory," Lee Maracle describes the Stó:lo process of "study" as a method for bringing communities, colonizer/settler and Indigenous, together to do the honest, hard, and painful work of communicating with one another. The making of story together, she observes, is a powerful approach to keep colonial stories from erasing Indigenous ones, but it is uncomfortable. It hurts. It requires us to sit, to remove our masks (our preconceptions, our usual filters), and listen and, when we encounter an idea that is painful, to track back to the origins of that pain in order to understand it. I think this is exactly the kind of conversation that needs to be had, or the concept of working together that can be used as a guidepost. It's work we all have to do. And having "storied that up," as I hope I have begun to help do here, we can take action.

For those preparing to engage with Indigenous rhetorics on these sensitive topics, the first step is to do the self-education to perceive their masks in the first place. This is precisely what didn't happen with the person who asked me to say a prayer on Thanksgiving. In answer to their query, Joy, Julie, and I first explained why an uncritical use of the "found" prayer would hurt more than it would help, and in its stead we crafted a land-acknowledgment-as-prayer for them to use:

> In an attitude of thanks and contrition, we recognize the indigenous peoples of this land, without whom the first Europeans here would have perished. We are the strangers here, befriended, and history reminds us we have rarely held up our obligations to that friendship or to the land itself. While today we gather in thanks, we also remember the harms and wrongs done, the promises broken, and the long road ahead to make ourselves the friends in this land we should have been. We recommit ourselves to recognizing the Cherokee and Muskogee peoples of this place in East Tennessee, and to recognizing the ways in which the land itself requires care in return for what it gives us. So may it be.

Joy also suggested her poem "Perhaps the World Ends Here" as part of the service (Harjo), though she declined to go there to read it; after all, she did not want the burden of being the "representative Indian."

What we tried to do here was help the caller see the narrative frame of appropriation for a Christian service that, while it wished to be inclusive, still enacted a kind of colonial violence by its very assumption that Thanksgiving means the same thing to everyone, and more so because the caller wished to have an "Indian" for spiritual decoration, not a dialogue, and certainly not as a survivor of colonial violence. The land-acknowledgment-as-prayer was the first step to reorient attendees to the history of the holiday and the long painful history enacted on this land. Moreover, there was still the possibility of friendship based on a new co-constructed narrative that begins with the land and Indigenous peoples, the acknowledgment of ongoing Indigenous presence, and a desire to acknowledge and put right historical wrongs. That was the decolonial possibility of the moment. We only hope they took it up. The caller thanked us for our email, suggested perhaps we ought to work together on a future project, and then . . . we never heard back.

Entry Points for Scholarship, Teaching, and Changing the Whole System

To be honest, I do not feel comfortable claiming that I teach this practice as religious rhetorics. Instead, I teach my students about Indigenous rhetorics, arguably another word for enacting lifeways, and I would argue that keeping this attention to land and respectful learning about individual histories and Indigenous traditions—not invasively—is one way to start. One key way to self-educate and to challenge colonial structures, if done well and thoughtfully, is the land acknowledgment. A land acknowledgment is a statement made at the opening of an event or gathering that pays tribute to and honors the land's original Indigenous peoples and the complex histories that got us all here today. "Acknowledgment is a simple, powerful way of showing respect and a step toward correcting the stories and practices that erase Indigenous people's history and culture and toward inviting and honoring the truth" (U.S. Department of Arts and Culture), and acknowledgment is becoming more common at sports events, academic conferences, and universities.

But like any gesture, it is easy for a short statement to become a superficial nod with little lasting impact. In the context of the university, and in the name of building better relationships that operate from an Indigenous epistemological perspective, a land acknowledgment done well requires the following:

1. Putting in the work to acquaint yourself with the history of the land you and your university are on, including treaty histories.
2. Recognizing the ways in which the land is not property but is itself the living foundation of Indigenous cultures wherever a given culture lives and has its being. (See Vine Deloria Jr.'s *For This Land* for an excellent cross-section of his work on the intersections among the land, Indigenous peoples, U.S. law, and Christianity; Robin Wall

Kimmerer's *Braiding Sweetgrass* provides an ethnobotanist's meditation on being in relationship with the land and what that means for all of us to live honorably.)

3. To avoid the trap of the token gesture, you can address some questions: "All settlers, including recent arrivants, have a responsibility to consider what it means to acknowledge the history and legacy of colonialism. What are some of the privileges settlers enjoy today because of colonialism? How can individuals develop relationships with peoples whose territory they are living on in the contemporary Canadian [and U.S.] geopolitical landscape? What are you, or your organization, doing beyond acknowledging the territory where you live, work, or hold your events?" (Native Land Digital).
4. In addition to the sources I've already named, consulting resources and Indigenous perspectives on what works well for reciprocal scholarship, teaching, and land acknowledgments and what does not, such as Debbie Reese's post on land acknowledgments (Reese) and Native Land Digital's full post on the subject.

Done well, the process of creating and then using a land acknowledgment can be transformative and can support the work of calling attention to and changing paracolonial frameworks.

In terms of practical steps, Nayantara Sheoran Appleton makes some thoughtful suggestions as an immigrant working on Indigenous land in Aotearoa (New Zealand), particularly for how to build toward a decolonized future in a fully paracolonial academy and how not to claim decolonization when we are far from it. Her list for beginning this work includes the following, with my own additions.

"*Diversify your syllabus and curriculum*": This is going to take more than an extra reading or two. This means fundamentally reorienting your syllabus to start with the land you are on, providing a diversity of materials from a variety of perspectives, and thinking about how these changes could be implemented across courses. A token reading, a token course is not enough. Use that land acknowledgment, too, and help your students connect it to the class.

"*Digress from the cannon* [sic]": This means going beyond the Big Five. It also means going beyond readings with the frame of religion or spirituality per se. For example, perhaps a unit on Standing Rock and the #NoDAPL protests as a sacred space that is specific to the Standing Rock Sioux but also an open space that welcomed other Indigenous nations and non-Indigenous peoples (including clergy from a variety of denominations) could be a start. (See "Standing Rock Syllabus.")

"*Decentre* [sic] *knowledge and knowledge production*": While scholarly sources can be useful, make use of Indigenous social media, YouTube, and tribal websites to help educate students. Support protests and local events sponsored by Indigenous communities. If you have contacts with your local tribal community, look to them (but also be prepared to financially support any speaker or contributor—don't ask them to labor for you for free).

"*Devalue hierarchies*": Start with yourself. Start with your institution. Assume a position of humility and learning and think in terms of relationships in order to take apart hierarchy. "At every stage, we have to ask ourselves, am I fulfilling my responsibilities to my relationships? Is this of benefit to the [Indigenous] community? Am I being true to my values? Am I being true to the values and wishes of the communities with whom I'm working? Is this research [or teaching] enacting an ethics of care?" (Wilson and Hughes 13). If you want to teach the work of a specific Indigenous scholar or speaker and you'd like them to visit, extend the invitation, be willing to answer all questions about your class/program, and center the invitation on giving them space to talk about what is important to them in relationship to lifeways/spirituality in a way that is comfortable to them. Be willing to support their visit financially. Don't ask them to talk about a specific ritual or ceremony and also be willing to hear the word "no." Any effort a speaker makes to come to your class will involve extra emotional labor on their part, and they may not have it to give you.

"*Disinvest from citational power structures*": Read the work of Indigenous scholars and community members. Listen to them. Learn from them. Cite them in whatever genre they are communicating. Specific to our field, engage with the work of Indigenous scholars and allies in rhetoric and composition even if it doesn't immediately look like it's discussing religion.

"*Diminish some voices and opinions in meetings, while magnifying others*": Pay attention to who is in the room, who gets to speak, and if the rest of the room is actually listening and taking up the suggestions of the most vulnerable who are present. This may also apply to your classrooms, where the dominant—even aggressive—voices will try to derail or delegitimize the discussion as the masks come off. This also applies to representation in organizational and administrative structures.

Perhaps for my purposes here, her suggestion to "design classes that have a '?' at the end of the title" is especially powerful. While it seems trivial, a class called "Religious Rhetorics?" with the question mark sets the stage for a different kind of discussion that does not immediately presume colonial hierarchies.

These suggestions are only the beginning, and I offer them to you the same way that Julie, Joy, and I offered the Thanksgiving caller a way to begin. I hope this is not the end of the story. I hope that there are ways we can build a better discussion between our communities, one in which good decolonial work can be done. I think it is possible, but much depends on you, dear reader. Please take this piece of the story, and carry it with you, for the sake of telling the hard truths and for making something better, together.

NOTES

1. The purview for this chapter is North America, but the same argument can be made for Central and South America, Polynesia, Micronesia, Australia, Africa, and elsewhere, more or less wherever European colonists have traveled, taking their own culture and religion with them.

2. I want to say a tremendous thank-you, *anushiik*, to my colleagues who have helped me in this project: Kristin Arola, Jill Hodges, Andrea Riley Mukavetz, Sarah Dees, Bernice Olivas, Christina Cedillo, Lydia Presley, and Caitlyn McKay; a particular thank-you to Joy Harjo and Julie Reed for their permission and support in telling the Thanksgiving caller story.

3. A quick explanation of names and naming: I use "Native American" to refer to Indigenous peoples in the United States, "Indigenous" more broadly to encompass North America as a continent since communities in Canada and Mexico have their own preferred general labels (for example, First Nations or Aboriginal), and wherever possible I use tribally specific names. Typically, tribally specific names are preferred.

4. To clarify: my move here is one that many have had to make to protect their time and energy in order to prevent being overwhelmed. It's not uncommon for sudden demands on Native American/Indigenous faculty members' time to emerge from Columbus Day/Indigenous Peoples Day all the way through Native American Heritage Month and Thanksgiving, and too often the request is actually an afterthought that requires a great deal of extra work on the part of the person being asked, with zero compensation and on a very short timeline. Frankly, it's frequently exploitive—hence my initial move to set it aside. Carefully made, mutually beneficial requests with enough lead time are a different matter.

5. Terminology is difficult here: "religion" and "spirituality" because they are concepts that do not necessarily reflect how Native American and Indigenous individuals, communities, and nations see their relationships with the world(s) around

them. I use "lifeways" here as something more all-encompassing and as a term I have seen Indigenous communities use; I include "spirituality" here as a commonplace for non-Native audiences, but please recognize that the term is only a tentative placeholder, as I address later.

6. When I use "Euro/American" I refer to peoples and cultures whose origins are or were European and who embarked on colonization around the globe and their descendants in the Americas, though in this article I am focusing primarily on North America. If a person born in North America is of European descent, then they are "Euro-American." Similarly, when I use "Christian" I am referring to all of the Christian traditions, sects, and denominations that are too numerous to list individually and that have participated in the colonial project, either officially through alliances with governments or in their individual missions, theologies, and attitudes toward Indigenous peoples. While other religious traditions—Judaism, Islam, etc.—can be complicit, the history of the United States is most thickly woven with Christian traditions of various iterations, and so is my focus here.

7. See also Harp for a good recorded discussion with Kim Tallbear, Candis Callison, Ken Williams, Brock Pitawanakwat, and Taté Walker.

8. Dees cites multiple excerpts from the work of the first director of the Bureau of Ethnology (later Bureau of American Ethnology), Major John Wesley Powell, such as this erroneous assessment of human development: "The age of savagery is the age of sentence words; the age of barbarism the age of phrase words; the age of civilization the age of idea words. In savagery, picture writings are used; in barbarism hieroglyphs; in civilization, alphabets. In savagery, there is no verb 'to be;' in barbarism there is no verb 'to read;' in civilization, verbs are resolved into parts of speech. In savagery, beast polytheism prevails; in barbarism, nature polytheism; in civilization, monotheism. In savagery, a wolf is an oracular god; in barbarism, it is a howling beast; in civilization, it is a connecting link in systemic zoology. In savagery, the powers of nature are feared as evil demons; in barbarism, the powers of nature are worshiped as gods; in civilization, the powers of nature are apprenticed servants" (qtd. in Dees [original source: Powell, J. W. "From Barbarism to Civilization." *American Anthropologist*, vol. 1, no. 2, 1888, pp. 97–123. Quotation taken from pp. 121–22]).

9. This "decolonization project" refers to the vast reorganization of power in the aftermath of World War II, when historically colonizing countries—the United States, Belgium, Great Britain, the Netherlands, France, Japan, and Portugal, for example—began a process of both forced and voluntary separation from their colonies in Africa, Asia, and the Caribbean. Note that the United States, once a series of colonies that declared independence from Britain, has a history as a colonizing force itself.

10. See also his work in Mignolo, *Darker Side*.

11. I want to acknowledge here the work of my colleagues, including Jo Hsu, Vani Kannan, Lisa Bailey, Christina Cedillo Perez, Joyce Rain Anderson, Andrea Riley

Mukavetz, and the excellent conversation they facilitated when I posed the question of what "decoloniality" and "decolonization" as terms meant to scholars in rhetoric and composition to my Facebook wall on October 7, 2019 ("Academic hive mind: On 'decoloniality' and 'decolonization'"). I'm grateful to my community.

WORKS CITED

Allen, Paula Gunn. *Sacred Hoop: Recovering the Feminine in American Indian Traditions.* Beacon Press, 1986.

Anderson, Kim. *A Recognition of Being: Reconstructing Native Womanhood.* Sumach Press, 2000.

Appleton, Nayantara Sheoran. "Do Not 'Decolonize' . . . If You Are Not Decolonizing: Progressive Language and Planning beyond a Hollow Academic Rebranding." *Critical Ethnic Studies* blog, 4 Feb. 2019, www.criticalethnicstudiesjournal.org/blog/2019/1/21/do-not-decolonize-if-you-are-not-decolonizing-alternate-language-to-navigate-desires-for-progressive-academia-6y5sg.

"Bears Ears Inter-Tribal Coalition: Who We Are." *Bears Ears Inter-Tribal Coalition,* 2019, bearsearscoalition.org/about-the-coalition/. Accessed 16 Sept. 2019.

Berkhofer, Robert F. *The White Man's Indian: Images of the American Indian from Columbus to the Present.* Vintage Books, 1978.

Bizzell, Patricia, and Bruce Herzberg, editors. *The Rhetorical Tradition: Readings from Classical Times to the Present.* 2nd ed., Bedford/St. Martin's, 2000.

Borja, Melissa. "How Has Ethnic Studies Changed American Religious Studies?" Anxious Bench Blog, 4 Apr. 2019, *Patheos,* www.patheos.com/blogs/anxiousbench/2019/04/how-has-ethnic-studies-changed-american-religious-studies/.

Child, Brenda. *Boarding School Seasons: American Indian Families, 1900–1940.* U of Nebraska P, 2000.

Corntassel, Jeff. "Re-envisioning Resurgence: Indigenous Pathways to Decolonization and Sustainable Self-Determination." *Decolonization: Indigeneity, Education & Society,* vol. 1, no. 1, 2012, pp. 86–101.

Coughlin, Richard W. "Interview—Walter Mignolo/Part 2: Key Concepts." *E-International Relations,* 17 Jan. 2017, www.e-ir.info/2017/01/21/interview-walter-mignolopart-2-key-concepts.

Cox, James. *From Primitive to Indigenous: The Academic Study of Indigenous Religions.* Ashgate, 2007.

Dees, Sarah. "An Equation of Language and Spirit: Comparative Philology and the Study of American Indian Religions." *Method and Theory in the Study of Religion,* vol. 27, no. 3, 2015, pp. 195–219.

Deloria, Vine, Jr. *American Indian Policy in the Twentieth Century.* U of Oklahoma P, 1985.

——. *For This Land: Writings on Religion in America*. Psychology Press, 1999.

Driskill, Qwo-Li. "Doubleweaving Two-Spirit Critiques: Building Alliances between Native and Queer Studies." *GLQ: A Journal of Lesbian and Gay Studies*, vol. 16, nos. 1–2, 2010, pp. 69–92.

General, Karla E. "Securing Rights to Sacred Places with the UN Declaration." *Indian Law Resource Center*, 2014, indianlaw.org/content/securing-indigenous-rights-sacred-places-un-declaration. Accessed 18 Sept. 2019.

Gross, Lawrence W. *Native American Rhetoric*. U of New Mexico P, 2021.

Harjo, Joy. "Perhaps the World Ends Here." 1994. *Poetry Foundation*, www.poetryfoundation.org/poems/49622/perhaps-the-world-ends-here.

Harp, Rick. "Episode 171: An Indigenous Chronicle of Christianity." *Media Indigena* (podcast), 28 July 2019, mediaindigena.libsyn.com/ep-171-an-indigenous-chronicle-of-christianity.

Irwin, Lee. "Freedom, Law, and Prophecy: A Brief History of Native American Religious Resistance." *Native American Spirituality: A Critical Reader*, edited by Lee Irwin, U of Nebraska P, 2000.

Kelley, Dennis. *Tradition, Performance, and Religion in Native America: Ancestral Ways, Modern Selves*. Routledge, 2014.

Kimmerer, Robin Wall. *Braiding Sweetgrass: Indigenous Wisdom, Scientific Knowledge, and the Teachings of Plants*. Milkweed Editions, 2013.

Lynch, Paul, and Matthew Miller. "Twenty-Five Years of Faith and Writing: Religion and Composition, 1992–2017." *Present Tense: A Journal of Rhetoric in Society*, vol. 6, no. 2, 3 Aug. 2017, www.presenttensejournal.org/volume-6/twenty-five-years-of-faith-in-writing-religion-and-composition-1992-2017/.

Maracle, Lee. "Oratory on Oratory." *Memory Serves: Oratories*, edited by Smaro Kamboureli, NeWest Press, 2015.

Masuzawa, Tomoko. *The Invention of World Religions; or, How European Universalism Was Preserved in the Language of Pluralism*. U of Chicago P, 2005.

McKenna, Phil. "Standing Rock Asks Court to Shut Down Dakota Access Pipeline as Company Plans to Double Capacity." *Inside Climate News*, 20 Aug. 2019, insideclimatenews.org/news/20082019/standing-rock-dakota-access-pipeline-impact-assessment-court-double-capacity.

Mignolo, Walter D. *The Darker Side of Western Modernity: Global Futures, Decolonial Options*. Duke UP, 2011.

Native Land Digital. "Territory Acknowledgement." *Native Land Digital*, native-land.ca/resources/territory-acknowledgement/. Accessed 24 Feb. 2023.

Newland, Bryan. *Federal Indian Boarding School Initiative Investigative Report*. United States Department of the Interior, May 2022, www.bia.gov/sites/default/files/dup/inline-files/bsi_investigative_report_may_2022_508.pdf.

Pearce, Roy Harvey. *Savagism and Civilization: A Study of the Indian and the American Mind.* U of California P, 1988.

Pernot, Laurent. "The Rhetoric of Religion." *Rhetorica: A Journal of the History of Rhetoric*, vol. 24, no. 3, 2006, pp. 235–54.

Powell, Malea, et al. "Our Story Begins Here: Constellating Cultural Rhetorics." *Enculturation: A Journal of Rhetoric, Writing, and Culture*, 25 Oct. 2014, enculturation.net/book/export/html/6096.

Pratt, Richard H. "'Kill the Indian, and Save the Man': Capt. Richard H. Pratt on the Education of Native Americans." *Official Report of the Nineteenth Annual Conference of Charities and Correction.* 1892, pp. 46–59. Reprinted in Richard H. Pratt, "The Advantages of Mingling Indians with Whites," *Americanizing the American Indians: Writings by the "Friends of the Indian," 1880–1900*, Harvard UP, 1973, pp. 60–271, historymatters.gmu.edu/d/4929/. Accessed 16 Sept. 2019.

Reese, Debbie. "Are You Planning to Do a Land Acknowledgement?" *American Indians in Children's Literature* (blog), 9 Mar. 2019, americanindiansin childrensliterature.blogspot.com/2019/03/are-you-planning-to-do-land.html.

Ritskes, Eric. "What Is Decolonization and Why Does It Matter?" *Intercontinental Cry*, 21 Sept. 2012, intercontinentalcry.org/what-is-decolonization-and-why-does-it-matter/.

Smith, Linda Tuhiwai. *Decolonizing Methodologies: Research and Indigenous Peoples.* Otago UP, 2012.

"Standing Rock Syllabus Project." *NYC Stands with Standing Rock Collective*, 2016, nycstandswithstandingrock.wordpress.com/standingrocksyllabus/. Accessed 16 September 2019.

Treat, James. *Around the Sacred Fire: Native Religious Activism in the Red Power Era.* Palgrave Macmillan, 2003.

Tuck, Eve, and K. Wayne Wang. "Decolonization Is Not a Metaphor." *Decolonization: Indigeneity, Education & Society*, vol. 1, no. 1, 2012, pp. 1–40.

"UNDRIP FAQs." *United Nations Department of Economic and Social Affairs: Indigenous Peoples*, 2019, www.un.org/esa/socdev/unpfii/documents/faq_drips_en.pdf. Accessed 16 Sept. 2019.

"United Nations Declaration on the Rights of Indigenous Peoples." United Nations, 2007, www.un.org/development/desa/indigenouspeoples/wp-content/uploads/sites/19/2018/11/UNDRIP_E_web.pdf.

U.S. Department of Arts and Culture. "Honor Native Land: A Guide and Call to Acknowledgment." *USDAC*, usdac.us/nativeland. Accessed 24 Feb. 2023.

Walsh, Catherine E. "The Decolonial For: Resurgences, Shifts, and Movements." *On Decoloniality: Concepts, Analytics, Praxis*, by Walter D. Mignolo and Catherine E. Walsh, Duke UP, 2018, pp. 15–32.

Wilson, Shawn. *Research Is Ceremony: Indigenous Research Methods*. Fernwood Publishing, 2009.

Wilson, Shawn, and Margaret Hughes. "Why Research Is Reconciliation." *Research & Reconciliation: Unsettling Ways of Knowing through Indigenous Relationships*, edited by Shawn Wilson et al., Canadian Scholars, 2019, pp. 5–20.

Interlude

PATRICIA BIZZELL

By the late 1990s, I felt that religious rhetoric was oddly neglected in U.S. rhetorical studies—"oddly," both because religious appeals were increasingly powerful in our national discourse and because religious persuasion foregrounded the classical triad rhetoricians are taught to analyze: pathos and ethos as well as logos. I tried to move the field in this direction when I set the theme for the 2004 Rhetoric Society of America (RSA) conference, "Rhetorical Agendas: Political, Ethical, Spiritual." I aimed my scholarship at faith-based rhetorics to elucidate what they can teach us about appeals involving emotion, and I chose particular areas because of personal connections, to Jesuit rhetoric, Jewish rhetoric, and nineteenth-century activist rhetoric.

How so? Well, by the time I retired in 2019, I had spent forty-two years teaching at a Jesuit college, but initially, I didn't know much about the tradition. In 1999, I eagerly agreed to contribute the keynote to Virginia Chappell's conference on Jesuit rhetoric (possibly the first in the United States) since the assignment required that I learn just what Jesuit rhetoric might be. I argued that it distinctively features the *cura personalis*, which legitimates attending to the affective, ethical, and cultural dimensions of persuasion. How do these dimensions mesh? I learned more at a workshop on Jesuit rhetoric at RSA's first Institute in 2005. Thus, the contemporary field was launched and, ten years later, populated Cinthia Gannett and John Brereton's magisterial collection, *Traditions of Eloquence* (Bizzell, "Historical Notes"). Cinthia and John organized the first international conference of the Society for the Study of Jesuit Rhetoric in London in July 2017, where I presented on Jesuit rhetorical pedagogy ("Jesuit Rhetoric"), and I also prepared an addition on Renaissance Jesuit rhetoric for the third edition of my coedited history/anthology, *The Rhetorical Tradition*.

As for my interest in Jewish rhetoric, it came upon me as a surprise. An ardent convert to Judaism many years ago, I finally found time to embark on graduate work in Jewish studies at Hebrew College in 2005, eventually achieving an MA in 2013. I undertook this work "for love," not for any anticipated professional advantage, but apparently, I cannot study anything without approaching it rhetorically, and so I was drawn to the workshop on Jewish rhetoric at the 2007 RSA Institute, co-lead by Steve Katz, David Metzger, and Janice Fernheimer.

Fascinated by the multicultural world of medieval Spain and by one of its great rabbis, Moses ben Nachman, known as Nachmanides, I eventually published on his argument style, where, again, I detected the role of ethos and pathos in persuasion, even within overtly "logical" arguments ("ץובש (Shibutz)"). Nachmanides understood the importance of displaying cultural references that would enhance his credibility and arouse favorable emotions in his audience, be they Spanish inquisitors in Barcelona ("Rationality") or recalcitrant rabbis in the south of France (in an important collection coedited by Michael Bernard-Donals and Jan Fernheimer, *Jewish Rhetoric: History, Theory, Practice* ["Rabbi Moses"]).

However, puzzlement dominated reactions to my keynote address at the 2006 RSA conference ("Religion and Rhetoric"). Few had heard of the philosopher Moses Mendelssohn, but he interested me because in attempting to provide "proofs" to justify religious faith, he argued that favorable emotions and seductive sensory experience are at least as important to conviction as rationally persuasive arguments. Mendelssohn addressed primarily his fellow Jews, who were still beleaguered in eighteenth-century Europe, but he attracted the attention of Immanuel Kant, who invited Mendelssohn to speak in his lecture hall. The Jew was hissed by the students as he walked forward.

Whether Jewish or not, white women and Black people struggled for their rights in nineteenth-century America, and in the first edition of *The Rhetorical Tradition*, I concentrated on their advocacy. But eventually I realized that I had to attend to the religious dimensions of their arguments: many activists were inspired by religious faith, and women confessed their inspiration to justify emerging from the domestic sphere. So, I added material on these arguments to the 2001 edition of *The Rhetorical Tradition*, featuring Methodist activists Phoebe Palmer and Frances Willard ("Frances Willard"). I learned more, too, at the 2009 RSA Institute, where I codirected a workshop, "Women, Religious Persuasion, and Social Activism in America, 1780–1940," with Jane Donawerth, Shirley Wilson Logan, and Roxanne Mountford. I soon published on how women adopted a religiously inflected oratorical stance, acting as preachers and risking the accusation that their chastity was compromised by seeking a public forum ("Chastity"). Nineteenth-century novelists also explored, and typically condemned, the morally ambivalent position of the woman public speaker, and I studied these texts, too ("Damnation"). One of the Institute participants was Lisa Zimmerelli, and she and I have recently edited a collection, *Nineteenth-Century American Activist Rhetorics*, which includes several chapters on religion and rhetoric.

Underlying my work in all three areas are twin theoretical problems. First, attending to ethos and pathos as well as logos embeds rhetorical analysis in context-bound elements such as shared cultural history, embodied experience, and more. We know that these elements are crucial to persuasion, but how do they translate to audiences who don't participate in the context? What happens when audiences recognize the rhetor's signals to a cultural context that does not include them or may even be hostile to them? If "outsider" audiences attempt to enter into discourse not aimed at them, are their efforts worthy, or intrusive? Second, attending to ethos and pathos as well as logos reveals the extent to which many discourses are founded on absolutes to which the rhetor and her/his target audience are firmly attached. If an "outsider" audience simply cannot accept these absolutes, is persuasion blocked?

Religious rhetorics pose both theoretical problems, and I explored them in my "faith-based initiative" essay challenging Peter Elbow's "Believing Game" ("Faith-Based Worldviews"). I argued that Elbow's Believing Game is a powerful antidote to traditional academic skepticism (which often assumes an agnostic posture) because the Believing Game requires being as open as possible to alien ideas and disturbing emotions. The Believing Game requires knowing an opposing position deeply, not simply pointing out its supposed logical errors, and therefore may help improve the academy's hospitality toward religious viewpoints, to which one should be as open as to any other position, however unfamiliar. But still, I argued that what I called "faith-based worldviews" pose a challenge to the Believing Game because, ultimately, one cannot simply *pretend* to inhabit these worldviews. For the person of faith, believing is not a game.

Hoping to find a rhetorical project that could engage religious believers and nonbelievers together, I posed these questions: What difference does it make to anyone's intellectual work if they are religious believers? What if there is crucial rhetorical knowledge that can be generated only by what we might call the Christian mind, or the Jewish or Muslim mind? Exploratory answers to these questions can help build bridges between "outsiders," I suggest, as well as producing important new rhetorical analyses.

WORKS CITED

Bizzell, Patricia. "Chastity Warrants for Women Public Speakers in Nineteenth-Century American Fiction." *Rhetoric Society Quarterly*, vol. 40, no. 4, 2010, pp. 385–401.

—. "The Damnation of Frances Willard: Women Public Speakers in Hawthorne, James, and Frederic." RSA Institute, Nov. 2010, University of Tennessee.

—. "Faith-Based Worldviews as a Challenge to the Believing Game." *Journal of the Assembly for Expanded Perspectives on Learning*, vol. 14, 2008–2009, pp. 29–35.

—. "Frances Willard, Phoebe Palmer, and the Ethos of the Methodist Woman Preacher." *Rhetoric Society Quarterly*, vol. 36, no. 4, 2006, pp. 377–98.

—. "Historical Notes on Rhetoric in Jesuit Education." *Traditions of Eloquence: The Jesuits and Modern Rhetorical Studies*, edited by Cinthia Gannett and John C. Brereton, Fordham UP, 2016

—. "Jesuit Rhetoric for the Modern Student." International Society for the Study of Jesuit Rhetoric, 26 July 2017, London.

—. "Rabbi Moses ben Nachman, Sophist?" *Jewish Rhetoric: History, Theory, Practice*, edited by Michael Bernard-Donals and Janice W. Fernheimer, Brandeis UP, 2014, pp. 131–46.

—. "Rationality as Rhetorical Strategy at the Barcelona Disputation, 1263: A Cautionary Tale." *College Composition and Communication*, vol. 58, no. 1, 2006, pp. 12–29.

—. "Religion and Rhetoric: Reason, Emotion and the Sensory in Religious Persuasion." *Sizing Up Rhetoric: Proceedings of the 2006 Rhetoric Society of America Conference*, edited by David Zarefsky and Elizabeth Benacka, Waveland Press, 2007.

—. "ץובש (Shibutz) as a Conciliatory Rhetorical Style in Nachmanides' 'Letter to the French Rabbis.'" *Advances in the History of Rhetoric*, vol. 17, no. 2, 2014, pp. 109–30.

Bizzell, Patricia, and Bruce Herzberg, editors. *The Rhetorical Tradition: Readings from Classical Times to the Present*. 1st ed., Bedford/St Martins, 1990.

—, editors. *The Rhetorical Tradition: Readings from Classical Times to the Present*. 2nd ed., Bedford/St. Martin's, 2000.

Bizzell, Patricia, et al., editors. *The Rhetorical Tradition: Readings from Classical Times to the Present*. 3rd ed., Bedford/St. Martin's, 2020.

Bizzell, Patricia, and Lisa Zimmerelli, editors. *Nineteenth-Century American Activist Rhetorics*. Modern Language Association of America, 2020.

2. Feminist Rhetorical Historiography and Religion

LISA ZIMMERELLI

"Well-behaved women seldom make history." I have a bracelet that bears this slogan; you are most likely familiar with it, a recognizable saying on bumper stickers and T-shirts, too. The author of the quotation is not Margaret Thatcher, nor Marilyn Monroe, nor Eleanor Roosevelt, as it is sometimes attributed. Rather, early American historian Laurel Thatcher Ulrich wrote the phrase in 1976 in a relatively obscure academic journal on the topic of Puritan funeral orations ("Vertuous Women"). In that original context, Ulrich was articulating a desire that historians pay closer attention to women otherwise considered "conservative" or "religious." Basically, Ulrich was arguing that conservative or religious women seldom make *the history books.*

Now, I've no problem with women using this quotation to express support for counter-normative, rebellious attitudes and behaviors. Nor does Ulrich! In fact, the misappropriation and popularization of the quotation inspired her to write a book in keeping with the modified meaning, titled *Well-Behaved Women Seldom Make History.*[1] I invoke the saying at the start of this chapter, however, as a tongue-in-cheek reminder of the alluring feminist historiographic impulse we all know well: finding and celebrating the women who make some noise for causes with which we agree, but giving less notice to the ones who agitate within what we consider to be conservative or limited spheres.

This chapter is about the treatment of religion within feminist historiographic scholarship: religious motivations, religious subjectivities, religious identities, religious movements. First, I briefly explore the genesis of feminist historiography up to its current centrality within the field, focusing on the familiar anthologies, edited collections, monographs, and theories of women's rhetorics that came out of this commitment to writing women into histories of rhetoric. As I do so, I consider how religion is invoked, cast, or ignored in these conversations and seminal feminist historiographic texts.

Second, I provide the historiography—what I claim is a storiography (borrowing the term from Janice Lauer)—of Frances Willard as a cautionary tale of what may happen if we don't carefully take into account religion in our feminist methodologies. I suggest what a feminist historiographic practice might look like when religion is used as a fruitful, generative lens for understanding the texts, motivations, and sensibilities of the people we examine as scholars of rhetoric. I close with a few methodological and pedagogical recommendations. For my colleagues who *do* feminist rhetorical history, it is my hope that this chapter encourages increased attention to religion as an identity, lens, ideology, opportunity, and constraint. And for my colleagues who use feminist rhetorical history in their scholarship, I offer this chapter as a reminder that any history should be seen as contested and evolving.

My definition of religion for the purposes of this analysis is inclusive, but not without boundaries. To borrow from Ken Wilber, the American philosopher known for "Integral Theory," his attempt to unify all systems of theory, religion, and spirituality into one single framework: "One, [religion] acts as a way of creating meaning for the separate self: it offers myths and stories and tales and narratives and rituals and revivals that, taken together, help the separate self make sense of, and endure, the slings and arrows of outrageous fortune" (par. 1). Wilber argues that religion as such is a way of "translating" the world; he continues, as many other religious philosophers have, to argue that religion can also be a source for "radical transformation and liberation . . . at the deepest seat of consciousness itself" (par. 2). Wilber and others suggest that the latter is preferable and sometimes speak with disdain toward those traditions that take a more literal approach to their religious texts and the application of those texts to their lives. In studying historical figures and the religious tenets they ascribe to, I would argue that we should suspend judgment; I define religion as any belief system that helps a person understand themselves as part of a more complicated, mysterious whole. Religion then, for me, encompasses a range from literalist traditions to more spiritual, mystical traditions.

I wish also to distinguish between critique and opportunity. In what follows, I try to name the collective work thus far, speak humbly to what I see as some shortcomings, and offer suggestions for progress. My own stance certainly is not agonistic, and I hope what follows is not perceived as antagonistic. Rather, this essay is an invitation. Specifically, when religion is made visible through the kind of recovery work I attempt to do in my articulation of the development of feminist rhetorical historiography and in my exploration of the treatment of Frances Willard, the consequences are significant. Adding religion as another layer of identity and analysis provides opportunities for even greater understanding—helping us explore new motivations, enabling us to see connections, and allowing intertextualities to rise to the surface. The decision—conscious or unconscious—to sideline religion in feminist rhetorical historiography does our scholarship a great disservice. Rather, what may result if feminist scholars accept my invitation to enfold religion in their historiographic practice is a fuller picture and better understanding of women's texts, lives, hearts, and dreams in history.

Where in the Feminist Rhetorical Historiographic Scholarship Is Religion?

In this section, I offer some observations and insights into how religion is covered and treated within feminist rhetorical histories. First, however, I wish to give the briefest (and I hope not reductive in its brevity) overview of feminist historiographic practice in rhetoric and composition studies. The Octalog of 1988 (a panel at the Conference on College Composition and Communication published in *Rhetoric Review* that same year) is a good snapshot of the emergence of feminist work in rhetorical historiography; panel members identified the need for women to be recognized within the history of rhetoric and signified the beginning of what Pat Bizzell and I call the "remarkable 1990s" (5). By the time the second Octalog was formed in 1997,[2] the publication of essays, anthologies, edited collections, and monographs that were expressly engaged in feminist historiographic practice served as models and set a course for feminist rhetorical historiography.[3] Moreover, feminist historiographic methodologies were also more explicitly named, described, and invited, as was the feminist rhetorical scholar's subjectivity as researcher and teacher.[4]

The next wave of feminist rhetorical scholarship[5] answered this call for (1) meta-awareness—both for researcher and subject—of identity politics (and I use that term in its celebratory, not pejorative, sense) and (2) more methodological inter- and trans-disciplinarity.[6] Feminist rhetorical scholars purposefully wrote histories that challenged any presumption that women were simply responding to masculinist, hegemonic discourse; rather, these histories highlighted women consciously and creatively crafting their own counter-discourses.

For the sake of argument, let's mark the third wave with the third Octalog (2010) and "Octalog Retrospective" (2011), both published in *Rhetoric Review*, and a special issue on "Practicing Histories" in *Advances in the History of Rhetoric* (2012). Among the variety of perspectives, subjects, and methodologies presented in these collections, feminist rhetorical scholars universally presented a disposition—a way of doing historiography—that was primarily concerned with structures of power and was highly embodied, situational, and contested.

Today, feminist rhetorical historiography is ubiquitous within the field of rhetoric and composition studies; we would be hard-pressed to find a general collection, monograph, or issue in any journal that does not in some way include, use, or at least reference feminist rhetorical historiographic scholarship.[7] Collectively, these theoretical, ideological, and methodological conversations about historiographic practice and the resulting essays, chapters, and books that are the fruit of this labor demonstrate agreement around key underlying principles: feminist rhetorical historiography is accessible, reflexive, inclusive, diverse, embodied, political, self-conscious, tolerant of ambiguity, embraces dissension, and marked by fluid boundaries. And the work is always in process, never complete; feminist rhetorical historiographers are attentive to the "rhetoricity" of history even as we shape these histories.

However, in the theoretical/methodological historiographic conversations outlined above, although gender and race, and sometimes class and sexuality, are named expressly as identity categories that must be taken into consideration as we write these histories, religion—as a subject position, as a belief system, as a sociohistorical political construct, as a dialectic, and as a driver of sociopolitical movements—is notably underrepresented. This is antithetical. As my cursory history of feminist rhetorical historiography demonstrates, its ideological, theoretical, and methodological premises are inherently inclusive and varied. That is to say, feminist rhetorical historiography is set up to embrace religion as another site of identity, as another generator of rich rhetorical discourse.

As early as 1973, in what Andrea Lunsford and Cheryl Glenn identify as one of the first essays practicing and naming feminist rhetorical history, Cheris Kramer wrote, "Age may be another important interacting factor, as religion might be" (37). Kramer was prompting rhetorical scholars to be sure to consider a wide range of factors in their writing of histories. But the point largely ended there. In what follows, I explore the anthologies of women's rhetorics and monographs and edited collections expressly committed to feminist rhetorical historiography to investigate how religion is identified, referenced, invoked, or ignored—and sometimes misunderstood, misapplied, or underexplored.

What follows is not intended to be an exhaustive study; it is more like random sampling than qualitative coding. I see my role in this section as a kind of observant curator. I grabbed books off my shelf, ordered others through interlibrary loan, searched indexes and tables of content in Google Books. I limited my search to histories; that is to say, I did not include feminist rhetorical scholarship like Beth Daniell's *A Communion of Friendship* because it is concerned with contemporary subjects. I offer the following notes and ruminations as someone who is deeply grateful to my community of feminist rhetorical historiographers. But, friends, we have some work to do.

FIRST-WAVE FEMINIST RHETORICAL HISTORIOGRAPHY: 1980S–1990S

Within the anthologies of women's rhetorics, individual religious female rhetors are represented, but religion as a warrant and motivation is fairly limited. Karlyn Kohls Campbell includes Lucretia Coffin Mott's *Discourse on Woman*; however, as I explain in the next section on Frances Willard, her treatment of religion overall in the text is problematic. Shirley Wilson Logan's *With Pen and Voice* situates Black women's voices within their religious context, but she does not engage deeply with how that religious context may have shaped the women's rhetoric. Overall, when religion is identified in these anthologies, it is predominantly used as a data point, with no more rhetorical relevance than, say, where the rhetor was born or how many children she had. Moreover, the texts selected from these women rarely have an explicit religious message (even though the rhetors had also written and/or delivered religious texts).

Among the collected editions of first-wave feminist rhetorical historiography, religion is more widely represented. Catherine Hobbs's collection on American literacy has two chapters expressly devoted to religion—one on Cherokee female seminarians and the other on gendered constructions of religion in nineteenth-century hymnody. In their collection on the rhetorics of Renaissance women, Carole Levin and Patricia Sullivan include chapters on the religious discourse of Christine de Pizan and Anne Askew. Andrea Lunsford's *Reclaiming Rhetorica* includes essays on Margery Kempe, Mary Astell, and Sojourner Truth. Molly Wertheimer includes a four-chapter section titled "Authorized by Faith." Sutherland and Sutcliffe include a chapter on St. Catherine of Siena and Hester Ann Rogers.

Religion is neglected, however, in the monographs of this period, notably absent in Nan Johnson's otherwise comprehensive *Nineteenth-Century Rhetoric in North America* and Lucille Schultz's otherwise comprehensive treatment of nineteenth-century American schooling and expectedly absent from Susan Jarratt's feminist classical recovery work (sophists were known secular atheists and skeptics). And even though most of the rhetors included in Martha Watson's work on activist autobiography (Elizabeth Cady Stanton, Frances Willard, Anna Howard Shaw, Mary Church Terrell) were devout religious women, only Frances Willard's religious warrants are discussed at length. The exception is Cheryl Glenn's chapter on medieval rhetoric in *Rhetoric Retold*, which contains an extensive discussion of early modern Christianity, Carol Mattingly's *Well-Tempered Women*, which explores the roots of evangelicalism and church clubs for the Woman's Christian Temperance Union, and Logan's "*We Are Coming*," which examines the rhetorical discourse of women in the Black Baptist women's movement.

In this first wave of feminist rhetorical historiography—scholarship mainly committed to recovery work—religious women share a fair proportion of the stage. However, *how* their religion is addressed is somewhat reductive, treated as superfluous or incidental, or even negatively as a stumbling block. When it is addressed more explicitly, religious tenets are positioned as a static backdrop to more meaningful rhetorical engagement. In other words, religion is often cited as a factor that women were working *against*, not as a site of rhetorical power and agency.

SECOND-WAVE FEMINIST RHETORICAL HISTORIOGRAPHY: 2000S

The anthologies of the second wave have relatively fair representation of women's religious rhetorics. Joy Ritchie and Kate Ronald include eight texts they consider "Rhetorics of Spirituality," dating from the fourteenth century to the twentieth century. The second edition of Bizzell and Herzberg's *The Rhetorical Tradition* includes Margaret Fell, Maria Stewart, Phoebe Palmer, and Frances Willard as representative of women engaging in religious discourse. Similarly, Jane Donawerth includes several female religious activists in her anthology *Rhetorical Theory by Women before 1900*: Margaret Fell, Jennie Willing, and Frances Willard.

However, unlike the first wave, within collected editions of original scholarship, religion barely gets mention; for example, aside from Jane Donawerth's chapter, religion is absent from Hildy Miller and Lillian Bridwell-Bowles's *Rhetorical Women*. Similarly, of the many monographs of this period, most focus on literacy and activism (e.g., Kates; Hollis; Sharer; Bordelon). A few exceptions that also address religion: Jacqueline Jones Royster acknowledges the role of the Black church for literacy; Carol Mattingly includes a discussion of Quaker attire in *Appropriate[ing] Dress*; and Jessica Enoch in *Refiguring Rhetorical Education* analyzes Lydia Maria Child's rhetoric through the lens of her faith. The exception, of course, is Roxanne Mountford's *The Gendered Pulpit*, the first monograph devoted in its entirety to religion, a fact universally acknowledged as an oversight of the field in reviews of the book. Mountford attends specifically to the fifth canon of delivery in her investigation of women preachers in the rhetorical space of the pulpit. Vicki Tolar Burton's *Spiritual Literacy in John Wesley's Methodism* followed a few years later. Remarkably, despite the significant numbers of women preaching, exhorting, and lecturing in Protestant circles in the early nineteenth century, women preachers are absent from Buchanan's *Regendering Delivery*.

THIRD-WAVE FEMINIST RHETORICAL HISTORIOGRAPHY: 2010S–PRESENT

Fewer anthologies of women's rhetorical history have been published in the last ten years; of them, *Mestiza Rhetorics* (Enoch and Ramírez) contains one text arguing against religious conservatism: "A Woman of This Century, 1888." Among the many edited collections that were published at the start of this wave, religion as a subject, as a consideration, is virtually absent. Exceptions: Ann George, M. Elizabeth Weiser, and Janet Zepernick's collection, *Woman and Rhetoric between the Wars*, includes a chapter considering the religious rhetoric of Dorothy Day and Nannie Helen Burroughs, and David Gold and Catherine Hobbs's *Rhetoric, History, and Women's Oratorical Education* includes a chapter on Catholic education.

A few monographs have been published expressly devoted to women's religious rhetoric. Carol Mattingly's *Secret Habits* explores the rhetoric of Catholic women; Rhea Lathan's *Freedom Writing* examines the importance of what gospel literacy meant for men and women's civil rights literacy activism; and Lisa Shaver's *Beyond the Pulpit* considers deathbeds as symbolic pulpits, and her *Reforming Women* locates the American Female Moral Reform Society as inspiring a distinct women's rhetoric.

Other scholars include chapters or sections within their books that engage with religion: Donawerth's *Conversational Rhetoric* has a chapter on women's defenses of their preaching, and Kimberly Harrison's *The Rhetoric of Rebel Women* has a chapter on Confederate women's prayers. Tarez Graban analyzes three case studies (Anne Askew, Anne Hutchinson, and Helen M. Gougar) of women's blended political-religious discourse between 1600 and 1900 in *Women's Irony*; and Michael-John DePalma in *Sacred Rhetorical Education in 19th Century America* traces how Austin Phelps sponsored and mentored the intellectual and ethical development of his daughter, Elizabeth Stuart Phelps.

Although not expressly feminist collections, several other edited collections in rhetoric contain chapters that engage with feminist rhetorical historiography. For example, *Renovating Rhetoric in Christian Tradition* (2014), edited by Elizabeth Vander Lei, Thomas Amorose, Beth Daniell, and Anne Ruggles Gere, contains chapters expressly concerned with historical challenges to Christian doctrines and gender roles: "The Rise of Christian Sects" and "The Rise of Female Rhetors." Similarly, Michael-John DePalma and Jeff Ringer's *Mapping Christian Rhetorics* (2014) includes chapters on defenses of women's preaching, evangelical masculinity, and the deaconess movement. Pat Bizzell's edited collection *Rhetorical Agendas* (2006) pointedly weaves spirituality and issues around faith and religion throughout the collection. In my edited collection with Patricia Bizzell, *Nineteenth-Century American Activist Rhetorics* (2020), Martin Camper uses stasis theory to analyze women's defenses of their preaching. And within the present collection, the chapters by Bizzell, Daniell, Vander Lei, Brereton and Gannett, and Geiger II draw on and contribute to feminist rhetorical historiography.

What has emerged is a feminist rhetorical historiographic practice that is trying to be inclusive and responsible but, when it comes to religious rhetorics, falls short on attending to religious motivations and factors. A few trends are clear: (1) Most scholarship on women's religious rhetorics is in the Christian tradition, and the American Christian tradition at that. Although there is a nod to the inherent spirituality of Indigenous rhetorics, it is not fully explored, and Jewish rhetorical studies tends to focus on contemporary practice. (2) Religion is often referred to as a contextual backdrop for analysis, invoked as a constraint that women needed to actively work against. (3) In feminist recovery work, known religious women get a fair amount of attention, but it is singular, rarely extended to larger movements or influences. (4) In third-wave feminist rhetorical historiography, the move to interdisciplinarity (applying, for example, queer theory, geopolitical theory, disability studies) neglected to include religious studies. Indeed, I would argue that the clear move away from an emphasis on individual rhetors to studying structures of power coupled with the prevailing disposition of secular humanism created a kind of perfect storm for the exclusion of religion in feminist rhetorical historiography.

In sum, rarely is religion called up as a primary generator of discourse, both generative and motivational. *Theoretically*, feminist rhetorical historiography absolutely allows for women's religious identity and the expression of that identity. For example, when I read Joy Ritchie and Kate Ronald's introduction to *Available Means*, I'm struck by how apt it is for religious women: "As they claim the means of representing themselves, many women rhetors construct an alternative subjectivity for women and in the process claim what minority women writers have helped us identify as oppositional identities, providing a new set of discourses, making available a new set of 'means' on which women can draw in order to continue to define women's subjectivity" (xxv). Religion is one identity category that is often diminished or even erased from rhetorical treatments of women in history. Our scholarship doesn't assume that race or gender is simply a trope to be called upon as it suits the rhetor; we also don't relegate race and gender to the private, the unverifiable. In every historical era, religion has played at least an important, if not a primary, role—institutionally, ideologically, and for some rhetors, personally. And if they weren't ascribing to a particular religion, rhetors were certainly aware of the prevailing religious discourse and responding to it.

In the next section, I explore the historiography of one rhetor who claimed a religious identity, used religious warrants with abandon, and constructed her own religious and rhetorical theory; Frances Willard was also (dare I say, therefore) greatly misunderstood by contemporary feminists. What follows presents the dangers of limiting our vision when we read texts and study rhetors, as well as the benefits of encouraging our field to see religion not as periphery to, but as central to, rhetorical discourse.

A Cautionary Tale: Frances Willard's Competing Storiographies in Biography and Feminist Recovery

Several years ago, Lisa Mastrangelo challenged our field to attend more carefully to the master, hero narratives of our disciplinary history. In "Lone Wolf or Leader of the Pack? Rethinking the Grand Narrative of Fred Newton Scott," Mastrangelo explores the canonization of Fred Newton Scott and suggests that composition scholars may have become a bit blinded by the hero glow of Scott, leaving other potential players in our collective history in the unexplored dark. Writes Mastrangelo, "There is great importance in acknowledging that a larger tradition existed around Scott, one that supported him and one that he himself contributed to. He is not a lone wolf. He might have been the head of the pack, but there clearly was a pack" (264).

Many of us may know Frances Willard as another historical lone wolf figure—the leader of the Woman's Christian Temperance Union (WCTU). Thanks largely to the work of Carol Mattingly, the WCTU is now considered a vibrant and multivocal movement that helped launch an entire generation of female reform leaders. In simultaneously acknowledging the work of Willard in building up the organization, but also disabusing us of the notion that the temperance movement was, essentially, the Frances Willard movement, Mattingly's balanced scholarship resists Mastrangelo's cautionary lone wolf syndrome. But Mastrangelo's historiographic concern is twofold, and she adds, "We must also step out of the hero-villain dichotomy that we continue to embrace, and instead opt for a 'real man/woman' approach that explores the messy and divergent interests and teaching approaches of various historical figures. We must not be afraid of complex stories" (264).

As I demonstrated in the previous section, feminist rhetorical historiographers have indeed grappled with not only the complex stories of individual rhetors but also with the sometimes messy story of our historiography of those rhetors. Taking Frances Willard as a kind of emblematic case study, I explore a dramatic turn in the perception and reception of one rhetor in the span of a century. Indeed, I argue that the inverse of what happened to Scott happened to Willard: Willard was systematically de-canonized over the course of the twentieth century. I am concerned by the historiographic motives and methods that allowed this to happen. How does a woman known as "Saint Frances" in her time become so vilified by our time? The answer, I assert, is our discomfort with her religious affiliation and our misunderstanding of her personal theology.

I find Janice Lauer's articulation of storiography to be a helpful starting frame. As part of Octalog II, Lauer's "Storiography and Rhetoric and Composition" takes issue with some ways in which histories in our field are both constructed and consumed. Lauer warns against "woven master narratives" that create "straw persons against which to authorize [a scholar's] own accounts instead of representing another's work in its own time and exigencies" (31). Lauer's critique is of composition history in particular and how composition as a field can become a kind of ahistorical storiography. My application is to Willard's place within nineteenth-century activist movements and religious communities; I use the concept of storiography to explore the way in which some female religious rhetors persistently get fixed or affixed—pinned, that is—to a certain ideology. I investigate two (his)story(ies) of Frances Willard as an example of this: first, that which emerges from the dozens of Willard biographies and encomiums written in her lifetime and in the fifty years following her death and, second, that generated by our field during early feminist rhetorical recovery work in the 1980s and 1990s.

Holding both (his)story(ies) up against each other reveals much about the presumptions, preoccupations, and priorities of each culture and time, and such inquiry helps us explore the following questions: How do we construct and then rely on personas of our subjects? What happens when the master narrative of our discipline represents explicitly progressive values, and our subjects and texts seem antithetical (or, I would like to say, we read them as antithetical) to that narrative, particularly when they are overtly religious?

THE STORIOGRAPHY OF FRANCES WILLARD, PART ONE

A successful rhetor, Willard embraced the public forum to advance the various causes she was committed to. She was trained by one of the leading elocutionists of the day, R. L. Cumnock of Northwestern University, and was one of the most prolific writers of her time, producing a handful of books, publishing dozens of articles, and delivering countless speeches on a variety of topics, including temperance, suffrage, social purity, labor rights, the social gospel, bicycle riding, women's preaching, and what she termed "Gospel Socialism." Willard was very active in the publishing industry, serving as associate editor of the serial *Dawn*, an organ of the Social Gospel movement, and establishing her own journal, *The Union Signal*.

Because Willard's volume of work spanned a variety of genres—autobiography, biography, novel, conduct literature, speech, and editorial—and appealed to a broad range of audiences—religious, conservative, liberal, socialist, and most notably her middle-class base—the attention she received was extensive. In her lifetime and in the half century following her death, Willard was enormously popular. Fellow evangelist Henry Ward Beecher called Willard "the best known and best beloved of women" (qtd. in Slagell 159), Bernie Babcock considered her "the foremost woman of the age" (10), and Congregational minister Newell Dwight Hillis wrote that Willard's "achievements for God and home and native land . . . rank her as one of the most famous women of this century" (361). "Saint Frances" was a fixture in popular compilations of famous men and women and the subject of over a dozen biographies; remarkably, from 1898 until 1944, Willard is the subject of a publication *every year*.

Within these publications two dominant and intersecting articulations of Willard emerge—(1) Willard as religious: morally upstanding and heavily influenced by her Methodist faith; and (2) Willard as activist: having a passionate commitment to a broad agenda. In describing Willard's faith, there is quite a spectrum. On the one hand, some writers use highly devotional language. For example, literary critic and author Lilian Whiting describes Willard as "a spirit strayed from the celestial kingdoms" (188), belonging to "the angelic order . . . fashioned of diviner quality than is often revealed in this stage of life's progress" (190), and "a heavenly visitant, sent to earth, divinely commissioned" (191). On the other hand, several writers acknowledge Willard's gradual acceptance of religion; for example, Babcock portrays Willard as challenging and questioning her devout Methodist father as a child and maintaining her skepticism through college, only converting fully at the age of twenty (116–17).

What is remarkable about the majority of the early biographical treatments of Willard is their recognition of the breadth of Willard's activist agenda and the role of Willard's faith in inspiring her to advance social causes. For example, poet and feminist Kate Sanborn: Willard was remarkable "as an educator of women in the wider sense, as an emancipator from conventionalities, prejudices, narrowness, and as a representative on a spiritual plane of the new age upon which we are entering" (714); educator Sherman Williams: "[Willard] was not interested in temperance alone, but worked for equal suffrage, social purity, labor reform—for whatever she believed stood for the uplifting of humanity.

It was not so much a movement or a cause that interested her as the welfare of mankind. Her sympathies and views were broad" (96); Louis Banks: "Miss Willard's great career as a reformer had its roots and growth in the religious character of the family and in the religious development of her own character and life" (224). Biographer Mary Earhart: "she was more than the leader of a temperance organization. . . . [S]he was the general of the whole woman's movement, seeking the emancipation of her sisters from all legal, traditional, and economic bonds" (11). Mary Parkman: "There were those who objected to the very breadth and inclusiveness of her sympathies and interests, and who protested against the 'scatteration' policies, what would, they said, lead to no definite goal" (114). And although Whiting was rather hyperbolic in her assertions of Willard's divine qualities, she also credited Willard with a range of political and social accomplishments: "The world of scholarship, of reform, of philanthropy, of religious progress, each brought to her its tribute" (207). Willard, she argued, was "a scholar among scholars; a thinker among those who devote time to philosophic thought; a researcher in the secrets of nature in the zealous spirit of the scientist; a beautiful example of cultured, Christian womanhood, to lead and guide college students; or a pastor" (193).

In other words, Willard's contemporaries attributed her commitment to social causes to her religious faith and understood her activism to be seated in temperance but not limited by it. Moreover, they often spoke of Willard as a religious scholar and a theologian who made notable contributions to the Social Gospel movement; indeed, she was considered "the Social Gospel theologian of the age" (Buhle 64).

Unfortunately, this rather broad view of Willard's activism and recognition of her intellectual engagement with Methodism was not shared by the one person who would most shape the public perception of her in the century following her death: Willard's close friend, biographer, and WCTU president replacement, Anna Gordon. According to Willard biographer Mary Earhart, writing in 1944, the posthumous Willard that Gordon editorialized in the *Union Signal* and created in her 1898 biography was idealized and almost mythological. Earhart critiqued Gordon's rhetorical construction of Willard as obsessively focused on temperance and as saintly: "For forty years the leaders of the Union followed Miss Gordon's example of emphasizing Frances Willard's saintliness until the members have acquired the same hallowed reverence for her that medieval mystics exhibited for some blessed patron" (5). Earhart considered the resulting injury to Willard's place in history "a form of intellectual perjury" (5). Lilian Whiting likewise observed as early as 1915, "no woman has been less adequately interpreted" (200).

A similar critique is made in 1968 in the biography compilation *Pioneer American Educators*. Placing Willard in the company of Thomas Jefferson, Horace Mann, Susan B. Anthony, Clara Barton, and Booker T. Washington, the preface author, Joy Morgan, claims that "[w]e are so accustomed to thinking of Miss Willard as an international temperance leader that we sometimes forget her '13 seasons' of teaching and school administration" (89) and that "Miss Willard did not limit her goal to temperance . . . she worked for woman suffrage, the right of women to hold property, a single standard of morality" (96). Earhart, Whiting, and Morgan identified a storiography already taking shape—crediting Gordon's narrow interpretation of Willard's field of activism and theology, they anticipated the decline in Willard's popularity in the second half of the twentieth century.

THE STORIOGRAPHY OF FRANCES WILLARD, PART TWO

Earhart's predictions came true. Willard slowly fell out of popular favor and recognition and, in the feminist recovery work of the 1970s on, became hardly more than a footnote in the histories of feminism, suffrage, the Methodist Episcopal Church, and education reform.[8] There was a marked hiatus for publications on Willard from Earhart's biography in 1944 until Ruth Bordin's biography in 1986. Devoting a chapter to Willard's theology, Bordin carefully traces Willard's targeted, aggressive engagement with the Methodist establishment over social reform causes and her significant contributions to social gospel thought and activism. Like Earhart, Bordin also remarks on the broad scope of Willard's activism and regrets the reductive nature of most treatments of her:

> Frances Willard played a much larger role in nineteenth-century America than her leadership of the temperance cause. . . . Willard's beliefs and contributions, which spanned a wide variety of reform causes, were reduced after her death to a single dimension, temperance, and that dimension of her life's work was repudiated unequivocally by a later generation. (xiv, 6)

Two things happen, says Bordin: Willard gets reduced to temperance, and temperance becomes rather unpopular in feminist circles. And I'll finish the enthymeme: Willard is largely left out of the historical narratives that get constructed by feminist scholars doing recovery work in the 1980s and 1990s.

That later generation included nineteenth-century scholars across the fields of history, communication studies, rhetoric, and women's studies, fields that today still tend to valorize the "radical" and more secular work of suffragists like Ida B. Wells, Elizabeth Cady Stanton, and Susan B. Anthony, and to discount the contributions of women involved in projects that seem, through a late-twentieth or twenty-first-century lens, to be conservative, sentimental, overly religious, or simply quaint. Mattingly makes this point in "Woman-Tempered Rhetoric," arguing that scholars have a "natural inclination to value the ideas and motives of those most like us" (58). Because of this inclination, Willard came to represent Barbara Welter's articulation of the "Cult of True Womanhood." As Prudence Flowers points out, Welter's argument has been problematized in terms of race and class; yet, it remains a primary rationale for explaining the activities of nineteenth-century white, middle-class, religious women (15). This stance is evident in most of the scholarship on Willard in the late twentieth century.

One of the first and few rhetorical scholars to treat Willard at length is Karlyn Kohrs Campbell, who includes Willard in her seminal *Man Cannot Speak for Her.* Characterizing Willard as socially and "religiously conservative," Campbell provides a rhetorical analysis of Willard's speech "A White Life for Two" and claims that this speech is representative of Willard's rhetoric generally (123). According to Campbell, Willard's "real achievement was in making suffrage acceptable to more conservative women, but she did so at a cost of making other reforms—reforms that would have attacked the tenets of true womanhood—far more difficult, if not impossible" (128). "Willard," writes Campbell, "stands in sharp contrast to the other great speakers of the woman's rights movement. . . . In her extraordinary efforts to be persuasive and adapt to her audiences, she ended up generating discourse which was suited only to reinforce existing beliefs. . . . Frances Willard's career, although significant for early feminism, was independent of that movement" (129–31). In Campbell's collection, Willard's speech is presented as the anomaly in nineteenth-century activist rhetorics and as a powerful but unfortunate digression from the feminist progressive agenda of her contemporaries.

Interestingly, the text that Campbell chooses to represent women's religious public speaking is Lucretia Mott's *Discourse on Women*. I would argue that *Discourse on Women*, although an important and significant work, is not representative of the vast numbers of defenses of women's preaching but is rather representative of the few scriptural defenses of women. Campbell presents Mott as a foil to Willard; however, Mott's scriptural defense of women shares many of the arguments of Willard's *Woman in the Pulpit*, including a hermeneutical reinterpretation of Paul and biblical models of women speaking. Moreover, although Mott relies on natural rights rhetoric, arguing that women are equal to men, like Willard, she does so carefully, still maintaining "the difference, that our great and beneficent Creator has made, in the relation of man and woman" (492).

I select Campbell as a representative text for this early feminist rhetorical recovery period for a few of reasons: first, it is hard to overstate the importance of her text in feminist rhetorical studies; second, Campbell is one of the only feminist rhetorical scholars of this period who treats Willard at all; and third, current references to Willard often still cite Campbell as their primary secondary source (Nan Johnson, for example, in *Gender and Rhetorical Space*). I am not suggesting that Campbell's reading of Willard has single-handedly contributed to our misperception of her; however, within rhetorical history, when Willard is mentioned, Campbell is still most often cited as the definitive text.

And the consequences are significant: as opposed to so many of the rhetors that share space with Willard in *Man Cannot Speak for Her*—Stanton, Mott, Sojourner Truth—who were subsequently taken up by rhetorical scholars for further analysis, Willard has received little attention. Do a database search of peer-reviewed literature, and you will be able to count on both hands the sum of substantive rhetorical scholarly work on Willard that has been generated over the past forty years.[9] And when she is mentioned by other scholars, Willard is still often characterized or caricatured as the conservative, religious temperance zealot, at odds with other female activists of her day.

For example, historians Barbara Epstein and Suzanne Marilley represent Willard and other temperance women as unquestioningly accepting separate spheres ideology, and although Patricia Bizzell, Jane Donawerth, Bonnie Dow, Janet Zolinger Giele, and Alison Parker nuance this view by conceding that there was a consciousness to Willard's use of the domestic, they claim, like Campbell, that such use was still nonetheless grounded in a middle-class True Womanhood ethic. Indeed, inherent in the very title of Giele's book *Two Paths to Women's Equality: Temperance, Suffrage, and the Origins of Modern Feminism* is the assumption that a woman activist of the nineteenth century had to adopt either a separate spheres/morality or equality/natural rights rhetoric.

Additionally, most treatments of Willard harbor a tacit condemnation of the fervent religious foundation to her social activism. She is therefore discounted, and her religion is portrayed as stifling and anti-intellectual. In fact, and as I indicate in my own scholarship on Willard, religious identity in the nineteenth century was remarkably generative; moreover, the prevailing religious discourse of her time, the social gospel, was a lively theo-intellectual movement that intertwined activism and religious purpose. Willard was referred to when she was alive and posthumously as a "Christian Philanthropist."

What is going on here? One of Willard's early biographers, Louis Banks, may have hit the nail on the head when he wrote, in the preface to his compilation *The Religious Life of Famous Americans*,

> The political biographer is not likely to make much of the personal religious character of the man the story of whose political honor and ambitious career he seeks to narrate. So that it often happens that a public man whose religious life was most devout and who drew the nourishment for his most splendid deeds from the hidden springs of worship and communion with God, stands in the eye of the multitude as an unknown quantity religiously. (1)

I suggest that the same is true for the feminist rhetorical historiographer. Willard's so-called feminine feminism has become a handy foil. She has become not a lone hero, as Fred Newton Scott, but rather a lone villain. And she represents villainous ideologies: the cult of true womanhood, republican motherhood, separate spheres ideology, evangelical Christianity.

If we question our reading of Willard, then we necessarily have to question our understanding of nineteenth-century ideology. If we unfix Willard, return to and read her texts (and not just a sample essay or speech here or there), and consider her articulation of the social gospel, then we potentially disrupt the paradigm of the nineteenth century that we have become so accustomed to as the landscape, the backdrop, the scenography of our historiography of this period. That is to say, although the discourses of separate spheres, true womanhood, and republican motherhood certainly were dominant nineteenth-century discourses, they were also in flux, and rhetors had very nuanced understandings of those discourses, Willard included.

I ask you now: Might the same be true for other eras in our history? Might attention paid to the religious sentiments, motivations, and theology of the times and the women we study disrupt otherwise codified narratives of those histories? In her history of her hometown, *A Classic Town: The Story of Evanston by an Old-Timer*, Willard writes, "History-writing is a dissecting process; therefore, before tearing apart the petals, let us mark for a moment the flower as a whole" (13). The whole of any historical moment is certainly inflected by religion. It is a petal essential to the flower as the whole.

In "Practicing Histories," Christa Olson calls historiographic practice a kind of leap of faith. Religion, belief, is a place of vulnerability for many people. I posit that feminist rhetorical historiography is an innately spiritual act, as we collectively look for the full expression of humanity. Let's assume, as feminists, that the personal is political. This is no longer a radical notion. But when it comes to religion, we stop short, we clam up, we become uncomfortable or apologetic. Why do we still insist that radical, revolutionary work is incompatible with deeply held and practiced religious beliefs? Why are we okay with women in the suffrage movement or in poverty reform being "called" to engage in that work, but we dismiss the call to preach as an unsubstantiated warrant or as a kind of indication of mystical nuttiness? Religion often originates a rhetor's desire to engage rhetorically and provides her with a community to support that engagement. Let's consider religion and religious identity as central to rhetorical impetus and motivation. Perhaps the most radical, feminist thing we could do is to honor it all.

Entry Points: Five Practical Suggestions for Scholarship and Teaching

Embracing religion as another critical identity category, I offer in this final section some recommendations for how we might extend the work of feminist rhetorical historiographic practice more meaningfully and more intentionally to include religion. These suggestions apply to our own research as well as to our teaching and mentoring of students working with historical texts and rhetors.

> *Asking important questions—of the rhetors and subject matter but also of yourself.* My first suggestion begins with the early work of inquiry, when we are newly diving into a research subject. I try to ask questions that prompt me to fully engage with the religious discourse of the time I am studying: What is the religious affiliation of the person I am researching? Of the major leaders of the movement I am studying? What religious discourse was "in the air" at the time? For example, if I am researching a subject who lived during the period of the 1790s until the 1840s in the United States, I always consider the effects of the Second Great Awakening, the Protestant religious revival in which tent revivals, camp meetings, and circuit riders were so prevalent on the western frontier that central and western New York was known as the "burned-over district." I would wager that any reference to fire or burning (spark, lit, afire, etc.) is an opportunity for rhetorical, intertextual, and discourse analysis. Even if religion is not the primary focus of my research, I remain open to the idea that it may have been a primary identity for my subject. And so I look for religion, am open to it, understand and appreciate the religious sensibilities of the age as a backdrop to my subject.
>
> For example, when I considered the theology of Frances Willard in *Woman in the Pulpit,* I had to do a deep dive into the social gospel of the Progressive Era. Reading the theology of the time helped me to see how Willard was both contributing to and challenging some of the premises of that religious theory.

As we do this, we may need to check our assumptions. It can be easy to allow religion to become a straw man or a foil—a constraint rather than an opportunity. I try to suspend secular humanistic judgment when considering religious tropes and warrants and remember that religious texts are considered credible—divine even—by some.

Adopting a stance of reasonable suspicion and archival curiosity. When I read accounts of history, I also now consider what Lauer calls the storiography of these histories. I know them to be complex, living things that are shaped by the propensities of the times in which they are written. And so I do not assume the current, "recovered" version of history is the correct version, is the most generous version, is the most progressive version, is the most *feminist* version. It very well may be. But if I am going to lean on that history for my rhetorical analysis, I do due diligence to figure that out, which often means returning to the archives, to the original, primary material and documents surrounding the rhetorical event I am studying.

I'll give one brief example of why this can matter so much. When I was studying the religious rhetoric of nineteenth-century preacher Julia Foote, I decided I wanted to see the original copy of her text (even though she has been anthologized quite a bit). I wanted to experience the text as close to how it may have been experienced when she self-published and circulated it to fund her itinerate preaching career. As I sat in the Library of Congress and thumbed to the back, I was surprised to see that what had always been published as a poem was, in fact, a hymn set to music. For whatever reason, perhaps simply because publishers said it was too expensive, the music got dropped when the text was anthologized. But poetry and hymn are distinct genres, and that discovery helped me see and make a compelling case for Foote's text as a kind of circulating sermon, the hymn closing out the de facto religious service her text creates.[10]

In primary research or when teaching historical texts, I recommend reading accounts of moments in history *in their own time* and in the years directly afterward to gain historiographic perspective. What does a rhetor's contemporaries say about him or her? Obituaries, for example, can be quite revealing. Also interesting is reading a text in its original publication, with the advertisements, op-eds, and pictures contained therein. For example, for a unit on women's suffrage, I pointed my students to an entire issue of *The Crisis* (vol. 10, no. 4, August 1915). I asked them to focus on the "Votes for Women" editorial section but also to peruse the rest of the issue cover to cover in search of other rhetorical cues that would shape how readers might receive these arguments for women's suffrage. Included in this issue are Christian missionary reports and contributions throughout from Black church leaders, and this prompted students to ask questions of the editorials they may not have otherwise asked.

Being mindful of where you are searching and where you are publishing. In any time period in history, religious presses are rich generators of rhetorical discourse, which often engaged deeply with the social issues of their time. Those who do research in literacy, for example, will find many books published by religious presses that were used in schools. In our secondary research, journals that engage with religious rhetorics (e.g., *Journal of Communication and Religion*) can be helpful, as can the Religious Communication Association or the Rhetoric and Religious Traditions Standing Group, as we explore the intersections of religion with our subject matters.

Attending to religious cues and signals. I try always to be aware of religious signals and cues: a depiction of a rhetor with a crucifix around her neck, a biblical inscription in the margins of a text, the Qur'an listed among her belongings in the archive of her things—these are not minor details to be ignored but rather signals that she experienced the world as a religious person. And so even if the rhetor does not directly invoke religion, it is incumbent upon us, writers of history, to at least explore the possibility that his/her arguments might be influenced by religion, might be inflected with religion.

Moreover, religious cues are often subtle. If I have an intuitive sense that the rhetor may be making a religious reference, I will often ask a colleague in theology or a friend I know to be well versed in that religion. In my teaching, I have asked colleagues from theology to visit my class as a guest lecturer and speak to the prevailing religious ideologies of the time. This is a wonderful way to engage the students with the religious dimension of rhetorical practice.

Welcoming the intersections of religious thought and feminist rhetorical theory. I try always to remember that religion was often the seat for other activist rhetorics, and rhetors therefore consciously engaged in rhetorical and theological multiplicity. Their texts, for example, might simultaneously be defenses of women's religious discourse; evangelical calls to Christ; and abolitionist, suffrage, and temperance texts. Therefore, it is important to consider that religious theory and feminist rhetorical theory might inform each other. Religious theory—with its impulse toward reflection and introspection and its attention to the ethics of what we do and why we do it—might offer us methodological prompts and model ways to engage with texts. For example, discussion of religion is absent in Jess Enoch's articulation of spatial rhetorics, but certainly the theory is quite useful as we apply it to churches, synagogues, mosques, and other religious spaces (*Domestic Occupations*).

NOTES

1. *Well-Behaved Women Seldom Make History* demonstrates how Rosa Parks, Christine de Pizan, Elizabeth Cady Stanton, Harriet Tubman, and Virginia Woolf shaped history.

2. The composition of the second Octalog indicates the degree to which feminist research practices and feminist scholars moved to the center of disciplinary conversations around historiography; of the eight panelists, six were women who had to some degree engaged in feminist historiographic practice (Janet Atwill, Linda Ferreira-Buckley, Cheryl Glenn, Janice Lauer, Roxanne Mountford, and Kathleen Welch).

3. See Campbell; Johnson; Glenn; Hobbs; Levin and Sullivan; Logan, "We Are Coming," *With Pen and Voice*; Lunsford; Wertheimer; Jarratt; Mattingly; Schultz; Sutherland and Sutcliffe; and Watson.

4. See Bizzell; Gordon; and Meyer.

5. The majority of this scholarship was published through the Studies in Rhetorics and Feminisms series that Cheryl Glenn and Shirley Wilson Logan started with Southern Illinois University Press; see http://www.siupress.com/series/studies-rhetorics-and-feminisms.

6. See Royster; Kates; Ritchie and Ronald; Donawerth; Johnson; Mattingly; Hollis; Buchanan; Miller and Bridwell-Bowles; Mountford; Sharer; Enoch; Burton; and Bordelon.

7. The sheer volume of edited collections devoted to feminist rhetorical history supported this sentiment. Following shortly on the heels of Buchanan and Ryan's collection was Eileen E. Schell and K. J. Rawson's *Rhetorica in Motion: Feminist Rhetorical Methods and Methodologies*, Jacqueline Jones Royster and Gesa Kirsch's *Feminist Rhetorical Practices: New Horizons for Rhetoric, Composition, and Literacy Studies*, and Cheryl Glenn and Andrea Lunsford's *Landmark Essays on Rhetoric and Feminism, 1973–2000*. See also Bessette; Bizzell and Zimmerelli; Buchanan; DePalma; Donawerth; Enoch, *Domestic Occupations*, *Refiguring Rhetorical Education*; George, Weiser, and Zepernick; Gold and Hobbs; Graban; Harrison; Hayden; Hallenbeck; Johnson; Lathan; Mattingly; Shaver, *Beyond the Pulpit*, *Reforming Women*; Skinner; and Wood.

8. The exceptions are the following histories of suffrage, each of which accounts for Willard's significant contribution: Jean Baker, *Sisters: The Lives of America's Suffragists*; and Shelley Mosley and John Charles, *Suffragists in Literature for Youth*.

9. For example, Pat Bizzell, Jane Donawerth, Bonnie Dow, Amy Slagell, Sarah Hallenbeck, Maegan Parker.

10. See Zimmerelli, "Itinerant Book."

WORKS CITED

Atwill, Janet. "Changing the Puzzle." In "Octalog II: the (Continuing) Politics of Historiography." *Rhetoric Review*, vol. 16, no. 1, 1997, pp. 23–25.

Babcock, Bernie. *An Uncrowned Queen: the Story of the Life of Frances E. Willard Told for Young People*. St. Louis Christian Advocate Company, 1902.

Baker, Jean. *Sisters: The Lives of America's Suffragists*. Hill and Wang, 2005.

Banks, Louis Albert. *Religious Life of Famous Americans*. American Tract Society, 1904.

Bessette, Jean. *Retroactivism in the Lesbian Archives: Composing Pasts and Futures*. Southern Illinois UP, 2017.

Bizzell, Patricia. "Frances Willard, Phoebe Palmer, and the Ethos of the Methodist Woman Preacher." *Rhetoric Society Quarterly*, vol. 36, no. 4, 2006, pp. 377–98.

—. "Opportunities for Feminist Research in the History of Rhetoric." *Rhetoric Review*, vol. 2, 1992, pp. 50–58.

—, editor. *Rhetorical Agendas: Political, Ethical, Spiritual*. Lawrence Erlbaum Associates, 2006.

Bizzell, Patricia, and Bruce Herzberg, editors. *The Rhetorical Tradition: Readings from Classical Times to the Present*. 2nd ed., Bedford/St. Martin's, 2000.

Bizzell, Patricia, and Lisa Zimmerelli, editors. *Nineteenth-Century American Activist Rhetorics*. Modern Language Association of America, 2020.

Bordelon, Suzanne. *Feminist Legacy: The Rhetoric and Pedagogy of Gertrude Buck*. Southern Illinois UP, 2009.

Bordin, Ruth. *Frances Willard: A Biography*. U of North Carolina P, 1986.

Buchanan, Lindal. *Regendering Delivery: The Fifth Canon and Antebellum Women Rhetors*. Southern Illinois UP, 2005.

—. *Rhetorics of Motherhood*. Southern Illinois UP, 2013.

Buchanan, Lindal, and Kathleen J. Ryan. *Walking and Talking Feminist Rhetorics: Landmark Essays and Controversies*. Parlor Press, 2010.

Buhle, Mari Jo. *Women and American Socialism, 1870–1920*. U of Illinois P, 1981.

Burton, Vicki Tolar. *Spiritual Literacy in John Wesley's Methodism: Reading, Writing, and Speaking to Believe*. Baylor UP, 2008.

Campbell, Karlyn Kohrs. *Man Cannot Speak for Her*. Praeger Publishers, 1989. 2 vols.

Daniell, Beth. *A Communion of Friendship: Literacy, Spiritual Practice, and Women in Recovery*. Southern Illinois UP, 2003.

DePalma, Michael-John. *Sacred Rhetorical Education in 19th Century America: Austin Phelps at Andover Theological Seminary.* Routledge, 2020.

DePalma, Michael-John, and Jeffrey M. Ringer, editors. *Mapping Christian Rhetorics: Connecting Conversations, Charting New Territories.* Routledge, 2014.

Donawerth, Jane. *Conversational Rhetoric: The Rise and Fall of a Women's Tradition, 1600–1900.* Southern Illinois UP, 2011.

—. "Poaching on Men's Philosophies of Rhetoric: Eighteenth- and Nineteenth-Century Rhetorical Theory by Women." *Philosophy and Rhetoric*, vol. 33, no. 3, 2000, pp. 243–58.

—, editor. *Rhetorical Theory by Women before 1900: An Anthology.* Rowman and Littlefield Publishers, 2002.

Dow, Bonnie. "Frances E. Willard (1839–1898), Reinventor of 'True Womanhood.'" *Women Public Speakers in the United States, 1800–1925: A Biocritical Sourcebook*, edited by Karlyn Kohrs Campbell, Greenwood Press, 1993, pp. 476–90.

Earhart, Mary. *Frances Willard: From Prayers to Politics.* U of Chicago P, 1944.

Enoch, Jessica. *Domestic Occupations: Spatial Rhetorics and Women's Work.* Southern Illinois UP, 2019.

—. *Refiguring Rhetorical Education: Women Teaching African American, Native American, and Chicano/a Students, 1865–1911.* Southern Illinois UP, 2008.

Enoch, Jessica, and Cristina Devereaux Ramírez, editors. *Mestiza Rhetorics: An Anthology of Mexicana Activism in the Spanish-Language Press, 1887–1922.* Southern Illinois UP, 2019.

Enos, Richard Leo. "An Octalog Retrospective: Looking Forward to History." In "Rhetorical Historiography and the Octalogs." *Rhetoric Review*, vol. 30, no. 3, 2011, pp. 244–45.

Epstein, Barbara Leslie. *The Politics of Domesticity: Women, Evangelism, and Temperance in Nineteenth-Century America.* Wesleyan UP, 1981.

Ferreira-Buckley, Linda. "Serving Time in the Archives." In "Octalog II: The (Continuing) Politics of Historiography." *Rhetoric Review*, vol. 16, no. 1, 1997, pp. 26–28.

Flowers, Prudence. "White Ribboners and the Ideology of Separate Spheres, 1860s–1890s." *Australasian Journal of American Studies*, vol. 25, 2006, pp. 14–31.

George, Ann M., et al. *Women and Rhetoric between the Wars.* Southern Illinois UP, 2013.

Giele, Janet Zollinger. *Two Paths to Women's Equality: Temperance, Suffrage, and the Origins of Modern Feminism.* Twayne Publishers, 1995.

Glenn, Cheryl. *Rhetoric Retold: Regendering the Tradition from Antiquity through the Renaissance.* Southern Illinois UP, 1997.

—. "Regendering the Rhetorical Tradition." In "Octalog II: The (Continuing) Politics of Historiography." *Rhetoric Review*, vol. 16, no. 1, 1997, pp. 28–30.

Glenn, Cheryl, and Andrea Lunsford, editors. *Landmark Essays on Rhetoric and Feminism, 1973–2000.* Routledge, 2015.

Gold, David, and Catherine Hobbs. *Educating the New Southern Woman: Speech, Writing, and Race at the Public Women's Colleges, 1884–1945.* Southern Illinois UP, 2013.

—. *Rhetoric, History, and Women's Oratorical Education: American Women Learn to Speak.* Routledge, 2013.

Gordon, Annie A. *The Beautiful Life of Frances E. Willard.* Chicago, 1898.

Gordon, Linda. *Woman's Body, Woman's Right: The History of Birth Control in America.* Grossman, 1976.

Graban, Tarez Samra. *Women's Irony: Rewriting Feminist Rhetorical History.* Southern Illinois UP, 2015.

Hallenbeck, Sarah. *Claiming the Bicycle: Women, Rhetoric, and Technology in Nineteenth-Century America.* Southern Illinois UP, 2015.

Harrison, Kimberly. *Rhetoric of Rebel Women: Civil War Diaries and Confederate Persuasion.* Southern Illinois UP, 2013.

Hayden, Wendy. *Evolutionary Rhetoric: Sex, Science, and Free Love in Nineteenth-Century Feminism.* Southern Illinois UP, 2013.

Hillis, Newell Dwight. *Great Books as Life-Teachers; Studies of Character, Real and Ideal.* New York, 1899.

Hobbs, Catherine. *Nineteenth-Century Women Learn to Write.* U of Virginia P, 1995.

Hollis, Karyn L. *Liberating Voices: Writing at the Bryn Mawr Summer School for Women Workers.* Southern Illinois UP, 2004.

Jarratt, Susan. *Rereading the Sophists: Classical Rhetoric Refigured.* Southern Illinois UP, 1998.

Johnson, Nan. *Gender and Rhetorical Space in American Life, 1866–1910.* Southern Illinois UP, 2002.

—. *Nineteenth-Century Rhetoric in North America.* Southern Illinois UP, 1991.

Johnson, Wendy Dasler. *Antebellum American Women's Poetry: A Rhetoric of Sentiment.* Southern Illinois UP, 2016.

Kates, Susan. *Activist Rhetorics and American Higher Education, 1885–1937.* Southern Illinois UP, 2001

Kramer, Cheris. "Woman's Speech: Separate but Equal." 1974. *Landmark Essays on Rhetoric and Feminism, 1973–2000,* edited by Cheryl Glenn and Andrea Lunsford, Routledge, 2015, pp. 34–46.

Lathan, Rhea Estelle. *Freedom Writing: African American Civil Rights Literacy Activism, 1955–1967.* National Council of Teachers of English, 2015.

Lauer, Janice. "Storiography and Rhetoric and Composition." In "Octalog II: The (Continuing) Politics of Historiography." *Rhetoric Review,* vol. 16, no. 1, 1997, pp. 30–32.

Levin, Carole, and Patricia A. Sullivan, editors. *Political Rhetoric, Power, and Renaissance Women*. State U of New York P, 1995.

Logan, Shirley Wilson. *Liberating Language: Sites of Rhetorical Education in Nineteenth-Century Black America*. Southern Illinois UP, 2008.

—. *"We Are Coming": The Persuasive Discourse of Nineteenth-Century Black Women*. Southern Illinois UP, 1999.

—, editor. *With Pen and Voice: A Critical Anthology of Nineteenth-Century African-American Women*. Southern Illinois UP, 1995.

Lunsford, Andrea, editor. *Reclaiming Rhetorica: Women in the Rhetorical Tradition*. U of Pittsburgh P, 1995.

Marilley, Suzanne M. "Frances Willard and the Feminism of Fear." *Feminist Studies*, vol. 19, no. 1, 1993, pp. 123–46.

Mastrangelo, Lisa. "Lone Wolf or Leader of the Pack? Rethinking the Grand Narrative of Fred Newton Scott." *College English*, vol. 72, no. 3, 2010, pp. 248–68.

Mattingly, Carol. *Appropriate[ing] Dress: Women's Rhetorical Style in Nineteenth-Century America*. Southern Illinois UP, 2002.

—. *Secret Habits: Catholic Literacy Education for Women in the Early Nineteenth Century*. Southern Illinois UP, 2016.

—. *Well-Tempered Women: Nineteenth-Century Temperance Rhetoric*. Southern Illinois UP, 1998.

—. "Woman-Tempered Rhetoric: Public Presentation and the WCTU." *Rhetoric Review*, vol. 14, no. 1, 1995, pp. 44–61.

Meyer, Michaela D. E. "Women Speak(ing): Forty Years of Feminist Contributions to Rhetoric and an Agenda for Feminist Rhetorical Studies." *Communication Quarterly*, vol. 55, no. 1, 2007, pp. 1–17.

Miller, Diane Helene. "The Future of Feminist Rhetorical Criticism." *Listening to Their Voices: The Rhetorical Activities of Historical Women*, edited by Molly Meijer Wertheimer, U of South Carolina P, 1997, pp. 359–80.

Miller, Hildy, and Lillian Bridwell-Bowles. *Rhetorical Women: Roles and Representations*. U of Alabama P, 2005.

Morgan, Joy Elmer. Preface. *Pioneer American Educators*, edited by Mildred Sandison Fenner and Eleanor C. Fishburn, National Education Association, 1944.

Mosley, Shelley, and John Charles. *Suffragists in Literature for Youth*. Scarecrow Press, 2006.

Mountford, Roxanne. *Gendered Pulpit: Preaching in American Protestant Spaces*. Southern Illinois UP, 2005.

—. "Looking for Rhetoric Where It Has Not Been Found: Definitions, Border Disputes, Future Directions." In "Octalog II: The (Continuing) Politics of Historiography." *Rhetoric Review*, vol. 16, no. 1, 1997, pp. 30–32.

Murphy, James J., et al. "The Politics of Historiography." *Rhetoric Review*, vol. 7, no. 1, 1988, pp. 5–49.

Parker, Maegan. "Desiring Citizenship: A Rhetorical Analysis of the Wells/Willard Controversy." *Women's Studies in Communication*, vol. 31, no. 1, 2008, pp. 56–78.

Parkman, Mary Rosetta. *Heroines of Service*. The Century, 1918.

Ritchie, Joy, and Kate Ronald. *Available Means: An Anthology of Women's Rhetoric(s)*. U of Pittsburgh P, 2001.

Royster, Jacqueline Jones. *Traces of a Stream: Literacy and Social Change among African American Women*. U of Pittsburgh P, 2000.

Royster, Jacqueline Jones, and Gesa Kirsch, editors. *Feminist Rhetorical Practices: New Horizons for Rhetoric, Composition, and Literacy Studies*. Southern Illinois UP, 2012.

Sharer, Wendy B. *Vote and Voice: Women's Organizations and Political Literacy, 1915–1930*. Southern Illinois UP, 2007.

Shaver, Lisa. *Beyond the Pulpit: Women's Rhetorical Roles in the Antebellum Religious Press*. U of Pittsburgh P, 2012.

—. *Reforming Women: The Rhetorical Tactics of the American Female Moral Reform Society, 1834–1854*. U of Pittsburgh P, 2019.

Schell, Eileen, and K. J. Rawson, editors. *Rhetorica in Motion: Feminist Rhetorical Methods and Methodologies*. U of Pittsburgh P, 2010.

Sanborn, Kate. "Frances E. Willard." *Our Famous Women. An Authorized Record of the Lives and Deeds of Distinguished American Women of Our Times*, edited by Elizabeth Stuart Phelps, Hartford, 1885, pp. 691–715.

Schultz, Lucille M. *The Young Composers: Composition's Beginnings in Nineteenth-Century Schools*. Southern Illinois UP, 1999.

Skinner, Carolyn. *Women Physicians and Professional Ethos in Nineteenth-Century America*. Southern Illinois UP, 2014.

Slagell, Amy R. "'Making the World More Homelike': The Reform Rhetoric of Frances E. Willard." *The Rhetoric of Nineteenth-Century Reform*. Vol. 5, Michigan State UP, 2008, pp. 159–94.

Sutherland, Christine M., and Rebecca Sutcliffe, editors. *The Changing Tradition: Women in the History of Rhetoric*. U of Calgary P, 1999.

Ulrich, Laurel Thatcher. "Vertuous Women Found: New England Ministerial Literature, 1668–1735." *American Quarterly*, vol. 28, 1976, pp. 20–40.

—. *Well-Behaved Women Seldom Make History*. Vintage Books, 2008.

Vander Lei, Elizabeth, et al., editors. *Renovating Rhetoric in Christian Tradition*. U of Pittsburgh P, 2014.

Watson, Martha. *Lives of Their Own: Rhetorical Dimensions in Autobiographies of Women Activists*. U of South Carolina P, 1999.

Welch, Kathleen Ethel. "Historiography of Technology and Gender in Rhetoric: Rhetorical HUTS, Logos-Users, and Neosophistic Performance." In "Octalog II: The (Continuing) Politics of Historiography." *Rhetoric Review*, vol. 16, no. 1, 1997, pp. 30–32.

Welter, Barbara. "The Cult of True Womanhood, 1820–60." *American Quarterly*, vol. 18, no. 2, 1966, pp. 151–74.

Wertheimer, Molly Meijer. *Listening to Their Voices: The Rhetorical Activities of Historical Women*. U of South Carolina P, 1997.

Whiting, Lilian. *Women Who Have Ennobled Life*. The Union Press, 1915.

Wilber, Ken. "A Spirituality That Transforms." *Trans4mind*, trans4mind.com/counterpoint/index-new-age/wilber.html. Accessed 7 Oct. 2020.

Willard, Frances. *A Classic Town: The Story of Evanston by an Old-Timer*. Chicago, 1892.

Williams, Sherman. *Some Successful Americans*. Ginn, 1904.

Wood, Henrietta Rix. *Praising Girls: The Rhetoric of Young Women, 1895–1930*. Southern Illinois UP, 2016.

Zimmerelli, Lisa. "'Heaven-Touched Lips and Pent-Up Voices': The Rhetoric of American Female Preaching Apologia, 1820–1930." *Mapping Christian Rhetorics: A Critical Reader for Writing Scholars*, edited by Michael-John DePalma and Jeffrey M. Ringer, Routledge, 2014, pp. 180–202.

—. "The Itinerant Book: Julia A. J. Foote's *A Brand Plucked from the Fire* as a Religious Activist Text." *Rhetoric Review*, vol. 33, no. 2, 2014, pp. 132–47.

—. "'The Stereoscopic View of Truth': Frances Willard's *Woman in the Pulpit* as a Feminist Rhetoric of Theology." *Rhetoric Society Quarterly*, vol. 42, no. 4, 2012, pp. 353–74.

Interlude

BETH DANIELL

My path to religion and rhetoric went through literacy and literacy theory. During my graduate studies, in the early to mid-1980s, I read everything I could find about literacy. I noticed that there was precious little about religion and literacy, except for one chapter by Jack Goody about literacy in traditional societies and one article by Daniel P. and Lauren B. Resnick about the incidence of literacy in Swedish Protestantism. I just knew that couldn't be right, since I had grown up in the South ("Christ-haunted," as Flannery O'Connor called it) and had attended a Baptist college (Mercer in Macon, Georgia). I knew in my bones that there was a deep connection between literacy and religion.

My dissertation turned out to be more or less a "deconstruction" of Walter Ong's Great Leap literacy-orality theory. Ong sets up a binary, wherein characteristics on each side oppose one another. As you might guess, Father Ong valorized the literate side of the literate-oral dichotomy (Daniell, "Against").

In Shirley Brice Heath's article "Protean Shapes," a prayer written in simple language becomes elaborated syntactically in the oral version. According to Ong, this shouldn't happen because literate language, he says, is more sophisticated and more complex than oral language.

To sum up what I learned: Literacy is not one thing. Literacy is diverse. Literacy depends on the community and the rules and customs about who can read what when and what can be said about the reading. The other thing I learned was that there are connections between literacy and power. And that in some societies, religion holds the power.

In such societies, there is a scribal elite, as Goody terms it. These are the people (mostly men) who can read and interpret what the sacred books say.

Illustrating the diversity and complexity of literacy and its relations to culture is Paulo Freire's book *Pedagogy of the Oppressed.* As I read *this* book, I noticed the Christian imagery—being born again with lower classes, "entering into communion with the people," "conversion to the people," "courage to love," and so forth.

At a conference in 1986, Ann Berthoff commented that Freire's literacy pedagogy was as much a result of his Catholicism as of his Marxism. This comment gave me permission to go forward. The next year I wrote a short essay asserting that composition and rhetoric needed to include religion as part of the mix.

Upon my returning to Austin after the conference, the car had to go to the shop (once again!). As I took my place in the waiting room with probably seven or eight other people, I noticed an older African American lady reading the Bible. Then I noticed a young man, who appeared to be a student at the University of Texas, reading a devotional book. A young woman was reading a novel that, by its title, was surely faith-based. A Hispanic gentleman across from me was reading his Spanish-language devotional book. Later that summer I moved to West Virginia for my first tenure-track job.

Because I had attended Al-Anon in Austin, I began attending those meetings in my new place. Because dissertation writers are often so focused on their subject, they miss things. In the Morgantown Al-Anon meetings, I saw the connection between literacy and spirituality writ large.

In 1993, Jan Swearingen, Joanne Campbell, and I organized a roundtable called "Spiritual Sites of Composing." We asked Ann Berthoff and James Moffett to chair and to respond, respectively. We were shocked that our audience almost filled a ballroom. But we were quite sure afterward that there was an audience for our work.

When I left West Virginia for Clemson, I wrote a research proposal to fund a trip back up to West Virginia to interview some of the women I knew there. These women were all members of Al-Anon. Both Alcoholics Anonymous and Al-Anon say that they are spiritual but not religious organizations, promising that if you "work" the Twelve Steps, you will have a spiritual awakening. While Al-Anon claims to be spiritual, it is also all about literacy. In meetings, women would say to one another,

"Have you read the section in *One Day at a Time* on letting go?" Or, "When I feel like that, I read page 37 over and over again."

Analyzing what the women told me and trying to make it make sense theoretically was far more intense than I had anticipated. Finally, however, I began to use my findings for talks at conferences and an article here or there. After one such talk, Robert Brooke, series editor for Studies in Writing and Rhetoric, wrote to ask whether I might be interested in turning this research into a book-length project. In 2004 that work was published as *A Communion of Friendship: Literacy, Spirituality, and Women in Recovery*, not a book about religion and literacy but rather about how spirituality and literacy worked together for the women I knew from Al-Anon.

What I had assumed would be the first chapter of the book I was working on appeared in *College Composition and Communication* in 1999 as "Narratives of Literacy: Connecting Composition to Culture." In this article, I used Lyotard's notion of the grand narratives of literacy to look at literacy, but I was now taking up more explicitly Freire's Christian beliefs.

Out of the blue, Elizabeth Vander Lei called me up and asked if I would be interested in being part of a symposium on Christianity and rhetoric. Yes, I would. The idea of having colleagues to work with was appealing, to say the least. We met at Calvin College in September 2002. There were five of us, and we spent an entire morning trying to come up with a name for our group. We finally decided on Rhetoric and Christian Tradition—not Christianity, which we thought might imply that we thought there is only one Christianity. The results of this symposium included several conference panels; a conference at DePaul in Chicago in 2005; a Special Interest Group of the Conference on College Composition and Communication; and, based on the papers from the DePaul conference, our collection was finally published as *Renovating Rhetoric in Christian Tradition* in 2014.

Moving once more, this time back to Atlanta, I began attending a lecture series at All Saints Church, where I found out about the January Adventure in Emerging Christianity, a weekend conference at Saint Simons Island. At both venues and elsewhere, I heard talks by Marcus Borg, John Dominic Crossan, Walter Brueggemann, Diana Butler Bass, Amy Jill Levine, Robin Meyers, and Elaine Pagels—and then I read their books. What I learned from these writers is that Christianity has always been diverse; like literacy, it is not one thing and never has been.

Its forms depend on tradition and culture. From Borg and Pagels, I learned that a major issue in both ancient and contemporary Christianity is reading. In ancient Christianity, it was more a matter of what you were allowed to read or what you had access to. In contemporary Christianity in America, it's how you read—the interpretation you come up with—through either of two frameworks according to Borg: natural literalism or historical-metaphorical. In my contribution to *Renovating Rhetoric*, I looked at reading, rhetoric, and Christianity—and how I have handled those issues in rhetorical theory classrooms because issues of what we believe always came up.

Recently, I have discovered Chris Keith, a Jesus scholar who is fascinated by the question of whether Jesus was literate or illiterate, as most Jewish peasants were illiterate in his time and place. Keith's response to the prior scholarship and to his dedicated reading of the New Testament is that Jesus was likely illiterate, but his explanations of scripture caused some in his audience to believe that he was one of the scribal elite, those who were credentialed to teach scripture in the synagogues. This is where Keith posits the beginning of the conflict between the Temple elite and Jesus and his followers. What I found satisfying about Keith's work was his immersion in the literacy scholarship and seeing in his account how literacy and power worked together and against each other in the first-century B.C.E. And, as we see around us, that conflict goes on.

WORKS CITED

Daniell, Beth. "Against the Great Leap Theory of Literacy." *Pre/Text*, vol. 7, 1986, pp. 181–94.

—. *A Communion of Friendship: Literacy, Spiritual Practice, and Women in Recovery.* Southern Illinois UP, 2003.

—. "Narratives of Literacy: Connecting Composition to Culture." *College Composition and Communication*, vol. 50, 1999, pp. 393–410. Rpt. in *Landmark Essays on Speech and Writing*, edited by Peter Elbow, Routledge, 2015, pp. 97–112.

Freire, Paulo. *Pedagogy of the Oppressed.* Translated by Myra Bergmann Ramos, Seabury Press, 1970.

Goody, Jack. "Introduction." *Literacy in Traditional Societies*, Cambridge UP, 1968, pp. 1–26.

Heath, Shirley Brice. "Protean Shapes: Ever-Shifting Oral and Literate Traditions." *Spoken and Written Language:*

Exploring Orality and Literacy, edited by Deborah Tannen, Ablex, 1982, pp. 91–117.

Keith, Chris. *Jesus against the Scribal Elite: The Origins of the Conflict*. Baker Academic, 2014.

Ong, Walter J. *Orality and Literacy: The Technologizing of the Word*. Metheun, 1982.

Resnick, Daniel, and Lauren Resnick. "The Nature of Literacy: An Historical Exploration." *Harvard Educational Review*, vol. 47, no. 3, 1977, pp. 370–85.

Vander Lei, Elizabeth, et al., editors. *Renovating Rhetoric in Christian Tradition*. U of Pittsburgh P, 2014.

3. "Joy Anyway!"

Narratives of Harm and Flourishing at the Intersections of Religious and LGBTQ+ Rhetorics

T J GEIGER II

On July 27, 2008, acquaintances of mine—retired university and community college professors—were, respectively, maimed and murdered in a church shooting. They had been connected to the Unitarian Universalist fellowship I belonged to in north Texas but had moved the preceding year or so to Tennessee. That summer day in 2008, Tennessee Valley Unitarian Universalist Church (TVUUC) of Knoxville had turned the Sunday morning service over to the children, who were staging the musical *Annie Jr.* On that day, a white man with a history of domestic violence walked into the building, removed a shotgun from inside a guitar case, and began firing his weapon in the sanctuary.

Not long after this shooting, evidence surfaced of the not-so-random nature of this violence. Years earlier, the shooter's fifth wife (who had received a protection order against him because of his threats) had been a member of the church. Officers also recovered a four-page letter from the shooter's vehicle that addressed his hatred for "the liberal movement," "[l]iberals in general, as well as gays" (qtd. in Hickman and Jacobs). Reports noted how the church was a "Welcoming Congregation" for lesbian, gay, bisexual, transgender, and queer (LGBTQ+) people. For example, one account observed that the church displayed a sign declaring an explicit greeting to LGBTQ+ members and visitors (Hickman and Jacobs); another article reported that the church hosted "several gay and gay friendly groups" ("Affidavit"). In this media coverage published almost fifteen years ago, an awkwardness abides in its pattern of reporting the attacker's hatred of liberals and gays, noting the "gay-friendly" position of TVUUC, and providing evidence that establishes the validity of the gay-friendly claim. The last move suggests the felt need to prove to the audience the reality of a church that actively promotes the human rights of LGBTQ+ individuals.

This gesture indicating a presumed tension (if not incompatibility) between religious and queer communities is unsurprising given findings in Debra L. Mason and Cathy E. Rosenholtz's 2012 *Missing Voices* report, a study supported by GLAAD (Gay & Lesbian Alliance Against Defamation), an LGBTQ+ media accountability group, and the University of Missouri Center on Religion and the Professions. In mainstream media reports, the vast majority of religiously identified sources commented negatively on LGBTQ+ issues, half of those sources were evangelical Christian–affiliated, and most LGBTQ+-affirming sources were not identified by religion. Indeed, the frequently told story is that liberal churches shrink because they're liberal and conservative churches grow because they're conservative. Given these trends, it follows that in 2008 there might have been some level of tentativeness regarding how to report the confluence of LGBTQ+ affirmation and religiosity found in a southern house of worship visited by terrorism.

This chapter responds to the problem of oft-reductive, yet-commonplace narratives that construct LGBTQ+ and religious rhetorics as joined only in binary opposition. It does so by examining how these rhetorics interact, in fact, as deeply blended sets of narratives. Narratives offer writers and readers spaces in which to meet and move. Specifically, this chapter explores narratives of religion-LGBTQ+ intersections that account for harm and flourishing—what perpetuates and remedies harm, what facilitates flourishing.

First, this chapter identifies how rhetoric and writing scholars have primarily examined the problems and possibilities of religion-LGBTQ+ intersections in public rhetoric, activism, and pedagogies. Within these examinations, scholars attend to recurring commonplaces in public rhetoric and activism (e.g., identification, resistance, universalizing claims, community, autonomy, oppositional framings); to pedagogies that foster binary-dismantling deliberation in contexts of vulnerability (even as teaching and learning are informed by larger forces of social normativity); and to complicated narratives of harm and flourishing. Second, building on this public, activist, and pedagogical work, this chapter encourages additional scholarship in the areas of researcher positionality through narrative frameworks and of archival/historical projects. Such efforts are important because they highlight potential impediments to, and opportunities for, deliberation within a group and among different constituencies. Deliberation seeks the *common good*, which is served by bringing values, emotions, and narratives to bear on the question "What should we do?" at religion-LGBTQ+ intersections. Third, this chapter's argument for increased work on history, archives, narrative frameworks, and researcher positionality holds broader implications for rhetoric and writing studies, especially regarding rhetorical conceptions of time (i.e., *chronos* and *kairos*) and the relationship of rhetorical practice and individual belief. Finally, the chapter closes by naming source material and questions for teaching purposes.

My reading and writing at religion-LGBTQ+ intersections are shaped by my positionality as a heterosexual, cisgender, white, Protestant, middle-class (with a working-class and rural background), academic man who strives to enact practices of solidarity with LGBTQ+ communities and by the relationships I have formed across civic, scholarly, religious, and social domains. Positionality shapes encounters, which come with responsibilities. Writing toward an ethics of responsibility when contending with LGBTQ+ discourses, Suzanne Holland critiques notions of liberal tolerance that resemble the sequential expression-without-listening of many political talk shows, urging instead the navigation of mutual vulnerability, a practice of risk that comes through concrete encounters with others. My encounters with others are shaped by the high level of privilege my embodiment yields in U.S. culture. By that, I mean certain dimensions of my identity and living do not by default provoke others to cause me daily difficulty, to discriminate against me, to question my competence or virtue, or to threaten my life and safety. To go through life is to experience harm, loss, and pain. Social arrangements, though, distribute pain and precariousness in ways that cause some to experience more than their share. Informed by awareness of my privilege, practices of solidarity, and what Lisa Blankenship has recently termed "rhetorical empathy," a mode of engagement shaped by listening, emotional awareness, narrative, and personal experience, I strive to resist either/or thinking regarding the blended forms that sexual and spiritual identities and ideologies might take.[1] A scholarly narrative that enacts rhetorical empathy and vulnerability might counter the oppositional framing that has long interrupted connections between religious rhetorics and LGBTQ+ rhetorics in the larger public.

Where Have We Been?

The oppositional framing readily available in the larger public may also appear to structure disciplinary engagement with the intersection of LGBTQ+ and religious discourses. For example, while two important annotated bibliographies published by the journal *Present Tense: A Journal of Rhetoric in Society* (one on LGBTQ+ rhetorics and one on religious rhetorics) include texts that address religion-LGBTQ+ intersections, they have no annotated sources in common. On the surface, Paul Lynch and Matthew Miller's "Twenty-Five Years of Faith in Writing: Religion and Composition, 1992–2017" (2017) and Matthew B. Cox and Michael J. Faris's "An Annotated Bibliography of LGBTQ+ Rhetorics" (2015) may seem to tell stories about religion-LGBTQ+ intersections that apparently have a little in common. Despite seemingly divergent treatments indicative of subfield silo-ing, when digging down into the sources in each bibliography, interwoven stories and salient points of connection emerge. This interweaving undermines false binaries or what Ann E. Berthoff called "killer dichotomies." Consequently, this section explores narratives of harm and flourishing that resist the shallow oppositional framing often applied to religious and LGBTQ+ discourses, an exploration supplemented with a few important sources published in and following 2015. What follows is not an exhaustive review of rhetorical scholarship about religion-LGBTQ+ discursive intersections. It is, rather, a discussion of some touchstone scholarly texts, central questions, and common threads at these intersections within religious rhetorics and queer rhetorics, two subfields that both wrestle with the binary tensions that tend to surround dominant narratives about LGBTQ+ and religion, especially in regard to public rhetorics, activism, and pedagogies.[2]

STORIES ABOUT PUBLIC RHETORICS AND ACTIVISM

Scholars of queer rhetorics attend to rhetorical practices for public and activist purposes as they examine particular case studies at religion-LGBTQ+ intersections, while considering limits and possibilities: of identification and resistance, of universalizing claims, and of community and autonomy—all contributing to complicated narratives of harm and flourishing. The sites of inquiry range widely: spiritual activist organizations that commit civil disobedience at institutions not fully affirming of LGBTQ+ members, ex-gay autobiographical discourse, biblical and spiritual literacies surrounding queer lives, legislative debates, and more. For instance, different readings of a spiritual activist organization indicate that identification strategies may help remedy harm by resisting oppositional framings while simultaneously universalizing new binaries that impede autonomy and stifle flourishing. Such tensions are in keeping with the stories queer rhetorics scholars tell of contradictory commonplace arguments at religion-LGBTQ+ intersections in public discourse.

Typical arguments universalize existing social arrangements, stymie empathy, and leverage oppositional framings even as the rhetorical strategies frequently employed highlight the instability of the categories and institutions upon which those arguments rest. For example, Ralph R. Smith and Russel R. Windes examine the relative fixedness surrounding policy discussions related to LGBTQ+ sexuality, a fixedness achieved in part through the interpretive activities of anti–gay rights traditionalists who appeal to culturally privileged institutions, including religious institutions that promote an LGBTQ+ versus Christianity binary. Other scholars likewise identify and critique commonplaces that fuse religious-social institutions, universalize heteronormativity as natural and unchanging, and assume liberal universalism and tolerance as paths to progress.

Although "ex-gay" or "conversion therapy" programs that seek to alter sexual orientation or lessen same-sex attraction have waned in recent years because of the harm done by this universalizing of heteronormative sexuality that frames Christian and queer desires as opposites, these programs have had a significant influence during the last fifty years. Through an analysis of the coauthored autobiography *Love Won Out* by John Paulk and Anne Paulk, Jeffrey A. Bennett ascertains key authorizing rhetorical moves within ex-gay identity performances and the instabilities that attend such performances. While asserting the universal, natural, and authentic status of heterosexuality against the assumed unnaturalness and inauthenticity of queer sexuality, the autobiography, Bennett argues, ultimately deconstructs the taken-for-granted-ness and stability of heterosexuality. Such deconstruction internal to oppositional framings provides an opening for resistance to community-imposed, universalizing claims.

With the tide turning against ex-gay operations, universalizing claims about the need for liberal tolerance were on the rise, a tolerance that might actually leave in place social structures, cultural attitudes, and political policies antithetical to LGBTQ+ flourishing. Echoing Holland's emphasis on the limits of tolerance, Kenneth Lythgoe examines the shortcomings of a 2011 anti-bullying bill in Michigan. The bill ultimately did not include a religious conscience exemption amendment that opponents argued would provide religious license for the bullying of queer youth. However, legislative efforts that fail to specify rights and protections for marginalized populations are unlikely to result in more safe or flourishing spaces for LGBTQ+ adults and children. Instead of focusing on isolated artifacts—such as viral videos that affectively resonate with the goals of queer liberation—Lythgoe urges an attention to the specifics of policy-making and the material outcomes of policy decisions, the terrain of deliberation. In other words, what specific policies facilitate flourishing, inflict harm, and serve the common good requires more attention.

Scholarly treatments of a particular activist organization tell stories of flourishing that resist oppositional framings of queerness and Christianity, resistance achieved through empathetic identification and vulnerability, and stories of harm through ostensible progress grounded in a universalism that reinscribes other oppositions and sacrifices autonomy. Queer rhetorics scholars both critique and praise Soulforce, an organization seeking policy changes through activism within religious communities. A spiritual activist organization that confronts institutions discriminating against LGBTQ+ people, Soulforce is significantly shaped by Christian discourse. Invoking the legacy of the civil rights–era Freedom Rides, Soulforce's Equality Rides involve buses of activists traveling to sites to have vulnerable dialogue, which might generate empathy. Such a campaign and its name seek to identify contemporary queer liberation work with historical social justice efforts. Offering a positive assessment, Leland G. Spencer and Joshua Trey Barnett argued in 2013 that Soulforce's Equality Rides question the queer versus Christian binary and the religious basis of discriminatory policies. Karma R. Chávez, however, writing in 2003, argued in a compelling piece that blends personal narrative and theoretical sophistication that Soulforce's discursive indebtedness to Christianity led these activists to frame their work in terms complicit with traditionalist evangelical rhetoric. Specifically, even as these activists attempted to undermine commonplace Christian assertions about queer sexuality being a simple choice, Soulforce's rhetoric still framed homosexuality as "natural" or "unnatural." Although universalizing the naturalness of queerness generates forceful arguments for LGBTQ+ affirmation within heteronormative spaces, accepting such a framing, Chávez contends, conceded rhetorical ground that would honor individuality and autonomy. Rather than seeking universal categories, which might render sexualities comprehensible across lines of difference, Chávez privileges autonomy in coalition-building and deliberation.

As LGBTQ+ people receive a range of messages about the incompatibility of their sexual orientations and gender identities with religious orientations, they and their allies forge creative forms of literate practice to heal harms and facilitate flourishing. Alexandra Cavallero documents an example of queer religious literacy practices for activist purposes that generate community, support autonomy, and resist heteronormativity. She studied a session, conducted by a pastor, which instructed participants in ways to defensively counter uses of so-called biblical "clobber passages" that religious adherents frequently cite as condemning queer sexualities and to reconstruct religious identity through disruptive reading practices. Such trainings produce community (i.e., a space of mutual vulnerability where participants undermine oppositional framings) while also honoring participants' autonomy (i.e., their own varied backgrounds, identities, choices, and motivations). Defensive and disruptive uses of spiritual literacies that enable agency-affirming re-narrations of experience can also be seen when Eric Darnell Pritchard examines the literacy practices through which Black LGBTQ+ people "enact self- and communal love by creating one's self and community as divine"; they counter normative uses of literacy that marginalize them within religious and spiritual contexts (155). Attentive to the harmful effects that religious literacy practices can have, Pritchard notes the spiritual violence that occurs when communities interpret religious scriptures as inherently opposing LGBTQ+ identities, justify abuse by appealing to religious beliefs, and silence queer and transgender people through religious instruction (154). Pritchard also examines how participants reconstruct their Christian identities, migrate to new religious communities, or produce individualized spiritual systems. Although religious communities sometimes undermine their efforts, many LGBTQ+ people find that spiritual literacies help them in their journeys away from harm and toward flourishing.

STORIES ABOUT PEDAGOGIES AND CLASSROOMS

If queer rhetorics has explored the contradictions in both explicitly anti-queer, status quo positions and apparently progressive stances, as well as the creative uses of spiritual literacy for remedying harm and facilitating flourishing, similar interests also arise in queer rhetorics and religious rhetorics scholarship addressing questions of teaching at religion-LGBTQ+ intersections. As Jonathan Alexander observes, teaching that takes up sexuality as a site of inquiry carries with it a certain "trickiness" (17). The complexity is compounded when simultaneously considering religion. When pedagogical scholarship in rhetoric and writing studies takes up the links between religious and LGBTQ+ discourses, the relationship is almost inevitably recounted as a site of anticipated or real conflict. Specifically, scholars observe how students and others opposed to—or hostile toward—LGBTQ+ people and rights often articulate this position in religious terms (De la Tierra; Downs; Patterson; Smart). At the same time, teachers' stories and scholars' narratives illustrate pedagogical responses that move beyond oppositional framings, demonstrate the deliberative possibilities of rhetoric in empathetic and vulnerable contexts, and account for flourishing-preventing and harm-inducing forces that trouble the classroom (e.g., universalizing heteronormativity, resistance to the responsibilities that vulnerability and empathy produce, and oppositional framing).

Pieces by Douglas Downs and Juanita M. Smart, which address commenting on student writing, exemplify how teachers might narrate their experiences teaching at the focal intersection of this chapter. In so doing, these teachers re-narrate intellectual understandings of, and affective encounters with, religious and LGBTQ+ discourse as primarily conflictual and oppositional. They ask questions about how to respond to student texts that trouble instructors or leave them grappling for ways to provide feedback. Their answers range from employing theoretical frameworks for response purposes to excavating teachers' lived experiences so as to identify resources for commenting. Providing a rare extended teacher's reading of student writing on an issue at the intersection of religious discourse and LGBTQ+ issues, Downs describes how he engaged with a student's paper that opposed adoptions by same-sex couples. Responding to the paper with intense disdain, Downs reflects on his reactions and turns to theorist James Gee to argue that the student and Downs himself were operating from divergent discourse frameworks—affirmation and inquiry, respectively. Taking a different approach while still focusing on teacher readings of student work, Smart explores the identity dynamics that may shape teachers' responses to student writing that performs a religiously grounded analysis. Raised in an evangelical context, Smart recognizes the religiously empowered self of her youth in a student's written comparison of Jesus Christ and Frankenstein's monster. Yet Smart also recounts how the Christian community that reared her rejected her when she disclosed her lesbian identity. Employing a reading stance grounded in her experiences with both evangelical and lesbian identities, Smart finds in the student's text a genuine struggle toward meaning and understanding, even as it is articulated in language that alienates audiences not already committed to a particular version of Christianity. These discursive intersections are sites that bear the marks of trauma—like the literary figure referenced by the student writer in Smart's piece. They are also sites for telling new stories.

Mark Alan Williams and I provide narratives of pedagogical approaches that examine student uptake of the religion-LGBTQ+ intersection in writing classes and that demonstrate the value of rhetoric, specifically oppositional-framing-resistant deliberative discourse, as a resource when moving away from universalizing claims and toward robust, vulnerability-practicing communities. Drawing on the work of Ann Pellegrini and Janet Jakobson, I argue for "the free exercise of rhetoric" as a means to privilege deliberation informed by values, narrative, and experience when students study or write about LGBTQ+ and religious topics. Extending this free rhetoric through a translingual framework, Williams elucidates the ways personal experience and community-authorized discourse may be used in LGBTQ+-affirming deliberative religious rhetoric (352–54). Ultimately, these two approaches suggest that rhetoric offers a way through apparently intractable conflicts and binary configurations that lock interlocutors into harmful patterns of interaction.

Despite the hopefulness forwarded in the arguments above, queer rhetorics scholars Casey Charles and G Patterson identify forces and configurations beyond classrooms (forces such as a universalizing heteronormativity and oppositional framings of difference as deplorable) that come to bear on classrooms as sites that may well hinder flourishing and foster harm. Like curricular and feedback decisions, the experiences and lives of teachers exist within larger patterns of interaction and of discursive circulation. Pedagogy exists within larger political and institutional contexts that present teachers—especially marginalized teachers—with a range of risks and potential harms. The patterns LGBTQ+ instructors encounter range from harassment by students and silencing by institutions to legal and political repercussions. Charles robustly accounts for these dynamics when describing a 1998 course on "Queer Stories" and the backlash the course received. Constituencies on campus, in the Montana state legislature, and from conservative Christian activist groups formed a diverse opposition to the course, with much of the concern focused on Charles's employing the label "queer." Patterson documents through interviews and observational research how English studies instructors navigate anti-LGBTQ+ harassment from students and others empowered by conservative Christian discourse and organizations. Patterson argues that marginalized teachers face institutional and disciplinary complicity with such efforts when encouraged to be silent about their experiences and expertise or to exercise a pedagogical neutrality that belies the harms that befall LGBTQ+ students and teachers. Charles and Patterson attend robustly to questions of harm and risk as well as to the different contexts with which pedagogies interact.

Where Do We Need to Go? Positionality and Archival Directions

As the survey above demonstrates, queer rhetorics and religious rhetorics consider religion-LGBTQ+ intersections from a range of angles. This section argues for more work that explores narrative frameworks for researcher positionality and that investigates archival and historical materials. Such a call surely does not emerge from an absence. Rather, it expresses a desire for a greater proliferation of discourses—more stories from more varied people might not only open new avenues for scholarly investigation but also invent additional opportunities for disrupting typical, oppositional narratives.

Researcher positionality and narrative emerges in compelling ways in research on queer rhetorics, on religious rhetorics, and on the intersection of these two areas. Smart and Chávez are exemplars in this regard. More work with narrative and positionality will further expand the possibilities for rhetorical empathy and deliberation. While this chapter opened with a narrative that signals some of my personal commitments in work at this discursive intersection, it focused on harm. Another story points to the possibilities for flourishing.

Even though I was raised without a religious background, I found Unitarian Universalism (a theologically eclectic religious movement) in college and was baptized and confirmed as an Episcopalian (a mainline Protestant denomination) during my doctoral studies. Starting in 1976, the Episcopal Church officially began articulating its positions regarding the place of gays and lesbians in the life of the church and society. One resolution declared that "homosexual persons are children of God who have a full and equal claim with all other persons upon the love, acceptance, and pastoral concern and care of the Church" (General Convention). Another resolution that year called for the protection of gays and lesbians in civil affairs. Living into these declarations has been a decades-long process. When I attended the summer 2015 triennial denominational decision-making gathering known as General Convention, the body voted to change church law to ensure same-sex couples' access to religious marriage ceremonies. This final vote took place mere days after the Supreme Court ruling that declared marriage equality in the United States is a civil right. On the day news broke of the Supreme Court ruling, a change occurred in the General Convention's morning worship program. An announcement indicated that we would greet the good news from the court with celebratory opening music. As we sang verses from the South African folk-song-cum-freedom-anthem "Siyahamba" (with lines like "We are marching in the light of God"), there was clapping and dancing. Dance lines formed with laypeople, bishops, monks, priests, and others moving through the aisles. This brief narrative involves personal engagement with deliberative rhetoric, community literacy, religious tradition, and histories of advocacy.

In the midst of this confluence, a secular institution's decision (i.e., the court ruling) recognizing the full and equal claims of LGBTQ+ persons to civil marriage served as an instigating incident for a Christian community's celebratory singing and dancing. Such a scene could easily be illegible as a religious moment. Even though it occurred in a church context, the prevalent oppositional framing of LGBTQ+ and religion discourses and the dearth of readily accessible language for telling different stories could lead an onlooker to understand it as a liberal celebration of a political victory. Yet, for those gathered—myself among them—this was a holy occasion and a spiritual experience. If this ground of community and individual religious self-recognition is neglected, then grounds for identification, persuasion, vulnerability, and empathy are lost.

The story of dancing Episcopalians is surely not an exception but one of many that speak to the interwoven nature of LGBTQ+ and religious discourses. Personal narratives and researchers accounting for their own positionality are, of course, rhetorical constructs rather than direct and unmediated renderings of experience. As such, these constructs both reveal and enact writers' commitments and beliefs. They provide writers and readers with ways into complexity and specificity, thus resisting a kind of universalism that empties experience of its particularity. At the same time, generating narratives from more, and more varied, standpoints increases the storehouse of available and trusted resources that support both in-group and cross-constituency deliberation.

The goals of more rhetorically empathetic deliberation and robust narratives are also served by increasing historical and archival research into the interactions of LGBTQ+ and religious discourses as more than reciprocally defining oppositions. Rhetoric scholar James Darsey has assessed the general recent history of activist appeals within LGBTQ+ civil rights and liberation rhetoric. Darsey helpfully charts the development of appeals within gay social change movements from 1977 to 1990: a late-1970s emphasis on unity, determination, and safety (48–50)—an emphasis that persisted with some differences into the early 1980s (51–55)—and a shift toward justice-oriented appeals during the 1980s AIDS crisis (56). Through social movement case studies, Darsey illustrates how LGBTQ+ activism often responds to religiously motivated activism, pointing to powerful histories of opposition. This important history provides a narrative of intense and mutually shaping oppositions. Stories of other configurations alongside this account are waiting to be told.

Even as queer rhetorics research considers historical and archival questions, possibilities abound for additional archival recoveries and analyses that attend more fully to the work of religion as a force for both harm and flourishing in the lives of LGBTQ+ people. For example, following the armed assault on the gay nightclub Pulse in 2016 during its "Latin Night," a few media accounts located that attack on LGBTQ+ people of color within a narrative history of violence against queer spaces, including the 1973 arson committed at the New Orleans UpStairs Lounge, a gay bar where part of the building housed a church space. That attack left thirty-two dead. Significantly, many of those victims were gay Christian men who had just been at the services of the Metropolitan Community Church, an LGBTQ+-affirming Protestant denomination. In 2009, writing about this event for communication scholars, Robert E. Goss critiqued the police, media, local churches, and gay businesses for the silence they enforced after the attack, and he praised activism designed to mourn and memorialize the dead. Additional historical and archival work may similarly enable other memorializations as well as provide pathways to source material that serve deliberative ends in the present.

Archival and historical research may help reframe contemporary and ongoing conversations within religious institutions about their policies related to the status of LGBTQ+ persons. For example, one set of institutions where such conversations continue are many religious colleges and universities. The issues addressed in these conversations—about the place of LGBTQ+ students and employees in the life of these institutions—are not new, as the story of Louie Crew Clay illustrates. Delving into Clay's history might help scholars gain a better understanding of how the stories of religion and LGBTQ+ lives have mutually informed one another not only to produce harm but also to facilitate flourishing and queer activism. From 1954 to 1958, Clay studied English as an undergraduate student at Baylor University, a research-intensive Protestant university with historical connections to Texas Baptists. Clay would go on to undertake significant writing and activism in English studies and in the Episcopal Church around LGBTQ+ recognition. One night during the General Convention I described earlier, an annual event called the Integrity Eucharist took place.[3] This particular Integrity Eucharist celebrated Clay's accomplishments. Clay held many academic appointments but retired after serving as an English professor at Rutgers University. In 1974, the year following the UpStairs Lounge fire, Clay founded Integrity. That same year, he married his husband, Ernest, and coedited with Rictor Norton a special issue of *College English* titled "The Homosexual Imagination" (see Cox and Faris for annotations of pieces from that special issue). The next year, Clay cofounded the lesbigay caucus of the National Council of Teachers of English, which Clay discussed in an interview with Mark McBeth in the collection *Listening to Our Elders*.[4]

On the evening of the 2015 Integrity Eucharist, to a long, standing ovation filled with applause, shouts, and alleluias, Clay stood with his husband before the crowd gathered for worship. As we clapped, Clay crossed himself, provoking more thunderous applause. And the couple kissed as another roll of celebratory noise made its way through the sanctuary made more sacred by their presence. That week, one of the goals to which Clay dedicated himself and Integrity became a reality: gay and lesbian couples' access to the sacrament of marriage within the Episcopal Church.

Clay's life illustrates how narratives—both personal and historical—work in overlapping ways to complicate easy dichotomies between religious and secular domains, between religiosity and queer sexuality. In addition to his scholarly, nonfiction, and poetic publications, Clay's collected papers housed in the Joseph A. Labadie Collection at the University of Michigan amply document the intertwining of religious and LGBTQ+ discourses in overlapping personal and historical narratives. Clay's archival materials contain correspondence, subject files, photos, and a range of other materials. The collection focuses on Clay's activism as a gay rights advocate across a number of religious and academic organizations. Much of the correspondence relates to Integrity and its journal. Of course, prior to all these religious, scholarly, and activist endeavors, Clay was a college student at a Texas Baptist university. He describes this time (from 1954 to 1958) in terms that held out little hope for blending Christianity—indeed, he went to college with ideas of becoming a Baptist minister—and his sexuality:

> When once at college I went for counsel about my incessant homosexual dreams, the preacher opened the door and asked his secretary to stay within earshot, so fearful was he of being closeted with someone even to discuss gay dreams. Four years later, this same preacher was fired for having an affair with his male choir director. . . . At Baylor I once slipped an anonymous note under the office door of my religion professor begging him to discuss homosexuality in our Christian ethics class; instead he gave a grim lecture on the Freudian terms *id*, *ego*, and *superego*, and suggested that his "anonymous caller" (I turned crimson) ought to see a psychiatrist, and a Christian psychiatrist at that. (5)

This story of a 1950s gay college student in the South repeatedly exercising tremendous vulnerability embodies a number of missed opportunities. In the midst of struggle and harm, throughout his life, Clay's mantra-cum-tagline and ceaseless prayer resounds: "Joy Anyway!" Even as they put on display practices and discourses that bring harm, narratives also help account for the forms of flourishing these interwoven discourses can enable.

Why It Matters

Thus far, this chapter has addressed the central problem of oppositional framings, pointed to interventions professionals in rhetoric and writing offer, and suggested lines for expanded inquiry. These expansions lead to two central issues of significance for the broader discipline. Historical and archival work points to implications related to rhetorical conceptions of time (i.e., *chronos* and *kairos*), and attention to narrative and researcher positionality raises questions about the relationship of rhetorical practice and individual belief (not just religious belief).

Since narratives unfold in time, considering different rhetorical orientations to time may help in thinking about religion-LGBTQ+ discursive intersections, and this thinking may yield broader insights into dichotomy-laden public discourse. In classical rhetoric, time appears as *chronos* and *kairos*, linear time and opportune time. Rhetorical scholarship tends to frame religious rhetoric in terms of kairos. For example, Richard B. Crosby argues for the primacy of "revelation—not persuasion" in kairotic moments (261). Kairos is a part of "the relationship between the rhetor and the divine," of how "divinity intervenes and may be invoked within and through discourse," and of "merging 'God's time' with human time" (266). Perhaps much harm-inducing rhetoric at religion-LGBTQ+ intersections is grounded, however, more in *chronos* than in *kairos*. Within some versions of Christianity, an understanding of salvation as bound up in going-to-heaven-and-avoiding-hell relies on a forward trajectory, moving toward one or the other eternal destination. This rhetoric relies on the relentless march of chronological time for its urgency, generating experiences that promote individual assent to a set of beliefs. By looking to archives and historical accounts that reveal how blended religious and LGBTQ+ discourses are, rhetoric scholars may well create kairotic moments in which to pull back the veil that appears to separate the past from the present and the future—bringing into question oppositional framings to religious and sexual desires, and putting the lie to universalizing claims of unidirectional forward progress in secular culture and of a thoroughly heteronormative past within religious communities.

The study of religion-LGBTQ+ intersection will also help scholars better understand how rhetorical practice may end up influencing and shaping belief (religious or otherwise)—rather than the more typical notion that beliefs and religious background inform rhetorical practice. In some ways, I follow Jeff Ringer, who examines a student's use of casuistry (a case-based form of reasoning that resolves problems by applying precedents to roughly similar situations) in an argument about the benefits of Christian schools. Ringer raises the concern that a lack of care when employing rhetorical practices, such as casuistry, may—without an evangelical student's full awareness—transform the student's faith because core principles of that faith are incompatible with the kind of self a form of address requires or implies. This topic—how rhetorical practice may contribute to demoralization, deconversion, or other shifts in belief—and its ethical implications warrant more attention. For example, the well-documented phenomenon of rhetorical inoculation entails exposing audiences to weak, easily refuted arguments in order to block later persuasion should audiences hear stronger versions of the argument. When it comes to religion and politics, inoculation as a rhetorical strategy can go terribly wrong. Inoculation is prevalent in much anti-LGBTQ+ discourse as a means to undermine potential identification with LGBTQ+ people (Stewart; Filip-Crawford and Neuberg). Not necessarily dangerous as a general strategy, when used to reinforce group insularity and caricature others, inoculation can produce negative consequences for public deliberation, harmful outcomes for LGBTQ+ persons who face much bias-motivated violence and harassment, and disorientation for religious practitioners if they realize the ethically suspect strategies used by those they hold in high regard. Realizing that trusted members of a community may have harmfully misrepresented others can lead to demoralization—and, potentially, to deconversion.

These questions of argumentative practice and its relationship to deliberation concern religious insiders, as well as scholars, as demonstrated in comments from Katelyn Beaty, former print managing editor of the flagship evangelical publication *Christianity Today*. During an April 2017 panel at the National Evangelical Press Association recorded and broadcast as an episode of the podcast *Quick to Listen*, Beaty claimed that a secular conservativism had crept into evangelicalism—similar to the long-standing claims by evangelicals and fundamentalists that secular liberalism has encroached upon and influenced mainline Protestantism. Beaty worried that the basis for many conservative evangelicals' decision-making had shifted from a traditional biblicism that treats the Bible as authoritative toward a blending of whatever mix of sources that would support the political or social conclusion already reached within the community or among its leaders ("How Should"). Consequently, scholars and religious communities express an interest in the implications of rhetorical practices and their potential contributions to community-internal and broader deliberations.

Recall the story of violence that opened this chapter. The Sunday following the shooting, that Knoxville church held worship and sang as a benediction a song that the community's children were meant to have performed the previous Sunday: "Tomorrow." With that hopeful tune from *Annie Jr.*, a religious community reclaimed sacred space. The day will come when all are invited to tell stories that acknowledge whatever harms have come their way while they are also supported in a journey toward their fullest flourishing. That day may still seem so far away. And yet, as an old hymn puts it, may it be here "soon and very soon."

Entry Points: Teaching LGBTQ+ and Religious Rhetorics

When considering how to effectively convey the deeply blended nature of religious and LGBTQ+ discourses, I have found documentaries especially useful throughout the entire curriculum, from first-year courses through graduate seminars, because of how they offer viewers narratives that intertwine these discourses. While any documentary—like any narrative—constructs a reality for viewers rather than presenting the transparent truth of a situation, these sources helpfully provide both background information and stories that serve as the starting point for engaging students in wide-ranging conversations and perspectives. They seem especially well suited to generate opportunities for rhetorical empathy because several films capture the everyday lives of those who participate in varied efforts within religious traditions to claim and inhabit sexual and gender identities in diverse ways.

Both religious and secular students bring with them ways of interpreting texts of all kinds, including those held as sacred by their own and others' communities. What interpretive reading practices might stymie or support rhetorical empathy at religion-LGBTQ+ intersections? *Trembling Before G-d* provides some potential answers. This film contains moments that reflect on religious adherents' interpretive practices. The documentary tells stories of LGBTQ+ Orthodox Jews. As students watch this film, they are disturbed by the trauma the documentary participants disclose—especially trauma induced by family members and religious communities because of their understandings of their sacred texts. In terms of rhetorical practice, students viewing this film observe what is sometimes referred to as the difference between particular orientations to religious law: reading by the letter versus reading by the spirit. Before viewing the film, most students from Christian and secular backgrounds tend to imagine a strict adherence to the letter of religious injunctions contained in scripture to result in no space for queer sexuality. Students tend to have encountered verses like Leviticus 18:22 as an all-encompassing ban on queer relationships for people of any gender. Consequently, they express surprise when a documentary participant describes avoiding a particular sexual act with other men (i.e., anal sex) because he views it as specifically forbidden in the Torah, but this strict textual reading does not from this interviewee's perspective preclude all forms of sexual activity with other men. Here, reading practices that support a strict adherence to sacred scripture open up possibilities for discussion.

Just as devout reading may result in divergent interpretations of scripture, theological orientations shape religious practitioners' uptake of religion-LGBTQ+ intersections. Does a traditionalist and theologically grounded stance on gender necessarily lead to particular positions regarding the enforcement of that gender ideology? Writing in a time of escalating global tensions and misrecognitions between the governments of Iran and the United States, I think it fair to say many U.S. residents likely imagine Iran as a space of "fundamentalism, fanaticism, and terrorism" (Satrapi ii). While many U.S. residents might know that same-sex attraction may be met with the death penalty in Iran, national policies have provided state subsidies for gender-affirming surgeries for transgender people. These policies within this theocratic nation find sponsorship in a religious opinion offered by Ayatollah Khomeini—the idea being that it is possible to change the body but not the soul. The documentary *Be Like Others* provides insight into the lives of people undergoing gender transition in Iran as well as the challenges they face. U. S.-based Christian students who have a similarly strict religiously sanctioned gender ideology (i.e., what's referred to as complementarianism) are often surprised by the inversion of their expectations: that the rigid maintenance of gender ideologies means denying any possibility of change or movement within the masculine/feminine binary. Secular and religious progressive students observe that both of these gender complementary theological programs seem to be two sides of the same normativity-reinforcing coin, with both sides troubling and limited. The conversations that follow raise questions for all students in terms of the relationship of gender identity, sexual orientation, and religiosity.

Like reading practices and theological positions, uses and re-appropriations of religious language also present occasions for reflection. How do LGBTQ+ people employ religious vocabularies for creative spiritual and social purposes in the context of their personal narratives? The documentary *Voices of Witness: Out of the Box* provides one answer. Produced by TransEpiscopal and the Episcopal Diocese of California, this thirty-minute film tells the stories of transgender Christians, including clergy members. In addition to providing a brief and accessible overview of gender identity as a concept, *Voices of Witness* helps students see how generally shared religious language and concepts may have specific resonances with particular groups, resonances informed by history and experience.

In one scene, the Rev. Carla Robinson, a Black trans woman who had been a pastor in the Lutheran Church–Missouri Synod, a conservative denomination, describes going into a clothing store for trans women early in her gender transition. The owner of Lydia's TV Fashions asked her name; Robinson replied with the masculine name she was given at birth: Carl. When asked again for her "femme name," Robinson said she didn't have one yet. Unaware that this customer had been a Lutheran pastor, the owner announced, "I hereby baptize you Carla." While the process of choosing a gender-affirming name is deeply personal, this moment was powerful for this Black trans Christian woman. Baptism is a significant ceremony in most Christian traditions, involving water and a dedication of one's life or of one's children to God. Nonreligious students are often struck by the idea that secular activities—such as clothes shopping—may carry spiritual or religious dimensions, something religious students readily take for granted. Students who come from backgrounds that do not affirm trans identities frequently express surprise that the things that matter to them from Christian tradition also matter to trans Christians, such as an experience of being called by name by the creator of the universe and having this call acknowledged in a community context.

NOTES

1. One of the case studies Blankenship uses to build a theory of rhetorical empathy centers on Justin Lee, a gay Christian man who has dedicated his life to having conversations with Christians who do not affirm LGBTQ+ sexuality or rights (5, 83–103). Refusing to accept culturally dominant discursive frameworks regarding LGBTQ+ identities and attending to embodied, vulnerable encounters across lines of difference have long been practiced within queer rhetorics scholarship.

2. Jonathan Alexander and Jacqueline Rhodes write "*that queer rhetoric names a constellation of discursive practices that emerge at different times for different groups in order to articulate resistance to regimes of sexualized normalization*" (n.p.). James Darsey and Joshua R. Ritter identify the 1960s as the beginning of a "Fifth Great Awakening" shaped by cultural turbulence involving questions of gender and sexuality; they observe that this mid-century awakening gave way to a contemporary "postmodern unraveling" (569). This unraveling means that increasing pluralism replaced long-standing notions of American civil religion as a binding social norm.

3. Eucharist is a religious ceremony structured by Jesus's final meal with his disciples and one that recalls this figure's death and resurrection; Integrity is an organization dedicated to achieving the full participation of LGBTQ+ Christians in the life of the Episcopal Church.

4. Annie S. Mendenhall also notes Clay's 1970s work to confront the racism in Georgia college literacy testing in *Desegregation State: College Writing Programs after the Civil Rights Movement*.

WORKS CITED

"Affidavit: Man Admits Church Shooting, Says Liberals Should Die." *CNN*, 28 July 2008, www.cnn.com/2008/CRIME/07/28/church.shooting/index.html.

Alexander, Jonathan. *Literacy, Sexuality, Pedagogy: Theory and Practice for Composition Studies*. Utah State UP, 2008.

Alexander, Jonathan, and Jacqueline Rhodes. "Queer Rhetoric and the Pleasures of the Archive." *Enculturation: A Journal of Rhetoric, Writing, and Culture*, vol. 13, 2012, enculturation.net/files/QueerRhetoric/queerarchive/Home.html.

Bennett, Jeffrey A. "Love Me Gender: Normative Homosexuality and 'Ex-gay' Performativity in Reparative Therapy." *Text and Performance Quarterly*, vol. 23, no. 4, 2003, pp. 331–52.

Berthoff, Ann E. "Killer Dichotomies: Reading In/Reading Out." *Farther Along: Transforming Dichotomies in Rhetoric and Composition*, edited by Kate Ronald and Hephzibah Roskelly, Boynton, 1990, pp. 12–24.

Blankenship, Lisa. *Changing the Subject: A Theory of Rhetorical Empathy*. Utah State UP, 2019.

Cavallaro, Alexandra J. "Fighting Biblical 'Textual Harassment': Queer Rhetorical Pedagogies in the Extracurriculum." *Enculturation: A Journal of Rhetoric, Writing, and Culture*, vol. 18, 2015, enculturation.net/fighting-Biblical-textual-harassment.

Charles, Casey. "Queer Writes." *Women's Studies in Communication*, vol. 28, no. 1, 2005, pp. 32–56.

Chávez, Karma R. "Beyond Complicity: Coherence, Queer Theory, and the Rhetoric of the 'Gay Christian Movement.'" *Text and Performance Quarterly*, vol. 24, nos. 3–4, 2004, pp. 255–75.

Clay, Louie Crew. "Growing Up Gay in Dixie." *Letters from Samaria: The Prose & Poetry of Louie Crew Clay*, edited by Max Niedzwiecki, Morehouse Publishing, 2015, pp. 3–10.

Cox, Matthew B., and Michael J. Faris. "An Annotated Bibliography of LGBTQ Rhetorics." *Present Tense: A Journal of Rhetoric in Society*, vol. 4, no. 2, 2015, pp. 1–161, www.presenttensejournal.org/volume-4/an-annotated-bibliography-of-lgbtq-rhetorics/.

Crosby, Richard B. "Kairos as God's Time in Martin Luther King Jr.'s Last Sunday Sermon." *Rhetoric Society Quarterly*, vol. 39, no. 3, 2009, pp. 260–80.

Darsey, James. "From 'Gay Is Good' to the Scourge of AIDS: The Evolution of Gay Liberation Rhetoric, 1977–1990." *Communication Studies*, vol. 42, no. 1, 1991, pp. 43–66.

Darsey, James, and Joshua R. Ritter. "Religious Voices in American Public Discourse." *The Sage Handbook of Rhetorical Studies*, edited by Rosa A. Eberly et al., Sage, 2009, pp. 553–86.

De la Tierra, Tatiana. "Coming Out and Creating Queer Awareness in the Classroom: An Approach from the U.S.-Mexican Border." *Lesbian and Gay Studies and the Teaching of English Composition*, edited by William Spurlin, National Council of Teachers of English, 2000, pp. 168–90.

Downs, Douglas. "True Believers, Real Scholars, and Real True Believing Scholars: Discourses of Inquiry and Affirmation in the Composition Classroom." Vander Lei and kyburz, pp. 39–55.

Filip-Crawford, Gabrielle, and Steven L. Neuberg. "Homosexuality and Pro-gay Ideology as Pathogens? Implications of a Disease-Spread Lay Model for Understanding Anti-gay Behaviors." *Personality and Social Psychology Review*, vol. 20, no. 4, 2016, pp. 332–64.

Geiger, T J, II. "Unpredictable Encounters: Religious Discourse, Sexuality, and the Free Exercise of Rhetoric." *College English*, vol. 75, no. 3, 2013, pp. 248–69.

General Convention. "Recognize the Equal Claims of Homosexuals." *Journal of the General Convention of The Episcopal Church, Minneapolis 1976*. 1977, pp. C-109, www.episcopalarchives.org/cgi-bin/acts/acts_resolution.pl?resolution=1976-A069.

Goss, Robert E. "Silencing Queers at the Upstairs Lounge: The Stonewall of New Orleans." *Queering the South*, special issue of *Southern Communication Journal*, vol. 74, no. 3, 2009, pp. 269–77.

Hickman, Hayes, and Don Jacobs. "Bill O'Reilly, Michael Savage, Sean Hannity on Accused Shooter's Reading List." *Knoxville News Sentinel*, 28 July 2008, archive.knoxnews.com/news/local/bill-oreilly-michael-savage-sean-hannity-on-accused-shooters-reading-list-ep-411278436-359830451.html.

Holland, Suzanne. "Levinas and Otherwise-than-Being (Tolerant): Homosexuality and the Discourse of Tolerance." *JAC*, vol. 23, no. 1, 2003, pp. 165–89.

"How Should White Evangelicals Respond to President Trump." *Quick to Listen* (podcast) from *Christianity Today*, 13 Apr. 2017, www.christianitytoday.com/ct/podcasts/quick-to-listen/live-how-should-white-evangelicals-respond-to-president-tru.html.

Lynch, Paul, and Matthew Miller. "Twenty-Five Years of Faith in Writing: Religion and Composition, 1992–2017," *Present Tense: A Journal of Rhetoric in Society*, vol. 6, no. 2, 2017, pp. 1–195, www.presenttensejournal.org/volume-6/twenty-five-years-of-faith-in-writing-religion-and-composition-1992-2017/.

Lythgoe, Kenneth. "Sleight of Hand: Michigan's Anti-Bully Law, (Un)acceptable Exceptions, and the Reversal of Policy Making Rhetoric." *QED: A Journal in GLBTQ Worldmaking*, vol. 1, 2013, pp. 115–40.

Mason, Debra L., and Cathy E. Rosenholtz. *Missing Voices: A Study of Religious Voices in Mainstream Media Reports about LGBT Equality*. University of Missouri Center on Religion & the Professions, 2012, www.glaad.org/files/GLAAD_MissingVoices_2012.pdf.

Mendenhall, Annie S. *Desegregation State: College Writing Programs after the Civil Rights Movement*. Utah State UP, 2022.

Patterson, G. "The Unbearable Weight of Pedagogical Neutrality: Religion and LGBTQ+ Issues in the English Studies Classroom." *Sexual Rhetorics: Methods, Identities, Publics*, edited by Jonathan Alexander and Jacqueline Rhodes, Routledge, 2015.

Pritchard, Eric Darnell. *Fashioning Lives: Black Queers and the Politics of Literacy*. Southern Illinois UP, 2017.

Ringer, Jeffrey M. *Vernacular Christian Rhetoric and Civil Discourse: The Religious Creativity of Evangelical Student Writers*. Routledge, 2016.

Satrapi, Marjane. *Persepolis: The Story of a Childhood*. Pantheon, 2003.

Smart, Juanita M. "'Frankenstein or Jesus Christ?': When the Voice of Faith Creates a Monster for the Composition Teacher." Vander Lei and kyburz, pp. 11–23.

Smith, Ralph R., and Russel R. Windes. *Progay/Antigay: The Rhetorical War over Sexuality*. Sage, 2000.

Spencer, Leland G., and Joshua Trey Barnett. "Touring Homophobia: Understanding the Soulforce Equality Ride as a Toxic Tour." *Southern Communication Journal*, vol. 78, no. 1, 2013, pp. 25–41.

Stewart, Craig O. "Social Cognition and Discourse Processing Goals in the Analysis of 'Ex-gay' Rhetoric." *Discourse and Society*, vol. 19, no. 1, 2008, pp. 63–83.

Vander Lei, Elizabeth, and bonnie lenore kyburz, editors. *Negotiating Religious Faith in the Composition Classroom*. Heinemann, 2005.

Williams, Mark Alan. "Transformations: Locating Agency and Difference in Student Accounts of Religious Experience." *College English*, vol. 77, no. 4, 2015, pp. 338–63.

Interlude

BEVERLY J. MOSS

I don't characterize my scholarly work as religious rhetorics—ironic, given the focus of this collection. When I'm asked to stake out my space in the field, I usually respond that I research literacy practices in African American community contexts and how those practices manifest themselves in composition classrooms. Those literacy practices sometimes take place in Black churches, Black women's social clubs (like my current research on the community group Phenomenal Women Incorporated), or the many other community spaces that Black people occupy. I am unapologetic in my scholarly agenda: to document and highlight the rich literacy practices that exist and thrive in Black community spaces, that highlight Black folk as meaning makers and knowledge producers whose literacies show them as more than orators and entertainers.

The Black church is one of those important community spaces where we witness these rich literacy practices. It is that Black community space where Black cultural production (including literacy activities), creative expression, civic engagement, and community and personal uplift often come together visibly in the missions of saving souls, fighting for social justice, educating the community, and creating a community identity. And while master narratives that circulate in popular culture and in discussions about and representations of Black churches have tended to focus on the powerful Black oral traditions that travel from pulpits to political and public arenas—the sermons and speeches of Martin Luther King Jr., Malcolm X, Sojourner Truth, Barbara Jordan, and Barack Obama come to mind—what is important to me is to show that these great rhetors, people who come from and were influenced by Black churches, were influenced also by the literacies in Black churches, whether they themselves were traditionally literate or not. Thus, given these interests, the Black church is one Black community space where my journey as a literacy scholar began.

I grew up in this Black community space, specifically in a southern, rural Black church, seeing and listening to local and national Black preachers and understanding Black churches as sites where the line that separated sacred from secular was often blurred, where silence when the minister was preaching often indicated a failed performance, where engaging politics and social action were/are considered necessary, where liberation of Black people was central to the church mission. It is in such contexts, beginning with my young childhood, that my initial scholarly interest in examining literacy in the Black church took root and developed.

Two specific moments come to mind that reflect how I began this work. First, when I was in graduate school at the University of Illinois at Chicago in Marcia Farr's Ethnography of Literacy seminar, we were reading Shirley Brice Heath's *Ways with Words*. As soon as I opened the book and saw the map of the Piedmont Carolinas and started to read about Trackton, I realized that I knew these people (maybe not literally). I knew the communities. I knew the area. I am from the Piedmont Carolinas. I grew up in Charlotte, but every Sunday we drove the thirty miles to the rural town of Clover in York County, South Carolina, to attend church. My relatives lived in areas like Trackton and in towns not just like Alberta and Gateway but, most likely, in Alberta and Gateway. The houses Heath described and photographed were almost identical to the ones that relatives lived in when I was a child. The old wooden church pictured in *Ways with Words* looked just like the one that my father and his family attended until his congregation raised enough money to build a small brick church and to tear the wooden one down. Several family members worked at the local mills, first on cleaning crews until, finally, the textile mills started hiring Black people.

Though I was troubled by Heath's seeming resistance to addressing the power of racism in the lives of the Black people that we meet in her book, what resonated most with me was Heath's presentation of the "preaching, singing, and praying [that] often depend on formal reading and writing, which coexist within a wide range of types of oral performance" and rhetorics (202). I recognized the "raising of hymns."

It happened every Sunday in my family's church. I remember when it was my father's turn to pray before his congregation. (My parents went to separate small Black Methodist churches in Clover, though they had the same pastor.) While I grew up in my mother's church, it just so happened that this particular Sunday, I went to my dad's church. Just like the schoolteacher in Heath's study, my father had written a short prayer of five or six sentences that turned into a much longer, more complex oral performance of his written text. His written prayer became a community text that made room for the call-and-response patterns and other rhetorical tropes that are associated with Black churches and Black rhetorical traditions. This memory became part of my reading of Heath's book. Mostly I remember thinking these are my people; this is the literate tradition that I come from. Why couldn't I tell my people's literacy stories in a way that made race, racialized spaces, and their rich literacy practices more central? Why were the master narratives about Black churches and community spaces fixated on them as oral spaces to the exclusion of the literacies that were also foundational? These questions opened up a space for me to see myself as a scholar and opened a disciplinary landscape (Royster) through which to enter scholarly conversations.

The second moment that led to my pursuing my scholarly work occurred almost simultaneously with the first. While I was in graduate school in Chicago, I attended a large, urban Black church, almost the complete opposite of my family's small, rural South Carolinian church. Of course, there were differences because of the size and urban location—resources that my little South Carolinian church didn't have, like a credit union, a large ministerial staff, multiple sermons during the week. Yet there was something going on there that resonated with my memories of my rural home church. Sunday after Sunday, I was enjoying the service, being spiritually edified, and constantly thinking about the kinds of literacy practices that we were engaging in, from the pulpit to the choir loft to the pews—similar kinds of literacy practices (maybe a bit more political in the big urban church) to the ones in my small, rural South Carolinian church. The singing, praying, and preaching were part of the literacy traditions—parts of the literate texts that are foundational to Black churches.

Almost twenty years ago (2003), I wrote about that moment when I became so fascinated with not just what the preacher was sayin' (though he could preach up a powerful storm!) or even how he was sayin' it (his words and his delivery stirred the congregation) but more so with the congregation's interactions with texts that were active parts of the service, the songs, the written program, and, of course, the sermon. As it was with my reading of *Ways*, something resonated. And it was more than a focus on the power of the Black preacher as orator, though, clearly, that was important. So for the next six or seven years, my scholarly path was set. I was going to church as both parishioner and researcher.

Not surprisingly, my ethnographic inquiry into the literacy practices in the church also meant that I was analyzing rhetorical strategies attached to those literacy practices, well-known ones like call-and-response patterns that helped me recast the sermon as a community text where the preacher—the rhetor—and the congregation—the audience—become co-composers or co-rhetors. I developed a heightened awareness of how Black churches interweave spoken, written, and musical texts seamlessly into a literate text that is foundational to Black church literacies and rhetorics (*Community Text*). I could not conduct an ethnography of literacy in Black churches without attending to the rhetorical traditions—secular and sacred—that operate in Black churches and that shape and are shaped by Black literacy traditions. Hence religious rhetorics in Black churches are inseparable from the literacy traditions in Black community spaces.

As I think about the future of religious rhetorics in Black community spaces at a time when most church services are taking place in virtual spaces, I wonder if or how digital technologies are reshaping the literacy and rhetorical practices within the spaces. What will Black cultural production look like post-COVID-19 in Black community spaces like the Black church? How will Facebook and YouTube change the nature of the community text? What will Black church literacies and rhetorics look like when we finally return to our physical community spaces?

WORKS CITED

Heath, Shirley Brice. *Ways with Words: Language, Life, and Work in Communities and Classrooms.* Cambridge UP, 1983.

Moss, Beverly. *A Community Text Arises: A Literate Text and a Literacy Tradition in African-American Churches.* Hampton Press, 2003.

Royster, Jacqueline Jones. "Disciplinary Landscaping, or Contemporary Challenges in the History of Rhetoric." *Philosophy & Rhetoric* vol. 36, no. 2, 2003, pp. 148–67.

4. "We Are Not Born for Ourselves Alone"

Jesuit Rhetoric for the Twenty-First Century

JOHN C. BRERETON AND CINTHIA GANNETT

Like the editors and other authors in this collection, we see this as a *kairotic* moment for bringing together (re)emerging discussions of the rich and powerful relationships between rhetorical studies and the discursive/symbolic expressions of multiple religious traditions, both historical and current. In the United States, scholar-teachers, certainly across most of the twentieth century, have been trained to see religious ideas and practices and rhetorical study and pedagogy as bordered and separate. Thus, this study is one of both discovery and recovery, the reclamation and adaptation of the intertwined histories of rhetoric and religion in the current moment. For starters, why would scholar-teachers in writing and rhetorical studies be interested in something called "Jesuit rhetoric"? For many of us who study and teach writing and rhetoric in the United States in the twenty-first century, the notion of Jesuit rhetoric has very little meaning, though we may know that there are some U.S. schools and colleges identified as Jesuit.[1] In this essay, we argue that understanding the continental origins of Jesuit rhetoric and its global educational reach across sacred and secular domains over nearly five centuries helps us create a richer and more productive view of rhetorical history, particularly rhetorical education, in the United States.

The explosion of scholarship on larger international and transnational histories of rhetoric from the 1960s onward restarted the project of recovering rhetoric and religion as intimately and mutually informing. This work has accelerated in the last few decades, as scholars seek to understand a host of rhetoric(s) in their larger cultural, social, and historical contexts and to develop historiographic approaches to religious and spiritual ideas and practices that are less polemic and confessionally bound. Our work on Jesuit rhetoric has been immensely aided by the convergence of several historiographic trends, including the renewal of interest in international histories of rhetoric from the 1960s on, as fostered by the International Society for the History of Rhetoric and the Rhetoric Society of America, which brought the integrated and multidirectional histories of regional/national rhetorics and religious orientations into sharp relief, moving historiographic orientations away from apologetic and polemic stances in historical works by and about the Jesuit tradition. This work joins with the Standing Group on Rhetoric and Religious Traditions of the Conference on College Composition and Communication to promote these conversations, along with Lynch and Miller's annotated bibliography of religious rhetorics in *Present Tense*. The convergence of these multiple communities of scholar-teachers is testimony to the vitality of this kind of work, and their output offers a useful set of resources for anyone who is interested in this area of inquiry.[2]

In this chapter, we offer a historical overview of the Jesuits that treats their "ministries of the word" and the ways in which their massive educational project enacted a distinctive transdisciplinary view of rhetoric. We briefly trace the particular historical trajectory of Jesuit education in the United States and the way it demonstrates both continuity and change in terms of structures, aims, and pedagogy. Perhaps most importantly for readers of the present volume, we trace the hidden Jesuit influence on modern rhetorical scholarship and teaching through two figures not usually associated with the Jesuits: Edward P. J. Corbett and John Bean.[3] Through these two figures and their key texts, we trace some of the subtle resonance of older Jesuit rhetorical principles, reframed in current parlance, as they interact with and enliven other modern rhetorical traditions in the United States. Finally, we suggest that aspects of the renewed Jesuit rhetorical legacy can contribute to American higher education and make an opening for further scholarly research.

The Jesuit rhetorical enterprise is captured by the phrase *eloquentia perfecta*, which Steven Mailloux defines as an adaptation of "the classical ideal of the good person writing and speaking well for the public good that promotes the teaching of eloquence combined with erudition and moral discernment" ("Good Person" 13). These principles focus on the development of personal, cultural, and critical consciousness in the service of action or, in Jesuit parlance, *cura personalis*, the formation and care of the entire person. Similarly, the cultivation of reflection, or "discernment," whether in spiritual terms or not, is joined with the central aim of engaging ethical and empathic principles in all social discourse—the imperative to use rhetoric for social justice, as in the Jesuit concept of "men and women for others."

Indeed, the Jesuits, unlike most other confessional orders, were described as "contemplatives in action," interacting with larger secular cultures and knowledge traditions from the beginning. From their own extended training in the language arts in the early sixteenth century at the University of Paris, one of the centers of Renaissance Christian humanism, the first Jesuits determined that education should focus on practice rather than precepts. In addition, active learning should engage all the senses—the "full sensorium," as Jesuit scholar Walter Ong describes it—in a clearly delineated developmental sequence. Their attention to reading and composing across all modes and media and their joining argument and persuasion with all the visual and performative arts to move the heart as well as the mind are principles that speak across the centuries directly to the current moment. This capacious, generative definition of rhetoric captures much of the Jesuit "way of proceeding," particularly the principle of "rhetorical accommodation," that is, attending and adjusting to the needs of others, which scholars like Marc Fumaroli ("Fertility and Shortcomings"), John O'Malley ("'Not for Ourselves'"; "Historiography"; *Saints and Devils*), Robert Maryks, (*St. Cicero*; "Rhetorical Veri-similitudo"), and Stephen Schloesser ("Accommodation as Rhetorical") have argued are at work in every aspect of the Jesuit enterprise.

We are, of course, aware that the Jesuit legacy is not unproblematic. There are all the serious issues of a nearly five-hundred-year-old, male-only religious order of European origin, as well as important questions connected to Jesuit global missionary activity, especially its engagements around gender and the colonial exploitation of subject peoples. There are always yawning gaps between divine principles and the human enactments of them. Yet there remain distinctive features of the Jesuit educational and rhetorical enterprise—then and now—worthy of our attention.

Sacred and Secular Rhetoric in the Old Society (1540–1773): "Ministries of the Word"

The Society of Jesus, the Jesuits, were formally founded in 1540 during the late Renaissance when rhetoric, both sacred and secular, was at the center of intellectual, cultural, and spiritual life. The Jesuits were (and remain) distinctive for their persuasive preaching and their famous devotional practice, the *Spiritual Exercises*, an extended set of meditations and conversations intended to cultivate a personal and discerning sense of spiritual awareness. Developed by St. Ignatius Loyola as he progressed in his own spiritual awareness and practice, they have been central to the formation of all Jesuits and the Jesuit enterprise as a whole. Identified by G. T. Tade as a form of *self-persuasion* as early as 1957, the *Exercises* are still amazingly popular as an ecumenical set of meditations after nearly five hundred years (see Endean; Pavur, "Jesuit Spirituality").

Along with their rhetorically rich spirituality, the Jesuits are probably best known for their rhetorically and spiritually infused pedagogy, delivered by the first worldwide network of schools. By 1773, according to O'Malley, "the Jesuit network of some 800 educational institutions had become the most immense [enterprise] operating under a single aegis on an international basis that the world had ever seen" (qtd. in Duminuco 65). Though the Jesuits did not at first aspire to become a teaching order, their high level of education made them attractive as faculty, and soon they were asked to open schools and colleges throughout Europe and, almost immediately, in Portuguese India. This early connection with education shaped the order from then on; they became the first Catholic order to commit to teaching both religious and lay students as a formal ministry.

The educational traditions of the Society of Jesus have always been deeply rooted in the rhetorical and discursive arts. From Loyola's founding of the order in 1540, Jesuit training was saturated with rhetoric, providing mastery of both theory and practice, and the Jesuits have always been identified as being—and creating—powerful rhetors across sacred and secular domains. Loyola himself was educated at the University of Paris, one of the centers of Renaissance rhetorical education. He wanted members of his order to be educated at excellent schools and fully capable of being "Ministers of the Word." The early Jesuits employed their rhetorical skills in art, architecture, theater, music, dance, emblem books (which fused images and scripts to inspire spiritual understanding), and, of course, oratory.

The course of study in Jesuit colleges consisted of humane letters, emphasizing the Greek and Latin classics, as codified by the *Ratio Studiorum* of 1599. This document, sometimes called the magna carta of Jesuit education, influenced the course of higher education generally in many ways.[4] Contrasting with and complementing the scholastic model of strict memorization of books of rules, and rigidly structured disputations, the new Jesuit college (*studia humanitatis*) focused on direct experience with classical literature as the prompt for humanistic learning. The Jesuit colleges emphasized active, developmental learning, arguing that the newly discovered great pagan texts could center all learning, providing models of style and grace as well as embodying wisdom and virtue and offering insight on the world and human nature. The Jesuits themselves produced innumerable texts and treatises on all areas of rhetorical inquiry (Conley; Kennedy; Mack; Kraus).

The rhetorical curriculum of a Jesuit college began with three years of grammatical study, wherein students developed competence in spoken Latin and sometimes Greek through readings and constant exercises. This was followed by two years of humanities, which included both poetry and history. The curriculum concluded with up to two more years of a capstone course in rhetoric. The Jesuits found in Cicero and Quintilian a deep connection with their own sense of the ministries and masteries of the word. "We are not born for ourselves alone. We as human beings are born for the sake of other human beings, that we might be able mutually to help one another" (*De Officiis* 1.7.22.) For Quintilian, the goal was "*vir bonus dicendi peritus*" (*Institutio Oratoria* 12.1.1). While the extended Jesuit curriculum included advanced study of philosophy and theology, this seven-year curriculum with its aim of *eloquentia perfecta* was considered full training for most learned occupations, as well as preparation for full citizenship. The centrality of rhetoric for the Jesuits is summed up cogently by Marc Fumaroli: "Far from being a trite technique of manipulation or pretence [*sic*], the rhetoric of the Humanists, and, later, the Jesuits was the creative driving force of their ethics, spirituality, exegesis, anthropology, and theology" ("Fertility and Shortcomings" 91). Or as John O'Malley put it, "Rhetoric in the humanistic tradition was not simply a discipline, not simply the culminating discipline, but the discipline that imbued the whole system with its finality and gave it a life-shaping force" (Foreword xi).

However, the great successes of the Jesuits also brought them many rivals and enemies. Considered too lax and flexible by more conservative Catholic orders and too bound to Rome and confessionalism by Enlightenment figures, emerging nation-states, and the rise in secularism, the Jesuit order was universally suppressed between 1773 and 1814, and the Society of Jesus with its schooling project was nearly extinguished. At the same time, older notions of oral public rhetoric were being transformed by the movement to print, scientific preferences for plain language, and the growing influence of belles-lettres.

The History of the Jesuits and Jesuit Rhetorical Education in America

The Society that had served as the "schoolmasters of Europe" contributed some of the great orators, preachers, and thinkers of the sixteenth and seventeenth centuries and provided tutors and confessors to the nobility in many European states, but the Jesuits played a very different and much more modest set of roles in America. Having been displaced or expelled from most European countries and parts of the new world during the Suppression, Jesuits were sent primarily to serve the spiritual and educational needs of the masses of immigrant Catholics in the nineteenth and early twentieth centuries, a marginalized group often excluded from educational and social opportunity in this very Protestant land.

U.S. Jesuits were acutely aware that they served Catholics in a predominantly Protestant, often anti-Catholic country. Though by 1820 Roman Catholics were increasing in numbers, they were still vastly outnumbered by their Protestant counterparts, as they still are today. The Jesuit schools would fill a serious need for those growing immigrant Catholic populations, which early on were often denied education or offered a Protestant version, with the King James Bible being the only sacred scripture permitted (Leahy; Mahoney; McKevitt). In 1789 the first Jesuit college, Georgetown University in Washington, DC, was founded by Jesuits affiliated with members of the order from White Russia.

The educational landscape that the Jesuits entered in America in the nineteenth century was one still very much in the classical tradition. Latin and Greek were taught almost everywhere; rhetoric was universal, mostly aimed at oral public discourse; and students wrote and practiced orations throughout all four years of college. The curriculum was almost entirely prescribed; colleges had neither departments nor electives. The small number of students who attended college were predominantly upper or upper-middle class, aspiring to the learned professions: medicine, law, or the ministry. The major rhetorical textbooks were, naturally, treatises by British Protestant divines: Hugh Blair, George Campbell, and Richard Whately, and there was still an emphasis on character formation in the larger institutional paideia.

The Jesuit schools established in the nineteenth century were both in and out of this tradition. While a comparison of the 1855 curriculum of Loyola College in Maryland with Harvard's reveals remarkable similarities, including a focus on the same limited set of classical authors and roughly equivalent ancillary coursework, these similarities conceal different curricular sources. Harvard's derived from English and Scottish approaches to classic authors and to rhetoric, whereas the Jesuits' curriculum drew on time-hallowed approaches that they themselves had developed in Catholic countries: Spain, Italy, Portugal, France, and southern Germany.

After the Civil War, the U.S. educational scene shifted dramatically. What had been explicitly Protestant institutions gradually became increasingly secular, and those seeking access to higher education grew exponentially. Thanks to a new continental import, the German research model, the American college curriculum became organized in and through departments, bringing increasing demand for specialization and the elevation of scientific knowledge production over perennial interest in the humanities. Culturally and educationally, interests in belletristic literary study as well as utilitarian agendas that valued written genres for the new print-centered society and new professions moved away from the emphasis on neoclassical public discourse and oratory toward "literature" and to more narrow forms of writing instruction, including the creation of first-year writing courses (freshman composition) by 1900.

These changes were generally resisted by Jesuit colleges. While accommodating in particular ways to the changing intellectual and educational American situation, Jesuit higher education retained key elements of its distinctive educational heritage. In doing so, Jesuits created new hybrid forms of curricula, texts, and educational practices, even while their curricula were increasingly vilified and denigrated as obsolete: in the words of President Charles William Eliot at Harvard, the Jesuit curriculum was "absurd," and he compared Jesuit schools to madrasas (Zaleski 159–60). However, the Jesuits continued to value extensive and immersive multilanguage training across classical and vernacular languages and to conceptualize all the receptive and expressive language arts as integrated, and integrative, habits of mind and heart as best they could for at least another fifty years. As one prominent Jesuit educator put it, "The apex of all studies was rhetoric. Mastery of *eloquentia perfecta*, or articulate wisdom, meant not only the ability to communicate with ease and elegance but 'the capacity to reason, to feel, to express oneself and to act, harmonizing virtue with learning'" (McKevitt 279). It is in this sustained emphasis on the integration of intellectual, civic, moral, and spiritual formation that we find some of the most distinctive Jesuit rhetorical thinking and practice at work.

The effort to sustain a Jesuit identity while accommodating the changing cultural conditions of American higher education can also be seen in the specific tradition of Jesuit rhetoric texts that were adapted or written for use in Jesuit schools and colleges in the United States. For example, while they certainly used the rhetoric texts from the larger Protestant culture from the beginning, they also used older Jesuit texts such as Martin De Cygne's 1619 rhetoric right into the twentieth century. German Jesuit Joseph Kleutgen's rhetoric text (in Latin) was used at Boston College into the 1920s. In addition, the late nineteenth and early twentieth centuries saw a series of rhetoric texts written in English by Jesuits Francis P. Donnelly, Francis X. O'Conor, and Sidney Smith that were used almost exclusively at Jesuit colleges.

But slowly and surely across the late nineteenth and first half of the twentieth centuries, the Jesuits separated their high schools and colleges, and they gave up much of their unified, concentrated curricular focus on language and literary and rhetorical study under pressure from accrediting organizations. They increasingly accommodated the disciplinary structures from the new German research-university models, as part of the broad secularization of American society by mid-century, and lost touch with parts of their own heritage, especially as more and more lay (and non-Catholic) faculty and administrators were needed to sustain the educational enterprise. The last holdout was Holy Cross, which eliminated the Greek requirement in 1958 and the requirement for four years of Latin in 1959 (Bizzell; Halloran; Leahy; Birnbaum and Meehan).

We focus our attention here on two important figures whose Jesuit connections are much less explicit than those of someone like Walter Ong. Edward

P. J. Corbett was a product of Catholic and Jesuit formation/education, and he brought that deeply embedded ethos with him to a large secular public institution and to his scholarly and pedagogical texts, particularly his *Classical Rhetoric for the Modern Student* (*CRMS*). John Bean, meanwhile, found himself at a Jesuit university and adapted some of its key educational principles and attitudes to modern composition studies. Whether consciously borrowing or not, both scholars offer a Jesuit-inflected emphasis on rhetorical and language studies, renewing it in subtle ways for new generations. These two examples demonstrate the profound, if often hidden, influence of Jesuit rhetorical traditions on modern theory and practice.

EDWARD P. J. CORBETT

Edward P. J. Corbett (1919–1998), one of twentieth-century America's most prominent rhetorical educators and a chief mover in the renewal of interest in classical rhetoric in the United States in the 1960s and 1970s, is referred to by Richard Enos as the "Quintilian of our era" (410). In addition to his major textbook, *Classical Rhetoric for the Modern Student*, which went through four editions (1965, 1971, 1990, and [with his student Robert J. Connors] 1999), Corbett published influential handbooks, teaching guides, and a variety of scholarly essays covering many areas of rhetorical inquiry. Corbett served as the president of the Conference on College Composition and Communication and helped found the Rhetoric Society of America. For most of his career he was at Ohio State University, where he played a formative role in training many generations of students in rhetoric who would form a key cohort of American rhetorical scholarship.

Our interest is in Corbett's Jesuit connections, both personal and professional, though he rarely mentions them, nor do others often acknowledge them in reference to his scholarly and pedagogical work. But these influences can be readily discerned. Indeed, Corbett's intellectual formation and his outlook on education were shaped by his early Jesuit training, particularly his commitment to the transformative moral power of humane letters (Nelms 202). Born to a very poor family in North Dakota, young Edward and his siblings moved to Milwaukee in his father's search for work, and Corbett attended Catholic primary school. He was selected to receive a scholarship to attend a Jesuit high school, Marquette University High School in Milwaukee, where he was immersed in a full Jesuit educational environment. The formal curriculum included four years of English, four years of Latin, three years of Greek, and a full year of public speaking. (For a full description of this classical kind of curriculum and the pedagogy at Marquette up into the 1950s, see Leigh.) As he was to put it, "Four years of Latin and Greek just turned my life around—and why me, Lord? Why me, Lord?" (Nelms 201). This work in classical languages and rhetoric translated through the lens of Renaissance Christian humanism and the Jesuit educational project was to lead eventually to his devotion to teaching classical rhetoric in the service of developing true eloquence, traits he shared with centuries of Jesuit teachers and scholars, both in America and abroad.

Corbett's integration of rhetoric and the language arts with religion continued with his seminary training at Venard College in Clarks Summit, Pennsylvania, a missionary training college run by the Maryknoll Fathers. There, Corbett, in preparation for a career as a Roman Catholic missionary, immersed himself in global rhetorics, studying Japanese, Chinese (speaking and ideographic writing), and French, as well as additional courses in Latin (Horace, Grammar, and Tacitus) along with philosophy, logic, theology, and metaphysics.[5] Corbett's deep focus on languages, religions, and cultures is in keeping with the training of most Jesuits across the centuries who believed that learning Latin and Greek was essential to achieving eloquence in the Christian humanist context of the Renaissance. Cultivating linguistic polymaths was also central to the Jesuit heritage, as they worked to form missionaries and public officials who could enter into the symbolic universes of the groups they encountered internationally.

Corbett went on to earn a master's in English literature from the University of Chicago, at the time one of the few universities that took rhetoric seriously. P. Albert Duhamel, who would later teach at Boston College, a Jesuit school, had taught there, as had Kenneth Burke. Other Chicago faculty included the rhetoricians Richard Weaver, Manuel Bilsky, Robert E. Streeter, Wilma Ebbitt, Henry Sams, and Wayne Booth. (Corbett would include an article by Bilsky, Streeter, and Weaver, "Looking for an Argument," in the second, third, and fourth editions of *CRMS*.) Rhetoric was in the air in Chicago's English Department, though Corbett claimed he didn't connect with it as a subject of interest until he was hired to teach at Creighton University, a Jesuit school in Omaha, where he discovered Hugh Blair. He explained that his Chicago MA training had prepared him to teach fourteen-line poems but not extended pieces of prose, a clear criticism of New Critical approaches prevalent at the time (Corbett, "Hugh Blair" 99). He credited Hugh Blair with introducing him to this method of rhetorical criticism, which he put to use in his literature courses at Creighton. When Corbett took a leave of absence from Creighton to get a PhD in English at Loyola University of Chicago, he wrote his dissertation on Blair's rhetoric, an unusual choice for the time, but one that would mark him out as claiming a place for the serious study of the eighteenth-century British foundations of rhetoric in America.

While these Catholic and Jesuit educational cultures assuredly influenced Corbett's interests (see Nelms), Corbett does not remark explicitly on the rhetorical education he had with the Jesuits, which is understandable because most Jesuit educators themselves did not call attention to it, given the significant effacement and loss of Jesuit traditions after the Suppression as well as the enormous pressure to "fit in" to American higher educational culture. Corbett's "A Survey of Rhetoric" might well be called "An English Major's Survey of Rhetoric," in that, like most American rhetorical scholars at the time, he omits most continental influences after the Renaissance. "Survey" is really a prolegomenon to Blair, Campbell, and Whately's rhetoric textbooks, which greatly influenced him and which he was to edit (Golden and Corbett). Yet Corbett continued his interest in joining religion and rhetoric, noting that the three key post-Renaissance rhetoricians for him, Thomas More, Samuel Johnson, and John Henry Newman, were all religious men. Interestingly, in his chapter on the history of rhetoric that Corbett included in all four editions of *CRMS*, he mentions the important French Jesuit preachers Bourdaloue and Massillon (560 [1965]), a clear gesture to that tradition.

There are two important ways in which Corbett's textbook fits nicely within the Jesuit textbook tradition: its compendious nature and its concentration on *belles lettres*. First, *CRMS*, like many Jesuit rhetoric textbooks of the sixteenth through the nineteenth centuries and so many that imitated them, is really a manual for teachers as well as a collection aimed at students. It contains theoretical statements forming a full-fledged system of instruction, plenty of illustrative readings, a range of exercises, passages for imitation, lists of rhetorical figures, and a long section on the topics for invention, quite unusual for a mid-twentieth-century textbook. These diverse treatments of different rhetorical elements are not fully woven together. In this way, they are aligned with the larger traditions of classical and Renaissance continental rhetorics. Indeed, they echo earlier American Jesuit rhetorics, such as Charles Coppens, S.J.'s 1885 textbook, *Practical Introduction to English Rhetoric: Precepts and Exercises*, and Joseph Wilhelm Kleutgen, S.J.'s *Ars dicendi* of 1847, both used in nineteenth- and twentieth-century American Jesuit colleges and intended to prepare students both for religious discourses such as preaching and for secular discourses of all kinds.[6]

Second, Corbett's readings often focus on classics of the eighteenth and nineteenth centuries (most by white males in keeping with the times), most on serious, "uplifting" subjects, the kind of readings intended to improve students' minds and characters as well as their ability to write. Corbett's readings are almost all literary in the broadest sense, reminding us that the Jesuits—along with many others—used literary texts as examples of moral formation as well as fine writing. Corbett's Catholic perspective can also be found in his frequent invocation of the works of Cardinal John Henry Newman, the Catholic intellectual who was not popular with non-Catholic secular rhetoricians of the time but was widely studied and emulated in Catholic higher education, particularly among scholars at Jesuit institutions, including Hughes and Duhamel at Boston College. Newman is cited ten times in the first edition of *CRMS*, more than any modern writer except Dr. Johnson, with thirteen entries in the index. Though the first edition of *CRMS* came out in 1965 at the height of the "New Journalism," there's nothing by Tom Wolfe or Gay Talese or Norman Mailer or Joan Didion. Instead, we get Macauley, Newman, Addison, Blair—a collection of "classics" of mostly English prose, the kind of writers Corbett had studied in graduate school. Corbett was never afraid to be seen as traditional; in fact, he welcomed that designation.

Corbett's later textbook collection of essays, *The Essay: Old and New*, 1974, done with his Ohio State student Sheryl L. Finkle, represents the side of Corbett that is open to more modern influences. Perhaps due to Finkle's collaboration, he includes many more contemporary essays and particularly essays by women and minorities. Despite its contemporaneity, however, it is distinctive for its very traditional opening essay by Abraham Cowley and its relatively rich collection of eighteenth- and nineteenth-century essayists, including two of Corbett's favorites, Johnson and Newman.

Corbett's Jesuit ethos is also revealed by his familiarity with a series of figures in twentieth-century American rhetoric associated with Jesuit institutions. He refers to his contemporaries Albert Duhamel and Richard Hughes of Boston College, as well as Francis Donnelly, S.J., Daniel Fogarty, S.J., and Walter Ong, S.J., all three of them influential Jesuits who wrote important rhetorical works, though Hughes and Duhamel and Donnelly, even Fogarty, are nowadays rarely identified as worthy of mention or discussion in the world of secular scholarship. Corbett is the only scholar of his era to display such awareness of the work of contemporary Jesuit or Jesuit-trained rhetoricians. Indeed, he mentions them in casual and informal ways, without supplying any identifying information about them, revealing that they were a comfortable part of his mental universe, assumed to be known to his readers as well.

Throughout his career Corbett displayed deep admiration for Quintilian and Cicero, just like the original Jesuits in their devotion to active, immersive learning over "praecepta"—and thus with frequent exercises in imitation and progymnasmata. Corbett displayed a great interest in style, once again in the 2020s becoming an important element of rhetorical studies. In fact, chapter five of *CRMS* became a separate textbook, *Style and Statement*, which Corbett published with his student Robert Connors. A glance at a Jesuit rhetoric textbook, whenever it was published, reveals that close attention to style was a crucial part of Jesuit education. It was too for Corbett and for the writers he most admired: Johnson, Swift, Blair, and Newman. And anyone who has worked with *Style and Statement*, for example, understands that for Corbett, the many forms of deep *imitatio* are intended to assist in the careful, ethical, and aesthetic education of writers; they are not exercises in superficial mimicry.

Another interesting example of Corbett's Jesuit-inflected sensibilities can be seen in his selection of two readings in the first edition of *CRMS* on the then-hot topic of censorship. What makes the paired readings distinctive is that they treat a specific Catholic controversy and do not posit simple pros or cons. One of the two essays, from *Harper's*, is an attack on a Catholic anti-censorship group. The second, from the Jesuit publication *America*, by John Courtney Murray, S.J., basically agrees with the point of the *Harper's* anti-censorship piece but takes issue with the way the argument is handled, in a very nuanced and sophisticated line of reasoning in the Jesuit casuistic manner. It's hard to imagine these two essays appearing in a comparable reader of the mid-1960s. Indeed, Corbett himself had written for the same Jesuit weekly magazine in 1961, involving a defense of *The Catcher in the Rye.* Similarly, it is important to note that Corbett wrote several essays for religious journals and magazines, including *Commonweal*, *America*, *Pastoral Life: A View from the Pews*, and *Homiletic and Pastoral Review.* By the time Corbett had moved from the Jesuit Creighton to the secular Ohio State, however, the religious essays had disappeared from the second edition. By 1961, Corbett had stopped publishing in Catholic journals altogether, and obvious signs of denominational affiliation had disappeared. What remained was the abiding connection to classical rhetoric, the centerpiece of the Jesuit educational enterprise. Corbett's work retains a view of rhetoric as deeply intertwined with moral development—as indispensable to human intellectual, social, and spiritual flourishing.

JOHN BEAN

A generation after Edward P. J. Corbett, John Bean became one of the premier figures in composition and rhetorical studies for his work in writing across the curriculum (WAC) and writing in the disciplines. His most influential work by far is a guide for faculty across all disciplines, *Engaging Ideas: The Professor's Guide to Integrating Writing, Critical Thinking, and Active Learning across the Curriculum*. First nationally published in 1996, this extraordinary work has been used for graduate student and faculty development in every disciplinary area, as well as for curricular and pedagogical reform and renewal for over fifteen years by colleges and universities across the United States and abroad. It has even been translated into Dutch and Chinese.

What is not well known, or perhaps not known at all, is that Bean initially developed this project with his colleagues at Seattle University, a Jesuit institution, starting in the mid-1980s with a variety of grants and curricular reform initiatives. In other words, this influential publication began as an in-house manual directly tied to the historical legacy of Jesuit educational and rhetorical principles and practices and was born out of the specific Jesuit ethos cultivated at Seattle University during that period. The materials of the unpublished manual explicitly set out the Jesuit foundation of the text before the published editions of the book both erased that Jesuit rhetorical and spiritual heritage and yet carried it forward in subtle but significant, even if unacknowledged, ways. Indeed, the interaction of Bean's earlier experience, expertise, and spiritual openness,[7] engaging the specific congenial—and Jesuit—educational environment at Seattle University, made this work possible. When John Bean arrived at Seattle University to help create what would become a nationally recognized WAC program, he already had fifteen years of teaching and WAC work under his belt. He also had earlier experience teaching at other Jesuit and Catholic universities, which he cites as influential on his experience at Seattle (personal email to authors).

Being at Seattle led to Bean's serendipitous discovery of the Jesuit Allan P. Farrell's 1938 work on the liberal code of Jesuit education. This discovery prompted him to find several productive alignments between principles codified in the 1586 version of the Jesuit educational guide, the *Ratio Studiorum*, and current educational precepts on the power of discursive education. In his preface to the in-house manual, of 1991, originally titled "Expecting Excellence: Writing and Active Learning across the Curriculum,"[8] Bean declares, "our program is rooted in a consistent pedagogy based on recent research and scholarship in composition and on *the traditional Jesuit ethos of an education aimed at the development of the whole human person*" (v; emphasis added).[9] Bean and coauthors address this history in part in their essay "Jesuit Ethos, Faculty-Owned Assessment, and the Organic Development of Rhetoric across the Curriculum at Seattle University," claiming that the Jesuit heritage of the in-house guide is explicit at every turn. In the manual's foreword, for example, Seattle's president, William J. Sullivan, S.J., explains the rhetoric- and values-centered nature of Jesuit education: "In a Jesuit university, the teaching of writing is among the most important things we do. . . . Writing is an active and fundamental tool: through writing, re-thinking and revising, students come to apprehend knowledge and to develop a complex system of personal values" (qtd. in Bean et al. 334).

Bean's preface focuses on this central aim of Jesuit rhetorical education, documented in the 1586 *Ratio Studiorum*, as one of "stimulating at every stage of development the power of written and oral expression in accordance with the highest ideals of the intellectual and moral order." ("Expecting Excellence" iv). The opening page of the preface makes this influence explicit through an 1893 quotation from Jesuit Superior General Luis Martin, which Allan P. Farrell also cites in *The Jesuit Code of Liberal Education*:

> Some have thought that though formerly the *Ratio Studiorum* was of value, it is so no longer. A statement of this sort, in my opinion, betrays a lack of understanding of the *Ratio* by taking account only of its curricular regulations and not of its spirit. . . . [This spirit is distinctive in] many individual elements, of which two only can be touched upon here: first, that activity be demanded of the students, and secondly, that insistence be placed on the genuine formation of the human faculties rather than on the amassing and learning of facts. (402)

"Through their emphasis on writing and active learning in the Core Curriculum," continues Bean, "Seattle University teachers are putting into practice these early Jesuit objectives" ("Expecting Excellence" iv).

The process of the creation of the original manual also bears a Jesuit ethos in that it was not the work of a single author but came from an intensive collaboration of both Jesuit and lay faculty to create a rich, revised core curriculum, which Bean coordinated by compiling and synthesizing the results.[10] In his preface to the in-house manual, for example, he explains that it "integrates my own scholarship in writing across the curriculum with the pedagogical work of more than 40 Seattle University colleagues," and he notes that the document is both a guide and a "testimony" to the individual and collective efforts of the whole faculty (iv). Bean mentions that the first in-depth writing assignment discussed at the first Seattle University WAC workshop was one from the Philosophy Department.

Interestingly, while Seattle University continued to call on its Jesuit rhetorical heritage as it undertook a variety of curricular, programmatic, and assessment reforms over the next full decade, the guide that Bean created with his colleagues would be stripped of all the overt Jesuit context and language when it became a commercial publication. About the conversion of the in-house manual into a national publication, Bean told us, "when the Jossey-Bass first edition was published, the Jesuit connections became opaque" (email, 16 Nov. 2020). The term "opaque" is an interesting one. Certainly, it makes sense to adapt the text to a national, later international, audience and to accommodate different academic cultures by eliding what is too "local" or too "parochial" to permit new and different uses of the text. And certainly, the resulting version was very successful in that regard. Still, it is interesting that almost every explicit trace of the long, and global, tradition of Jesuit rhetorical education was erased. It suggests that any explicit acknowledgment of confessional identity or source would not be acceptable. In her foreword to the second edition, Maryellen Weimer, the scholarship on teaching and learning (SoTL) scholar who promoted and sponsored the move to national publication, explains that upon encountering the first "incarnation" of the guide, she had found a "diamond in the rough" (vii). The stripping of *any* overt contribution from the Jesuit tradition in the exposition and framing leads us to think that it was the very Jesuit-ness of the original that, in part, was considered "the rough" rather than the diamond.

Indeed, a close reading of the entire preface offers no clue, no explicit trace of its origins at Seattle or from the larger tradition of the *Ratio*, no mention of the importance of developing the full human faculties of students by integrating their intellectual and moral/spiritual dimensions. What does get acknowledged as key resources/influences is evidenced in the preface's subheads: SoTL (xi), "Recent Scholarship in Rhetoric, Composition, and Writing in the Disciplines" (xii), "Quantitative and Scientific Literacy Across the Curriculum," the "Use of Classroom Technology" (xiii), and new work on "Teaching Undergraduate Research" (xiv). In the brief section "What Hasn't Changed," Bean references the long-term work on WAC and critical thinking and even quotes John Dewey (xiv). Near the end of this short section, he includes a claim that resonates, however fleetingly, with the Jesuit rhetorical traditions so fully articulated in the original guide: "Equally important are giving critical thinking problems to students, and for creating a course atmosphere that encourages inquiry, exploration, discussion, and debate, *while valuing the dignity and worth of each student*" (xiv; emphasis added).

Even with all this effacement, Bean's work brings that rich Jesuit rhetorical heritage to bear on the whole field of rhetoric and composition through its newer incarnations. We argue that there is strength in what remains, that the tacit foundation—the understory—remains. For example, even though the text recognizes disciplines as the privileged sites for writing development and instruction, many of the strategies, activities, and assignments are not simply discipline bound, though they are useful in disciplinary contexts. Rather, they act as transdisciplinary rhetorical practices that support the formation of the whole learner beyond disciplinary expertise, often calling on experiential attention and reflection.[11]

It is easy to find many examples and assignments/activities that are carried over from the original manual, and they engage all the language and symbolic arts, not just writing. Consider the wonderful metaphors for invention: *brouillon* and *plan*, which call on the imagination and the intellect and draw on the full "sensorium" (à la Walter Ong). The chapter "Reading Difficult Texts" has a special Jesuit feel in the way it offers a view of reading as the intimate counterpart of composition, and it positions the teacher and student as sharing responsibility with each other and to the text in the construction of rich, productive, and sophisticated readings (161–82).[12] Similarly, *Engaging Ideas* retains a deep respect for both teachers and learners as "whole humans" throughout, manifesting a kind of "care for the whole learner/teacher" in contrast to many other faculty guides that seem more instrumental in nature. Bean is mindful of helping faculty construct assignments that make room for the learner to find his/her way in and that care for the learner's developing consciousness, and he subtly promotes a sense of *accompanying* students on their educational journeys, rather than invoking a model of teaching *at* students, assigning work, and judging it.

Reflecting on these matters, Bean explained to us his relation to the Jesuit educational tradition. He told us in an email that at both Gonzaga and Seattle University, he sensed the Jesuit influence, especially in the "enormous emphasis on 'care of the whole person,'" "a spirit of open inquiry, conservation, and debate," and the prominence of writing instruction throughout the curriculum. But it wasn't until moving to Seattle that he discovered the source of these values:

> At Seattle U, when I discovered the *Ratio Studiorum*, I realized it was an historical current I could tap into. So the *Ratio* wasn't a pedagogical influence on me—the influences came out of the heady scholarship of those wonderful early years in comp with heroes like Linda Flower, Peter Elbow, etc.—but it was like the discovery of [a] powerful ancestor spirit. (email, 23 Dec. 2020)[13]

We see, however, Bean's commitment to the central aim of Jesuit rhetorical education as that of fostering students' proficiency in written and oral communication in alignment with the loftiest goals of intellectual and moral development, with its implication that language is not only for personal, social, commercial, or civic development but always for the greater good. This key Jesuit principle is reflected in multiple ways and in all the versions of his faculty guide. Bean's work speaks eloquently to the transformative power of the word, including the intimate interanimation of the rhetorical word with the spiritual Word, just as in Ong and others. In this way, we see Bean's work writ large as arguing that this capacious and generative notion of rhetoric can center the whole curriculum, no matter the subject, and that his is a guide not just for writing in all the disciplines but also a guide for using all the language arts for the genuine formation of all the human faculties for both students and teachers.

Entry Points: Renewing Jesuit Rhetoric for the Twenty-First Century

At a time when higher education struggles to find and sustain the place of the humanities and rhetoric is often invoked only as a negative term, scholars at many Jesuit institutions, or scholars who have been educated at Jesuit institutions, are working to recover these complex and variable histories to understand what is still vital about the enduring Jesuit tradition and what might be useful for addressing broader questions of the dis-integration of culture and curriculum in postsecondary schooling. (See Gannett and Brereton, *Traditions of Eloquence*, section three.)

Also, the revival of a rhetorical "usable past" and possible future at Jesuit schools, and beyond, will need to honor and understand more fully the works of American Jesuit rhetoricians, such as Charles Coppens, John Francis X. O'Conor, Sidney Smith, Francis P. Donnelly, Walter Ong, Daniel Fogarty, Henry Bean, and Albert Johnson, as well as Jesuit-influenced teachers and scholars, such as Albert Duhamel and Richard Hughes, Edward P. J. Corbett, Stephen Toulmin, Paolo Freire, Kate Adams, Frank D'Angelo, Michael Halloran, Mike Rose, James Slevin, Krista Ratcliffe, Janice Lauer Rice, Tom Conley, Steve Mailloux, Jack Selzer, Art Walzer, Kathleen Hall Jamieson, and so many others.

Most exciting, rhetorical scholars are creating a whole new interdisciplinary and transnational field of study that bridges rhetoric and religion. Steven Mailloux (Loyola Marymount) has written on nineteenth-century American Jesuit *eloquentia perfecta* as well as Jesuit enactment theory and is now examining the fascinating connections between Kenneth Burke and French Jesuit scholarship, especially his relationship with Gaston Fessard, S.J. (personal correspondence). Deborah Holdstein has been researching the complex interactions between Christian and Hebraic rhetorics in the early Jesuits, as several of the first Jesuits were *conversos*, who brought the Jewish intellectual and spiritual tradition into the whole rhetorical and educational enterprise ("Assimilation and Disappearance") on these inquiries. Paul Lynch at St. Louis University has written on the continuing importance of the Jesuit *Ratio Studiorum* and its new incarnation, Ignatian pedagogy, for scholarship and teaching (Johnson and Lynch; Lynch, "Best Training"), as well as the epideictic rhetoric of the new Jesuit pope, Pope Francis ("On Care"). Michelle Zaleski has written about the early twentieth-century controversies between Harvard and the Jesuits over confessional tensions in the curriculum, particularly the Christian humanist rhetorical curriculum that Harvard had recently abandoned ("Word Made Secular"), and has undertaken important rhetorical research on the Jesuits in Sri Lanka and South Asia. Renea Frey at Xavier University is researching the Jesuit history of

Renaissance emblematics (a common genre of persuasive religious devotional work that combines language and visual imagery in complex textual art forms) as rhetorical practice with applications for understanding and re-seeing the mixed media of visual/verbal texts today (personal correspondence). Thomas Farrell and Paul Soukup have published widely on Walter Ong's legacy and his final synthetic work, which is not well known yet, titled *Language as Hermeneutic: A Primer on the Word and Digitization*, edited by Thomas D. Zlatic and Sara van den Berg, which came out in 2017.

Scholars in anthropology, sociology, and across the arts and sciences are also bringing their expertise to new studies on the Jesuits' engagement with complex intercultural encounters across peoples and their cultural traditions. New journals, such as the *Journal of Jesuit Studies*, and research centers, such as the new Institute for Advanced Jesuit Studies at Boston College, have been established over the last decade to gather and sponsor global research resources for Jesuit and non-Jesuit scholars alike, including the rich emergent community of international scholars who are studying all aspects of the Jesuits' relation to rhetoric across time and place. Also, earlier Jesuit educational documents and texts are now being translated to make them available for English-speaking scholars (L. Flynn, *De Arte Rhetorica (1568)*, "*De Arte Rhetorica*," "Sources and Influence"; Pavur, *Ratio Studiorum*, *School of Ignatius*; Casalini and Pavur).[14] Studying the history and future of Jesuit rhetorics offers an important opportunity to test our collective assumptions about American rhetorical history (including its confessionalism), larger histories of rhetoric, and the possible pedagogical relationships that can be forged between religion and rhetoric in and beyond Jesuit institutions. This work includes many kinds of inquiries. We view the following as promising fronts of Jesuit-informed research in rhetoric.

First, we need to broaden our views of rhetoric. In light of the capacious view of rhetoric that the Jesuits embraced—which included oral, print, and visual literacies; drama, dance, art, and architecture; and education for the public sphere and discernment for heart and spirit and for argument and imagination—how can the field reconstruct more nuanced and robust local and global accounts of rhetorical history? How do we reintegrate all the language arts once again in theory and in practice? How can we invoke and actualize the Jesuits' rich and humanizing notion of rhetoric?

Second, we need to continue to promote the study of language and rhetoric globally. Given that the Jesuits were an inter- and transnational order from the beginning, they always had to negotiate across languages, cultures, and belief systems. Thus, the Jesuits themselves often had to be linguistic and cultural polymaths, working across a variety of country and cultural borders, such as their extended exchanges in Asia and the Americas. While they were not always successful or able to rid themselves of bias or prejudice, they did make many efforts to engage fully. How can we create classes in which we practice "being men and women for others"? How might we make the most of complex cultural engagements that require mutuality, value multiple language and cultural resources, and invite all students to enrich their discursive development as whole persons in this new global era?

Third, we need to join eloquence to civic action. For the Jesuits, developing *eloquentia perfecta* meant that learners understood their responsibility to be informed and to speak up and speak out on matters affecting whole communities (for the greater good) and especially for those without voice. In this regard, how might college courses foster deep experiential learning and "speaking up" (in speech or writing) in productive ways about important topics and themes within and across classes and for larger communities? How can they learn to use language eloquently, effectively, and ethically across the whole sequence of courses and in the larger educational and social paideia?

Finally, we need to recognize the connections among Jesuit rhetoric, religion, and reflection. One of the distinctive features of Jesuit rhetoric has always been its multiple nature: its public active face balanced by its focus on the inner spiritual, dialogic rhetorics of reflection and meditation, the moments of knowing the mind and heart at work and being fully present to oneself. How can rhetoric and composition regularly incorporate reflection as a means of learning and a way to care for the whole person? And how might we study and integrate the public and personal forms of rhetorical practice to support the whole learner and more integrated learning?

The twentieth-century revival of Jesuit rhetoric is an important stream of scholarly research and proof of how the 450-year-old capacious Jesuit tradition of educating for *eloquentia perfecta* lives on and informs contemporary thinking about education. It is a kind of education that, when enacted effectively, can connect moral and ethical formation with eloquent speech including thinking, reading, writing—indeed, all uses of language and symbolic forms—intended to cultivate phronesis, discernment, persuasive force, and a full commitment to the development of the whole person and the larger community.

NOTES

1. One might even have picked up random references to Jesuits as a powerful secret society engaged in conspiracies of world dominance (try googling the term "Jesuit").

2. The U.S.-focused work on Jesuit rhetoric has expanded rapidly, as we discovered a nascent international, indeed, global community of scholars engaged in research

related to the Jesuits and rhetoric. In 2017, we helped inaugurate the International Society for the Study of Jesuit Rhetoric, which meets as an adjunct to the biennial conference of the International Society for the History of Rhetoric. We express our grateful appreciation to the organizers of the "Rhetoric and Religion in the 21st Century" conference in Knoxville, Tennessee, October 4–7, 2018, who provided the opportunity for extended, ecumenical inquiry and conversation, and to the wonderful seminar participants, who discussed these materials with such insight and enthusiasm. We hope we have characterized some of their contributions to this emerging work attentively.

3. While Walter Ong, S.J., is by far the best-known twentieth-century American rhetorician associated with the Jesuit tradition, his contribution is far too varied and extensive to treat in this essay. (For a full bibliography of his work, see Farrell and Soukup, *Ong Reader*; Walsh, "Walter J. Ong Bibliography.")

4. Paul Shore attributes the tremendous influence of the *Ratio Studiorum* on the development of education to both the organization it provided to hundreds of schools that the Jesuits established worldwide and to its vision of the teacher.

5. His coursework from Venard College is laid out in his University of Chicago graduate transcript.

6. There is no question of imitation or even conscious or unconscious influence; we don't even know if Corbett had read or knew of either of them. It's just that, like generations of Jesuits before him, Corbett saw all aspects of classical rhetoric as worthy of interest, both to teachers and to students, and included as many as he could.

7. "I am not a Catholic, but am an active Episcopalian considering myself a 'seeker' rather than a 'believer.' I always felt welcome at SU because of the Jesuit openness to mystery and questions" (email from John Bean, 17 Nov. 2020).

8. We are very grateful to John Bean for his work on the essay in *Traditions of Eloquence* that treats some of these matters, as well as his generosity in sharing materials from the original in-house manual, "Expecting Excellence" (Seattle University 1991), and his own retrospective analysis and reflections communicated to us by email.

9. One might see this as part of the enduring legacy of cultural hybridity and rhetorical accommodation that the Jesuits were both famous and infamous for over the centuries.

10. As part of the new core curriculum, "particular linkages were established between first-year composition and first-year courses in philosophy and literature. Each of these courses was rhetorically rich, shaped by the Jesuit and Catholic intellectual tradition that valued both philosophic inquiry into the nature of the human person and the aesthetic, illuminating power of literature," explain John Bean and coauthors. "To help institute this writing-across-the curriculum mandate, the university hired John Bean . . . to create and sustain the necessary faculty conversations" (333–34).

11. See especially "Helping Writers Think Rhetorically," 46–51; chapter four: "Using a Range of Genres to Extend Critical Thinking and Deepen Learning," 52–65; chapter seven: "Informal Exploratory Writing Activities," 120–48; and chapter eight: "Designing Tasks to Promote Active Thinking and Learning," 149–60.

12. This view of reading resonates well with the important Jesuit tradition of "prelection," a process in which the teacher prepares students for engaging complex texts, often in Greek or Latin, ahead of time, then leads them through the "process" of careful reading, not only to get the most meaning and utility from a given text but also to model the multiple intellectual tasks that higher-level reading demands.

13. In our most recent correspondence, John Bean said he decided to acknowledge the original Jesuit contributions to the manual in the third edition of *Engaging Ideas*, which came out in 2021.

14. See Boston College's website for the Institute for Advanced Jesuit Studies, https://www.bc.edu/bc-web/centers/iajs.html. Its mission statement reads, "The Institute for Advanced Jesuit Studies seeks to deepen an understanding and appreciation of the history, spirituality, educational heritage, and pedagogical approach of the Society of Jesus through courses, workshops, publications, and scholarly symposia. The Institute offers collaborative opportunities for scholars from around the world in order to promote a network of scholars engaged in the expanding field of Jesuit Studies." See especially the "Portal to Jesuit Studies," which includes the *Jesuit Online Bibliography*. For more information about the new international work being undertaken by members of the International Society for the Study of Jesuit Rhetoric, please contact Cinthia Gannett and John Brereton.

WORKS CITED

Abbot, Don Paul. "Reading, Writing, and Rhetoric in the Renaissance." *A Short History of Writing Instruction from Ancient Greece to Contemporary America.* 3rd ed., edited by James J. Murphy, Routledge, 2012, pp. 148–71.

Banchoff, Thomas, and José Casanova, editors. *The Jesuits and Globalization: Historical Legacies and Contemporary Challenges.* Georgetown UP, 2016.

Bean, John C. *Engaging Ideas: The Professor's Guide to Integrating Writing, Critical Thinking and Active Learning across the Curriculum.* 2nd ed., Jossey-Bass, 2011.

Bean, John C., et al. "Jesuit Ethos, Faculty-Owned Assessment, and the Organic Development of Rhetoric across the Curriculum at Seattle University." Gannett and Brereton, pp. 332–45.

Birnbaum, Benjamin, and Seth Meehan, *The Heights: An Illustrated History of Boston College, 1863–1913.* Linden Lane Press, 2014.

Bizzell, Patricia. "Historical Notes on Rhetoric in Jesuit Education." Gannett and Brereton, pp. 39–59.

Casalini, Cristiano, and Claude Pavur, editors. *The Way to Learn and the Way to Teach*, by Joseph Jouvancey, S.J., Institute of Jesuit Sources, 2020.

Codina, Gabriel. "The 'Modus Parisiensis.'" *The Jesuit* Ratio Studiorum*: 400th Anniversary Perspectives*, edited by Vincent J. Duminuco, Fordham UP, 2000, pp. 28–49.

Conley, Thomas. *Rhetoric in the European Tradition*. U of Chicago P, 1990.

Coppens, Charles. *The Art of Oratorical Composition*. Schwartz, Kirwin, and Fauss, 1885.

—. *A Practical Introduction to English Rhetoric: Precepts and Exercises*. Schwartz, Kirwin, and Fauss, 1880.

Corbett, Edward P. J. *Classical Rhetoric for the Modern Student*. 1st ed., Oxford UP, 1965.

—. *Classical Rhetoric for the Modern Student*. 2nd ed., Oxford UP, 1971.

—. *Classical Rhetoric for the Modern Student*. 3rd ed., Oxford UP, 1990.

—. *Classical Rhetoric for the Modern Student*. 4th ed., Oxford UP, 1999.

—. "Hugh Blair as an Analyzer of English Prose Style." *College Composition and Communication*, vol. 9, no. 2, 1958, pp. 98–103.

—. *Selected Essays of Edward P.J. Corbett*. Edited by Robert J. Connors, Southern Methodist UP, 1989.

Corbett, Edward P. J., and Robert J. Connors. *Style and Statement*. Oxford UP, 1998.

Corbett, Edward P. J., and Sheryl Finkle, editors. *The Essay: Old and New*. Pearson, 1993.

De Dainville, François. *L'education des jesuites*. Les Editions de Minuit, 1978.

Donnelly, Francis P., S.J. *Imitation and Analysis,* Allyn and Bacon, 1902.

—. *Model English I*. Allyn and Bacon, 1920.

—. *Model English II*. Allyn and Bacon, 1919.

—. *Persuasive Speech*. P. J. Kenedy & Sons, 1931.

Du Cygne, Martin. *Ars Rhetorica*. 2nd American ed., Baltimore, 1866.

Duminuco, Vincent J., editor. *The Jesuit* Ratio Studiorum*: 400th Anniversary Perspectives*. Fordham UP, 2000.

Endean, Phillip. "The Spiritual Exercises." *The Cambridge Companion to the Jesuits*, edited by Thomas Worcester, Cambridge UP, 2008, pp. 52–67.

Enos, Richard Leo. Review of *Selected Essays of Edward P.J. Corbett*, edited by Robert J. Connors. *Journal of Advanced Composition*, vol. 10, no. 2, pp. 410–12.

Farrell, Allan P. *The Jesuit Code of Liberal Education: Development and Scope of the* Ratio Studiorum. Bruce Publishing, 1938.

Farrell, Thomas J., and Paul A. Soukup, editors. *An Ong Reader: Challenges for Further Inquiry*. Hampton Press, 2002.

—, editors. *Of Ong and Media Ecology: Essays in Communication, Composition, and Literary Studies.* Hampton Press, 2012.

Fitts, Karen, and Alan W. France, editors. *Left Margins: Cultural Studies and Composition Pedagogy.* State U of New York P, 1995.

Flynn, Lawrence J. *The* De Arte Rhetorica *(1568) of Cyprien Soarez, S.J.: A Translation with Introduction and Notes.* 1955. U of Florida, PhD dissertation. U of Michigan P, 2001.

—. "The *De Arte Rhetorica* of Cyprien Soarez, S.J." *Quarterly Journal of Speech,* vol. 42, no. 4, 1956, pp. 367–74.

—. "Sources and Influence of Soarez' *De Arte Rhetorica.*" *Quarterly Journal of Speech,* vol. 43, no. 3, 1957, pp. 257–65.

Fogarty, Daniel. *Roots for a New Rhetoric.* Teachers College Press, 1959.

Fumaroli, Marc. *L'age d'eloquence.* Droz, 1990.

—. "The Fertility and Shortcomings of Renaissance Rhetoric: The Jesuit Case." *The Jesuits: Culture, Sciences, and the Arts, 1540–1773,* edited by John W. O'Malley, S.J., et al., U of Toronto P, 1999, pp. 90–106.

—, editor. *Histoire de la rhétorique dans l'Europe moderne, 1450–1950.* Presses Universitaires de France, 1999.

Gaillet, Lynée Lewis, and Winifred Bryan Horner, editors. *The Present State of Scholarship in the History of Rhetoric: A Twenty-First Century Guide.* U of Missouri P, 2010.

Gannett, Cinthia. "Rhetoric(s) and *Eloquentia Perfecta.*" Worcester, pp. 677–78.

—. "Universities, 1540–1773." Worcester, pp. 804–6.

—. "Universities, 1773–Present." Worcester, pp. 806–8.

Gannett, Cinthia, and John C. Brereton, editors. *Traditions of Eloquence: The Jesuits and Modern Rhetorical Studies.* Fordham UP, 2016.

Ganss, George. *St. Ignatius' Idea of a Jesuit University.* Marquette UP, 1956.

Gleason, Philip. "The New Americanism in Catholic Historiography." *U.S. Catholic Historian,* vol. 11, no. 3, 1993, pp. 1–18.

Golden, James L., and Edward P. J. Corbett, editors. *The Rhetoric of Blair, Campbell, and Whately.* Holt, Rinehart and Winston, 1968.

Gorman, Margaret. "The Influence of Ignatian Spirituality on Women's Teaching Orders in the United States," *Jesuit Tradition in Education and Missions: A 450-Year Perspective,* edited by Christopher Chapple, U of Scranton P, 1993, pp. 182–202.

Halloran, S. Michael. "Jesuit Rhetoric at Holy Cross College, circa 1957–1958." Gannett and Brereton, pp. 252–56.

Hawley, John C. "A *Ratio Studiorum* for the Postcolonialist's Classroom." Fitts and France, pp. 255–68.

Holdstein, Deborah. "Assimilation and Disappearance: Hebraic Influences on Jesuit Rhetoric." Prospects for Research on Jesuit Rhetoric, International Society for the History of Rhetoric, 26 July 2017, Queen Mary University, London, United Kingdom. Panel presentation.

Johnson, Kristine, and Paul Lynch. "*Ad perfectum eloquentiam*: The 'Spoils of Egypt' in Jesuit Renaissance Rhetoric." *Rhetoric Review*, vol. 31, no. 2, 2012, pp. 99–116.

Kennedy, George. *Classical Rhetoric and Its Christian and Secular Tradition from Ancient to Modern Times*. U of North Carolina P, 1980.

Kleutgen, Joseph. *Ars dicendi priscorum potissimum Praeceptis et Exemplis*. Rome, 1847.

Kraus, Manfred. "Jesuit Rhetorics for Greeks: Greek Jesuit Progymnasmata in the Seventeenth and Eighteenth Centuries." *Horizons: Seoul Journal of Humanities*, vol. 7, no. 1, 2016, pp. 75–95.

Leahy, William P. *Adapting to America: Catholics, Jesuits, and Higher Education in the Twentieth Century*. Georgetown UP, 1991.

Leigh, David. "The Changing Practice of Liberal Education and Rhetoric in Jesuit Education, 1600–2000." Gannett and Brereton, pp. 125–37.

Lynch, Edward J. *The Origin and Development of Rhetoric in the Plan of Studies of 1599 of the Society of Jesus*. 1968. Northwestern U, PhD dissertation.

Lynch, Paul. "On Care for Our Common Discourse: Pope Francis's Nonmodern Epideictic," *Rhetoric Society Quarterly*, vol. 47, no. 5, 2017, pp. 463–82.

—. "The Best Training for Public Life: Reconciling Traditions; Jesuit Rhetoric and Ignatian Pedagogy." *Conversations on Jesuit Higher Education*, vol. 43, no. 1, 2013, pp. 6–10. epublications.marquette.edu/conversations/vol43/iss1/5.

Lynch, Paul, and Matthew Miller. "Twenty-Five Years of Faith in Writing: Religion and Composition, 1992–2017." *Present Tense: A Journal of Rhetoric in Society*, vol. 6, no. 2, 2017, www.presenttensejournal.org/volume-6/twenty-five-years-of-faith-in-writing-religion-and-composition-1992-2017/.

Mack, Peter. *A History of Renaissance Rhetoric, 1300–1620*. Oxford: Oxford UP, 2011.

Mahoney, Kathleen A. *Catholic Higher Education in Protestant America: The Jesuits and Harvard in the Age of the University*. Johns Hopkins UP, 2003.

Mailloux, Steven. "Enactment History, Jesuit Practices, and Rhetorical Hermeneutics." *Rhetoric's Pragmatism: Essays in Rhetorical Hermeneutics*, Penn State UP, 2017, pp. 71–85.

—. "A Good Person Speaking Well." *Conversations on Jesuit Higher Education*, vol. 43, no. 1, 2013, pp. 10–14.

—. "Rhetorical Ways of Proceeding: *Eloquentia Perfecta* in American Jesuit Colleges." Gannett and Brereton, pp. 162–74.

Maryks, Robert A. *St. Cicero and the Jesuits*. Ashgate, 2008.

—. "Rhetorical Veri-similitudo: Cicero, Probabilism, and Jesuit Casuistry." Gannett and Brereton, pp. 60–72.

Mazurek, Raymond. "Freirean Pedagogy, Cultural Studies, and the Initiation of Students to Academic Discourse." Fitts and France, pp. 173–88.

McGucken, William J. *The Jesuits and Education*. Bruce Publishing, 1932.

McKevitt, Gerald. "Jesuit Schools in the U.S.A., 1814–c. 1970." *The Cambridge Companion to the Jesuits*, edited by Thomas Worcester, Cambridge UP, 2008, pp. 278–97.

Murphy, James J., editor. *A Short History of Writing Instruction: From Ancient Greece to Contemporary America*. Routledge, 2012.

Nelms, Gerald, "Edward P.J. Corbett, the Revival of Classical Rhetoric, and the Jesuit Tradition." Gannett and Brereton, pp. 200–218.

O'Conor, John Francis Xavier. *Rhetoric and Oratory*. Boston, 1898.

O'Malley, John W. *The First Jesuits*. Harvard UP, 1993.

—. Foreword. Gannett and Brereton, ix–xiii.

—. "The Historiography of the Society of Jesus: Where Does It Stand Today?" *Saints or Devils Incarnate?*, pp. 1–36.

—. "Jesuit Schools of Humanities: Yesterday and Today." *Studies in the Spirituality of Jesuits*, vol. 47, no. 1, 2015, pp. 1–31.

—. "'Not for Ourselves Alone': Rhetorical Education in the Jesuit Mode with Five Bullet Points for Today." *Conversations on Jesuit Higher Education*, vol. 43, no. 1, 2013, pp. 3–5. epublications.marquette.edu/conversations/vol43/iss1/4/.

—. *Saints or Devils Incarnate? Studies in Jesuit History*. Brill, 2013.

O'Malley, John et al., editors. *The Jesuits: Cultures, Sciences, and the Arts, 1540–1773*. U of Toronto P, 1999.

Ong, Walter J. *Language as Hermeneutic: A Primer on the Word and Digitization*. Edited by Thomas D. Zlatic and Sara van den Berg, Cornell UP, 2017.

Padberg, John. *Colleges in Controversy: The Jesuit Schools in France from Revival to Suppression, 1815–1880*. Harvard UP, 1969.

Pavur, Claude. *In the School of Ignatius: Studious Zeal and Devoted Learning*. Institute of Jesuit Sources, 2019.

—. "Jesuit Spirituality and Catholic Higher Education," *Review for Religious*, vol. 52, no. 6, 1993, pp. 875–85.

—. *The* Ratio Studiorum*: The Official Plan for Jesuit Education*. Institute of Jesuit Sources, 2005.

Quintilian. *The Institutio Oratoria of Quintilian*. Translated by H. E. Butler, Heineman, 1979.

Rice, Janice Lauer. "Walter Ong: A Jesuit Rhetorical and Interdisciplinary Scholar and Educator." Gannett and Brereton, pp. 188–99.

Schloesser, Stephen. "Accommodation as a Rhetorical Principle Twenty Years after John O'Malley's *The First Jesuits* (1993)," *Journal of Jesuit Studies*, vol. 1, no. 3, 2014, pp. 347–72.

Shore, Paul. "The *Ratio Studiorum* at Four Hundred: Some Considerations from an American Perspective." *Ratio Studiorum da Companhia de Jesus (1599–1999)*, special issue of *Revista Portuguesa de Filosofia*, vol. 55, no. 3, 1999, pp. 319–30.

Smith, Sidney. *Precepts of Rhetoric*. Worcester, MA, 1936.

Soukup, Paul A. "Walter Ong, S.J.: A Retrospective." Farrell and Soukup, pp. 13–44.

Tade, G. T. "The *Spiritual Exercises*: A Method of Self-Persuasion." *Quarterly Journal of Speech*, vol. 43, no. 4, 1957, pp. 383–89.

Walsh, Thomas M. "The Walter J. Ong Bibliography." *Language, Culture, and Identity: The Legacy of Walter J. Ong*, edited by Sara van den Berg and Thomas M. Walsh, Hampton Press, 2011.

Worcester, Thomas, editor. *The Cambridge Encyclopedia of the Jesuits*. Cambridge UP, 2017.

Zaleski, Michelle. "The Word Made Secular: Religious Rhetoric and the New University at the Turn of the Twentieth Century." *College English*, vol. 80, no. 2, 2017, pp. 159–83.

Interlude

LAURENT PERNOT

A short tale by the French poet and playwright Paul Claudel (1868–1955) can be used to shed some light on the issue of religious rhetoric. The text, written in 1925, tells the story of a man and a woman living as a couple and bearing Latin names. His name is Animus, that is, "Spirit," the principle of moral and intellectual life, the ability to desire, judge, want, and conclude. Her name is Anima, "Soul," in the sense of vital breath and poetic inspiration. As one might suspect, Animus and Anima are a pair whose relationship is conflictual. The husband is a pedantic, suspicious, jealous man, tormenting his wife, while she consoles herself by singing gently and seeking solace in the divine (see Claudel).

This is as far as the story goes, and the couple is left struggling. Hence, this parable, whose aim is to portray poem composition, highlights the opposition between two approaches to man and world, one rational, the other inspired: between intellectualism and religious poetry, between immanence and transcendence, these two terms are not separated by a clear dividing line but are considered one from a dialectic perspective.

That is why this text, ever since I read it for the first time many years ago, served as a guide to me. May the late poet forgive me: even though this had not been his intention, he brilliantly raised the problem of the link between rhetoric and religion. Animus could symbolize rhetoric, as the art of analyzing and controlling the logical and psychological means of persuasion. Claudel says about him: "He taught himself to speak with a small pebble in his mouth, and now, when he speaks, he speaks so well that his friends say that one cannot speak better than he speaks." The detail about the pebble in the mouth, alluding to diction exercises done by Demosthenes, suggests that Animus is a disciple of this great orator. Anima, for her part, symbolizes religion of the soul turned toward God. On the one hand, method, scheme, intelligence, and human passion; on the other, exaltation and access to a dimension higher than the human one—thus making it difficult to link and blend the two ideas.

Exploring "rhetoric" with reference to religion is adding a deductive and almost scientific aspect to linguistic phenomena of faith and worship, which, by definition, refer to something beyond reason. It is reducing to art or artifice that which claims to comply with ultimate values. It is true that rhetoric is not only rational and religion is not only irrational, but there is still a certain audacity in relating them to each other in spite of all that distinguishes and opposes them. This is the reason why the concept of religious rhetoric might have seemed paradoxical, even subversive, and took time to become accepted. This concept was hardly conceivable in France some decades ago. To introduce it, a new approach had to be developed: one that was based on the Centre d'Analyse des Rhétoriques Religieuses de l'Antiquité, which I founded at the Université de Strasbourg in 1994 and ran with my colleagues Gérard Freyburger and Yves Lehmann successively, as well as the series Recherches sur les Rhétoriques Religieuses, published by Brepols Publishers, of which I am in charge with Gérard Freyburger and which to date consists of thirty-five volumes. The sixteenth congress of the International Society for the History of Rhetoric, which I had the honor of organizing in Strasbourg in 2007 as the president of the society, dealt with the topic of "Rhetoric and Religion." In my own research work, I have contemplated the link between rhetoric and religion mainly from a Graeco-Roman antiquity perspective, in line with my areas of interest, and have noted the wealth of the ancient field as a laboratory for the issue at hand (see "Saint"; "Prière"; "Christianisme"; "Au-delà"; "Le lieu"; "Rhetoric"; "Les mystères").

My research took the shape of an inquiry, with the aim of unearthing the religious and the sacred in ancient rhetoric. Apparently, these aspects were missing. Ancient rhetoric, as defined by Aristotle, Cicero, Quintilian, Hermogenes, and others, focused on debate among citizens with regard to the running of the city-state, the republic, or the empire, its subject matter being legal proceedings, political deliberations, and public and private tributes; it did not comprise a religious feature in its own right. Thus, a closer look had to be taken, without prejudice, in order to discover sensitive areas. Here are examples of probable avenues to be explored:

- *The authority of the word.* In antiquity, Persuasion (*Peithō, Suada*) could be regarded as a divinity. The Greek sophist Gorgias gave credit to speech for its magical effectiveness. Certain utterances were defined as "sacred speech" (*hieros logos*) and certain eloquent, wise men as "divine man" (*theios anēr*). Forms of rhetoric equipped with religious power included curses, oaths, prophecies, oracles, and revelation.
- *Encomium.* The epideictic genre (the third oratory genre, alongside the deliberative and the judicial) had the function of praising; when praise was divinely oriented, one was dealing, ipso facto, with religious rhetoric. Such was the case with hymns in honor of gods and heroes and panegyrics in honor of saints.
- *Prayer.* Prayer often took the form of a well-argued request. It included uttering the name of the divine and using sacred epithets (*epiklēseis*) or ritual acclamations.
- *Preaching.* The works of Greek and Latin fathers of the church comprise numerous sermons and homilies aimed at the faithful and devoting all the resources in persuasion to encourage listeners in their faith and to urge them to improve.
- *Controversy.* Religious rhetoric implied controversial reasoning intended for refuting opponents, whether one was dealing with pagans attacking Christians, Christian apologetics challenging pagans, or oral and written material meant for fighting heresy.

Thus, within ancient rhetoric we discover the religious field, which for a long time went unnoticed because it was denied and repressed in the name of a narrow definition of rhetoric. Some components of religious rhetoric had been acknowledged by the ancients but confined to a minor role; others had been excluded from the conventional definition of rhetorical arts; others still had not been acknowledged at all. Sometimes, in a flash, the importance of the subject is revealed in an aside: Plato describes the purpose of true rhetoric not as a means to speak to men but as "the ability to speak in a language pleasing to the gods" (*Phaedrus* 273e); Longinus, the author of the treatise *On Sublimity*, quotes the beginning of Genesis, "And God said, Let there be light: and there was light," as an example of sublime style, comparable to Homer's verses (9.9). The ancients caught a glimpse of what Kenneth Burke would call "Rhetorical Radiance of the 'Divine'" (294).

Research on these phenomena has hardly begun. The probable avenues listed above are the foundation for an epistemology in the field and a program for future research. These are not only new topics up for study, but they help push forward the frontier of knowledge and examine how rhetoric works in an activity—the religious one—that seems the most resistant to its influence. This entails reconceptualizing rhetoric, acknowledging that it is concerned not only with political and secular discourse, with which it is usually associated, and extending it to speech about divine subjects. This reconceptualization is currently under way in different fields: for instance, the epistolary genre, conversation, and visual arts are being considered from a rhetorical perspective, although these topics are not included in the conventional conception of rhetoric. Likewise, it is legitimate to approach the field of religion from a rhetorical perspective and in it perceive an art of persuasion determined by norms and codes relating to argumentation, disposition, style, and pronunciation, not to mention the deviation from norms and codes, which is a source of creativity.

This approach not only expands the field of rhetoric but also opens up a promising avenue to better understand religion. We cannot but notice that there is a linguistic aspect (in speech, in writing) to religion and that even, more profoundly, there is no religion without language and that any religion is, perhaps, at its core a linguistic phenomenon. This includes speeches about gods (the different ways of addressing gods or God, of expressing religious awareness or feeling, and of asserting theological concepts), speeches addressed to gods (such as prayer and hymn), and speeches coming from the gods (for example, prophecies and revelations).

From a strictly rhetorical sense, each religion has its distinctive features; at the same time, however, common characteristics can be identified. The study of antiquity offers a prime example of this since paganism and Christianity existed side by side without an insuperable boundary, and in the early centuries of the Roman Empire, there was a common language of religious experience found both in pagan and in Christian texts. Although they were bearers of irreconcilable faiths and traditions, pagans and Christians lived in the same world and shared forms of expression and languages. The issues religious rhetoric raises are whether there are universals of religious language, anthropological and psycholinguistic invariants, or at least fundamental and interdisciplinary concepts, for example, the praise of divine action and power, hymns of grace, persuasive prayers, argumentative structures, stylistic devices, and phraseology. I hope a rhetoric-based approach can offer a fresh new perspective on the study of religion.

This is why Animus and Anima still need each other.

WORKS CITED

Burke, Kenneth. *A Rhetoric of Motives.* U of California P, 1969.

Claudel, Paul. "Parabole d'Animus et d'Anima." *Œuvres en prose*, edited by Jacques Petit and Charles Galpérine, Gallimard, 1965, pp. 27–28.

Pernot, Laurent. "Au-delà de Babel: le langage de la louange et de la prière." *Millennium*, vol. 2, 2005, pp. 63–77.

—. "Christianisme et sophistique." *Papers on Rhetoric* IV, edited by Lucia Calboli Montefusco, Herder, 2002, pp. 245–62.

—. "Le lieu du nom (*topos apo tou onomatos*) dans la rhétorique religieuse des Grecs." *Nommer les dieux: Théonymes, épithètes, épiclèses dans l'Antiquité*, edited by Nicole Belayche et al., Brepols, 2005, pp. 29–39.

—. "Les mystères de la rhétorique." *Hommage à Jacqueline de Romilly*, edited by Marc Fumaroli et al., Académie des inscriptions et belles-lettres, 2014, pp. 61–76.

—. "Prière et rhétorique." *Papers on Rhetoric* III, edited by Lucia Calboli Montefusco, Clueb, 2000, pp. 213–32.

—. "The Rhetoric of Religion." *Rhetorica*, vol. 24, no. 3, 2006, pp. 235–54.

—. "Saint Pionios, martyr et orateur." *Du héros païen au saint chrétien*, edited by Gérard Freyburger and Laurent Pernot, Institut d'Études augustiniennes, 1997, pp. 111–23.

Section 2. Inventing Rhetorics

5. Creating Pathways for Ethical (Inter)Actions

New Directions for Jewish Rhetorics

JANICE W. FERNHEIMER

It is a pleasure to write about "New Directions for Jewish Rhetorics" as part and parcel of a larger conversation on religious rhetorics and their growing importance to both rhetorical studies and to contemporary politics. The need is ever more urgent as Jewish people across the globe experience a significant rise in anti-Semitism reflected in increased vandalism, violence, and vitriol against their persons, beliefs, and institutions. As I first drafted this essay, global attention focused on the unspeakably anti-Semitic representations at the Belgian city of Aalst's carnival, where some participants wore costumes representing Hasidic Jews as vermin (Cnaan), and the Spanish town Campo de Criptana's carnival representations, which included a dance troupe dressed as Nazi officers and concentration camp prisoners followed by floats shaped like a menorah and crematoria chimneys. These symbolic representations in Europe follow some of the most violent years in the United States for Jewish people, in which Jewish worshipers were tragically murdered at the Tree of Life Synagogue in the Squirrel Hill neighborhood of Pittsburgh, Pennsylvania, in 2018 and again six months later in Poway, California, in 2019. Throughout the Chanukah holiday season in 2019, violent attacks surged even in areas with large Jewish populations like New York (Ari Feldman).

The COVID-19 pandemic revived blood-libel-inspired conspiracy theories to blame Jews for the virus (Estrin). These claims have been exacerbated by negative perceptions of ultraorthodox Jewish communities, especially as these communities experienced significant spread of the virus in both Israel and throughout New York.[1] As protestors across the United States grew impatient with social distancing efforts, their protests often featured anti-Semitic tropes.[2] If such hatred stems in part from fear of the "other," one of the best weapons against this fear is to transform the unknown into the familiar, thereby making it less susceptible to "othering." One way to participate in such transformation is through increased attention to Jewish rhetorics, peoples, and practices.

To write about new directions in Jewish rhetorics implies that the field has already been established and can now be deepened and broadened to be even more comprehensive and inclusive. Looking back from the vantage point of my own entry into the field as a graduate student at the University of Texas at Austin in the early 2000s, including my experience of studying classical Jewish texts (Torah, Talmud, Midrash) in a *bet midrash* (traditional Jewish house of study) in Israel in 2000–2001, I am delighted to see both how far the field has come and to see how many interconnections remain to be explored. Some of the most compelling questions explored to date have been definitional and methodological. For example, what are Jewish rhetorics, pedagogies, and approaches to speaking, persuading, writing, and communicating? How are scholars defining both "Jewish" and "rhetoric"? Is the descriptor "Jewish" meant to delineate religious practices, rituals, prayers, and beliefs or a set of cultural practices, values, and ethics? Most importantly, who gets to decide who or what counts as Jewish?[3]

To begin to answer these questions, I argue that we must recursively return to the concept of "to-ness," a canon of Jewish rhetorics that emphasizes the way that Jewish rhetorics are fundamentally based on logics of relationship and juxtaposition, either between individual and community or between insiders and outsiders.[4] In Rabbinic conceptions, the very foundation of the world is relational, contingent, and dependent upon divine verbal utterance. To-ness expresses this orientation. Of the emerging canons of Jewish rhetorics, then, to-ness is best suited as a model for ethical research and ethical relations that seeks to recognize rather than write over difference and mutual influence. To-ness thus provides a historiographic method for building relationships among and between rhetorical traditions across both space and time and creating conversations that consider various traditions in relationship to one another rather than in isolation. For it is relationship that is central to to-ness. To operationalize to-ness as a method for inquiry, one must locate oneself—temporally, geographically, culturally—in relationship to/with the questions one poses, the framework one uses to investigate/theorize, and the people, cultures, and traditions one studies. One must work multidirectionally to pose questions of not only where concepts originate but also how they travel and change when they cross into new cultures, continuing to shift and transform as they traverse geography, time, and context.

One of the goals of this collection is to take up the relationship between religious rhetorics and different rhetorical traditions, to demonstrate the importance of this work, and to provide methods for accomplishing it. It is of course necessary for each tradition to develop what Hawhee and Olson call a "pan-historiographic scope," which recognizes that some historiography must reach beyond temporal eras and geographic areas, all the while resisting the temptation to reduce difference and erase specificity (90). But it is perhaps even more important at this moment to realize the future imagined by Sam Edelman, one of the first scholars to trace a pan-historiographic Jewish rhetoric, where "the rhetorics of the Greek, Chinese, Jewish, and other civilizations are taught comparatively and through that distinctively Jewish pattern of reasoning, Kal-ve-Chomer (juxtaposition)" (123). This essay pursues this project in three stages. It first maps the growth of Jewish rhetorics and then argues for the importance of studying Jewish rhetorics through the canon of to-ness—that is, as a part of (not apart from) "the" rhetorical tradition and in relational conversation with other religious traditions and rhetorics. Finally, it maps areas of future growth for Jewish rhetorics and discusses the teaching of Jewish rhetorics as a means of equipping students and citizens to deal ethically with others.

Jewish Rhetorics: A Brief History of the Field

Jewish people have dispersed across the globe since the destruction of the Temple in 586 B.C.E., and "Jewishness" has been defined variously by blood descent, cultural affiliation, and religious practice. As I've argued in more detail elsewhere,[5] these competing values interact in dissociative fashion, with one or another being privileged at various points in Jewish history, depending on who is doing the defining and for what purpose. Given the more than four thousand years of history, exile, and dispersal that accompany Jewish rhetorics, this transnational "tradition" presents several challenges of scope. Each of the aforementioned areas brings with it a set of methodological challenges and opportunities impacted by understandings of multiple languages—contemporary Hebrew, biblical Hebrew, Aramaic, Arabic, Yiddish, Ladino, Judeo-Arabic, among others.

Given the daunting challenges of studying Jewish religious traditions as a whole, let alone their rhetorical valences, it is perhaps not surprising that scholars' initial enactment of to-ness forged links to the familiar Greco-Roman rhetorical tradition. David Daube and Abraham Tauber, dating to 1949 and 1969, respectively, are two of the first to mention the term "Jewish rhetorics" and to establish Jewish rhetorics as an area of study ripe with possibility. These early essays studied the question of whether Jewish rhetorics were deeply enmeshed with the history and historiography of more widely known (then and perhaps even now) rhetorical Greco-Roman traditions. Published in the *Hebrew Union College Annual*, Daube's essay was aimed more at Jewish studies than rhetoric scholars, but its importance for both lay in the connection it drew between two theretofore separate fields. Daube claims that "Rabbinic methods of interpretation derive from Hellenistic rhetoric" (239) and that "in its beginnings, the Rabbinic system of hermeneutics is a product of the Hellenistic civilization then dominating the Mediterranean world" (240).[6] Right away, Daube's essay raises the question of what counts as Jewish rhetorics by asking whether Rabbinic methods for interpretation are "purely" Jewish or were also influenced by Hellenism. Moreover, his claim points to the deep interanimation of cultures once thought to be distinct and separate.

Twenty years later, Abraham Tauber's "Jewish Rhetoric," which grew out of a presentation to the Speech for Religious Workers Special Interest Group at the 1968 Speech Association of America Convention, argues that "Jewish rhetoric has had an influence on American preaching and the sermon to a greater degree than generally realized" (57). In addition, Tauber observes that "the sermon as a regular religious institution was a unique creation of Judaism, later adopted by other religions" (61). This pan-historiographic glimpse of Jewish rhetorical history, focused through the lens of preaching, demonstrated that Jewish rhetorics are responsible for the creation of the sermon, the most ubiquitous form of religious rhetoric. Both Daube and Tauber make significant claims for the importance of Jewish rhetorics, suggesting that there is something particular and unique to Jewish traditions, epistemologies, and rhetoric. Yet whatever that "something" is, it both influences and is influenced by the cultures in which Jews have lived and interacted for thousands of years. This study of what is both uniquely Jewish and the product of mutual influence demonstrates the importance of to-ness.

The importance of to-ness can be seen in the continuing development of the field, first through studies that emphasized connections between Jewish and Hellenistic traditions, then through studies that emphasized Jewish traditions on their own terms.

Through the 1980s, scholars in a range of fields (Jewish studies, communication, English, biblical criticism, and literary studies) increased the "presence" of Jewish rhetorics by connecting it to concepts already familiar from other disciplines and the Greco-Roman tradition.[7] In 1983, Yehoshua Gitay published "Isaiah and His Audience" in *Prooftexts*, offering rhetoric as a mode for better understanding Jewish prophetic traditions and the poetics of Isaiah specifically. That same year, Susan Handelman broke significant ground with her monograph *The Slayers of Moses: The Emergence of Rabbinic Thought in Contemporary Literary Theory*, which considered the influence of Jewish epistemology and Rabbinic hermeneutics on contemporary literary theory, thus linking ancient Rabbinic understandings with contemporary modes of critical interpretation. Arthur Lesley's 1984 essay, "A Survey of Medieval Hebrew Rhetoric" published in *Approaches to Judaism in Medieval Times*, broke equally important ground in a different geographic place and temporal era—that of Jewish communities under Muslim, Christian, Spanish, and Italian rule from the fifteenth century to the eighteenth century (111). In addition to laying out important methodological considerations for the study of medieval Hebrew rhetoric and literature, Lesley indicates the importance of studying Hebrew poetry across time and space in the context of local and majority culture and constraints. Continuing to call attention to the rich interconnections in this era, Isaac Rabinowitz's early and important bibliographic study, "Pre-modern Jewish Study of Rhetoric: An Introductory Bibliography" (1985), identifies primary Jewish rhetorical texts that warrant further study, especially those specifically rhetorical treatises authored by Jewish rhetors in the medieval and Renaissance periods.[8]

If the 1980s produced studies that focused on Jewish rhetorics in relation to Greco-Roman traditions, the 1990s featured scholarly attempts to identify what constitutes Jewish rhetorics on their own terms. Throughout the 1990s, the Preconvention Seminar on Jewish Rhetoric met regularly at the Speech Communication Association Convention.[9] Not surprisingly, substantive scholarship by communication scholars soon began to cultivate the tenets of Jewish rhetorics. Meanwhile, scholars in Jewish studies began pioneering work that shed light on Jewish preaching and pedagogical strategies among medieval Jews across Europe.[10] Early threads of this line of inquiry date back to Lesley and Rabinowitz's 1980s work, which focused on the period when Jewish rhetors and authors began to author their own treatises, such as the Nophet Sophim.[11] But in the 1990s, scholars such as Margaret Zulick and Marcia Falk built on Yehoshua Gitay's approach to look at the Tanach (Torah, Writings, and Prophets) through rhetorical eyes. These scholars began to demonstrate the presence of rhetorical theory and knowledge in ancient Jewish texts, even if they were expressed less explicitly than in a text like Aristotle's *Rhetoric*. Zulick's "The Active Force of Hearing: The Ancient Hebrew Language of Persuasion" from 1992 focused on the ways that hearing and audience function in Jewish rhetorics, giving significantly more power and importance to both than does Aristotelian rhetoric. Likewise, in "The Agon of Jeremiah: On the Dialogic Invention of Prophetic Ethos," she elucidates "a complex rhetorical consciousness which is . . . a native achievement in Hebrew culture" (126). She also distinguishes between biblical and Aristotelian conceptions of ethos, the former privileging "mastery of ethos in a mythic and personal vein" whereas the latter values "logical demonstration of credibility" (Zulick 126).

Meanwhile, in English/rhetoric/composition studies, Steve Katz published two key essays that began to shape how Jewish rhetorics would be studied both in connection and in contrast to the Greco-Roman tradition. The now-foundational "The Ethic of Expediency: Classical Rhetoric, Technology, and the Holocaust" argues that an "ethic of expediency" not only served as part of the moral fabric that enabled the Holocaust, but the ethic also "underlies technical communication and deliberative rhetoric, and by extension writing pedagogy and practice based on it" (258). A few years later, "The Epistemology of the Kabbalah: Toward a Jewish Philosophy of Rhetoric" argued that Kabbalah and Jewish mystical approaches to the aleph-bet and letters constitute a rhetorical tradition of their own with a distinct epistemology. Specifically, Katz argues that "Kabbalah embraces and constitutes a Jewish mystical theory of rhetoric which, although severed from the main trunk of that liturgical tradition, nevertheless seems to inform it" (111). Katz places this Kabbalistic Jewish tradition within the Western context and makes the case for Jewish rhetoric as a middle or third path between the sophists and the Greeks (108). Moreover, he suggests that this "strand of Jewish rhetoric shows us a philosophy of language in which ethical behavior and spiritual existence rather than referential signification and rational thought is the focal point and primary concern of its practitioners" (119). Making a related case for the ethics of Jewish rhetorics as an important alternative to Western Enlightenment thought, David Frank, in his 1997 "The New Rhetoric, Judaism, and Post-Enlightenment Thought: The Cultural Origins of Perelmanian Philosophy," claims Chaïm Perelman as a Jewish rhetor and the New Rhetoric as a type of Jewish rhetoric that grew out of the strong influence of Talmudic thinking on Perelman's conception of reason, which thus provides a "third way" between Enlightenment metaphysics and more extreme versions of postmodern thought.

Following these attempts to make the case for an explicitly Jewish rhetorical tradition, two scholars worked to develop Jewish rhetorical theory from ancient Jewish texts. Following Zulick's lead, Marcia Falk, in "Jewish Laws of Speech: Toward a Multicultural Rhetoric," looks back to ancient Jewish texts such as the Tanach to deduce Jewish rhetorical principles and precepts from prescriptive language about speech in the absence of explicitly rhetorical ancient treatises. Similarly, Susan Zaeske examines Jewish women's rhetorical practices in "Unveiling Esther as a Pragmatic Radical Rhetoric" from 2000. Like Falk, she works inductively from Jewish texts themselves, focusing her attention on the Book of Esther. Zaeske's article not only introduces rhetorical audiences to the full translated text of *Megillat Esther* but also reads it as a handbook for "exilic rhetoric" and thus a model of Jewish rhetorical theory. This distinctive theory values cautious and planned speech over the prideful and impulsive, privileges communal over individual survival, and empowers minorities to see how individual and community survival can be facilitated by well-timed, meticulous, and carefully executed rhetorical plans, even if they sometimes come at a cost to dignity.

These early projects looked at one or two individual aspects of Jewish rhetorics and argued they were in fact both explicitly Jewish and decidedly rhetorical when viewed on their own terms. But it was not until later in the 2000s, as "the" rhetorical tradition was complicated from a variety of directions,[12] that scholars worked to establish and codify Jewish rhetorical traditions in a more comprehensive fashion. This work was facilitated by several parallel scholarly tracks: special journal issues, scholarly seminars and meetings, and the formation in 2007 of Klal Rhetorica, a scholarly society dedicated to providing mentorship and encouragement for scholars in this growing field. These conscious attempts continued the development of Jewish rhetorical traditions as traditions in their own right. The timing of this effort was propitious: the turn to complicating "the" rhetorical tradition brought renewed energy to Jewish rhetorics as a worthy area of study. Much of the research from 2000 to 2015 worked to lay out parameters, further define both "Jewish" and "rhetorics," and establish additional heuristics, canons, and frameworks for future scholarship.

The fruits of this effort are evident in the publication of two special issues, two edited collections, and numerous monographs, essays, and articles. The first special issue, which appeared in 2003 in the *Journal of Communication and Religion*, focused entirely and explicitly on Jewish rhetorics. The four essays, along with the introduction by David Frank, all make significant contributions. Perhaps the most useful for scholars wishing to enter the field is Sam Edelman's "Ancient Traditions, Modern Needs: An Introduction to Jewish Rhetoric," which not only sketches the broad strokes of a pan-historiographic tradition of Jewish thought from biblical times to Emancipation to the twentieth century, but it also does so briefly (in a mere twelve pages) and in terms accessible enough for undergraduates, interested scholars, and laypeople alike. Equally important is David Frank's "The Jewish Countermodel: Talmudic Argumentation, the New Rhetoric Project, and the Classical Tradition of Rhetoric," which further develops the argument he began in 1997 that the New Rhetoric is girded by Talmudic argumentation strategies and conceptions of reason. By bringing together new essays by established scholars such as Frank, Katz, Zulick, and Amos Kiewe, this special issue laid the groundwork for future growth in the field.

Encouraged by this increased attention, Katz, David Metzger, and I led the first workshop on Jewish rhetorics at the 2007 summer institute of the Rhetoric Society of America (RSA), which brought together scholars from rhetoric/composition and Jewish and English studies to ponder how to further establish a distinctive field of Jewish rhetorics. This workshop, which also helped establish Klal Rhetorica, was quickly followed by Andrea Greenbaum and Deborah Holdstein's groundbreaking 2008 anthology *Judaic Perspectives in Composition and Rhetoric*, which was the first edited collection to focus explicitly on Jewish rhetorics. Dividing it into three sections, "Theorizing Jewish Rhetoric," "Jewish

Cultural Identity in Writing," and "Contexts for Judaic Rhetoric in Composition," Holdstein and Greenbaum imagine their collection as a "way to open a door to create more space for conversations that we have neglected in composition" (8).

Building upon their work as well as scholarship emerging from that first Jewish rhetorics workshop in 2007, I edited a second special issue dedicated to Jewish rhetorics in *College English* in 2010. This collection of five essays, written by scholars in Jewish and rhetoric and composition studies, continued the work of making legitimate space for Jewish rhetorics.[13] It was followed by a second Jewish rhetorics workshop at the RSA summer institute in 2011. This period also witnessed the publication of several important monographs and articles that advanced the field in terms of classical, Talmudic, and contemporary approaches. In Talmudic and Rabbinic studies, scholars began to recognize the Talmud and its constituent elements as a consciously composed text. Jeffrey Rubenstein's 2003 edited collection, *Creation and Composition: The Contribution of the Bavli Redactors (Stammaim) to the Agada*, did not use explicitly composition/rhetoric frameworks but did begin to investigate the way the *stammaim* helped shape the Talmud as a composed text.

Meanwhile, in 2009, rhetoric scholar Sergey Dolgopolski published *What Is Talmud? The Art of Disagreement*, which argues that Talmud offers an alternative to philosophy. In 2010, ordained rabbi and Jewish rhetorics scholar Richard Hidary published his essay "Classical Rhetorical Arrangement and Reasoning in the Talmud: The Case of Yershalmi Berakhot 1:1" in *AJS Review*, the publication of the Association of Jewish Studies, introducing rhetorical approaches to a broad audience of scholars in Jewish studies and arguing that the redactors of the Talmud were influenced by classical rhetorical forms and arrangement.[14] Also in 2010, Bruce McComiskey published his *Rhetoric Review* article "Laws, Works, and the End of Days: Rhetorics of Identification, Distinction, and Persuasion in *Miqṣat Ma'aśeh ha-Torah* (Dead Sea Scroll 4QMMT)," which investigates the rhetorical qualities of the Dead Sea Scrolls.[15] In 2013, Andrew Schumann published "Logical Cornerstones of Jewish Argumentation Theory" in *Argumentation*, which calls attention to Judaic inference rules such as "*qal wa-h omer, gezerah šawah*, *heqeš, binyan 'av*" and considers "the pragmatic limits of applying these rules" (305). Focusing on the way Jewish concepts and histories impact and shape contemporary rhetorical debates, my 2014 *Stepping into Zion: Hatzaad Harishon, Black Jews, and the Remaking of Jewish Identity* argues that the way we argue about identity generally and Jewish identity specifically is often dissociative and has the power to reshape what we take to be common ground. Further advancing biblical rhetorics, Davida Charney's 2015 monograph, *Persuading God: Rhetorical Studies of First-Person Psalms*, grew out of her earlier articles investigating the rhetorical power of the psalms and examines first-person psalms as explicitly rhetorical texts.[16] By this point, it was fair to say that Jewish rhetorics had already arrived as a legitimate, recognized, and distinctive mode of inquiry in rhetorical and religious studies.

The twin inquiries into both distinctly Jewish rhetorical practices and those related to the Greco-Roman tradition have led to productive interanimations. Relationship and preservation of difference through juxtaposition lie at the heart of these canons, and it is my hope that they will facilitate a new chapter in the research and teaching of rhetorical traditions and rhetorics of religion. It is only through acknowledging extant relationships and working to build new, more ethical ones that we may pursue the just development not only of Jewish rhetorics but of other religious rhetorics as well. The canon of to-ness offers these possibilities, which are further pursued in the next section.

The Importance of To-ness for Research and Teaching Alike

From 2016 forward, the trends in research open multiple, complementary paths to answer the dual calls to consider Jewish rhetorics on their own terms and to highlight their interanimation with other rhetorical traditions and histories; in other words, they move to strongly engage by virtue of to-ness. Scholars deepened attention to the way Jewish rhetorics differently consider speech and hearing (Koban) and the mutually constitutive relationships between the rabbis and classical rhetoric (Hidary, *Rabbis*). They also focused on the relationship between what Bernard-Donals and I term the "cross-pollinations" of Jewish rhetorics with other rhetorics, whether these relationships are constructed positively, negatively, or through an entirely different set of parameters of influence and reinvention. Not surprisingly, these trajectories were also followed by several important pedagogical innovations as well,[17] as veteran researchers introduced and began teaching courses at both the graduate and undergraduate levels that introduced Jewish rhetorics to official curricula.

The first major move in this direction was a third special issue dedicated to Jewish rhetorics, again edited by David Frank and appearing in the *Journal of Communication and Religion* in 2016. As Frank writes, this special issue was meant to complement the first one he edited in 2003 and this time provides a collection of essays that respond to Kiewe's 2011 book, *Confronting Anti-Semitism: Seeking an End to Hateful Rhetoric* ("Rhetoric of Judaism"). The issue's four essays and response from Kiewe all focus on anti-Semitism or anti-Judaism in some respect and call attention to how our consideration of rhetorics cannot be separated from the cultural environments that produce such rhetorics, environments often tainted by the anti-Semitic and anti-Judaic attitudes that produce them.[18] Given the uptick of global anti-Semitism that year and in the following years, this type of to-ness is an important type of relational inquiry to continue.

A second major turn to put Jewish rhetorics in broader conversation with other religious rhetorics came in 2017 when Paul Lynch and Matthew Miller published their comprehensive annotated bibliography "Twenty-Five Years of Faith in Writing: Religion and Composition, 1992–2017" in *Present Tense*. This bibliography continued the important work of putting Jewish rhetorics in conversation with other discourses about faith, religion, writing, and composition. This remarkable work annotates around two hundred articles, essays, and books that touch on a variety of aspects of religious rhetorics, while also providing a stirring introduction that cogently argues "religious encounters have led to productive rethinking of dominant attitudes and familiar assumptions," which have enabled scholars to understand religion itself as "a call and a resource for rhetorical invention" (Lynch and Miller). In addition to this bibliography, the 2018 Rhetoric and Religion in the 21st Century conference from which this essay and volume emerged put multiple approaches to religion and rhetoric in conversation. Those conversations are already beginning to bear fruit. Representing these forms of inter-religious to-ness, Moshin and Crosby's 2018 "Liminally White: Jews, Mormons, and Whiteness" provides a comparative case study of Jews and Mormons that argues that both groups are "liminal Whites," an identity that problematizes "notions of Whiteness as a natural, essentialized race" and is "uniquely well positioned to offer critiques of Whiteness" (448). This essay illustrates how similar outsider perceptions of two distinct religious peoples put groups usually not considered together in an important relationship.

A third shift exemplifies the turn to enact the very to-ness I suggest in our rhetorical historiographies. Jewish rhetorics scholars' attention to to-ness has brought new comparative approaches that put Jewish rhetors and rhetorics into conversation with elements of multiple rhetorical traditions. One of the most prolific of these scholars is Brandon Katzir, whose three-article series shows how Jewish-Muslim traditions in the medieval period are just as interanimated (if not more so) than Jewish–Greco-Roman ones under Hellenism. His award-winning 2017 "'The Truth of Reliable Tradition': Saadya Gaon, Arabic Rhetoric, and the Challenge to Rhetorical Historiography" showcases Saadya Gaon as "a particularly interesting example of the crosspollination of medieval rhetorical traditions, especially because of his defense of Jewish tradition with a rhetorical mode adopted from Islamic theology," as illustrated in Gaon's *Book of Doctrines and Beliefs* (167). In his insightful analysis, Katzir shows how Gaon's approaches reflect the way that "Jewish rhetoric functions not so much as a counter model to the rhetorical traditions of the Greeks, but as an interconnected rhetoric influenced by (and influencing in turn) Greco-Islamic ideology" (178). He followed this essay in 2018 with "Paths of Virtue: Legal Rhetorics in Judaism and Islam," which deepens his exploration and tracing of Jewish/Muslim "interconnectiveness" by comparatively investigating legal rhetorics in Judaism and Islam. This was one of the first articles to give rhetorical attention to more than fourteen centuries of Jews and Muslims who lived together "all over the world and especially in the Middle East and North Africa" (28). Finally, in 2019, he extends this line of inquiry with "Against the Philosophers: Writing and Identity in Medieval Mediterranean Rhetoric," which analyzes what he terms the "antiphilosophical texts" of medieval writers al-Ghazali, Halevi, and Ibn Arabi to show how they believed writing to be a mode of identity formation in the medieval Mediterranean (366).[19] That same year Richard Hidary published *Rabbis and Classical Rhetoric: Sophistic Education and Oratory in the Talmud and Midrash*, which deepens his earlier work examining the influence of Greek and sophistic thought on the rabbis who helped construct the Talmud. Hidary argues that the "cultural fluidity" between the groups led to "inevitable" and "unselfconscious" intertwinements (20), which make it difficult to distinguish among them, and that the "rabbis display significant integration with the sophistic tradition" (21). As Hidary notes, "Appreciating the place of classical rhetoric in rabbinic society according to this more complex, but realistic web of interactions, requires that we include the views of Jews, Greeks, Romans, Christians, and Persians and triangulate each with the others," while acknowledging, of course, that there are subdivisions within each of these groups who also "quarreled" with one another (21). Both Katzir and Hidary deepen our conceptions of two very different but related to-nesses—the relationship of Jewish to Muslim and of both to Greco-Roman rhetorics—and provide imitable models for how this work of teaching/researching with to-ness can progress. The growing field would benefit from the addition of a variety of additional approaches and voices, which I detail in the next section.

To-ness and New Directions in Jewish Rhetorics

Just as it is important to consider Jewish rhetorics on their own terms and in conversation with other traditions, it is equally important to move the conversation within Jewish rhetorics forward by including additional voices and approaches to who counts as Jewish and what counts as rhetoric. Six years ago, Michael Bernard-Donals and I called readers' attention to the gaps in our collection that needed to be filled. We recognized the strong "slants toward the Ashkenazi tradition" (xxv) along with the lack of attention to Mizrachi and Sephardi traditions (two essays notwithstanding).[20] As we noted, there is "much work . . . to be done before women's voices are fully incorporated into Jewish rhetorics, theory, practice" (xxvi). Despite the veritable outpouring of scholarship in Jewish rhetorics since then, and important work from Alexander Slotkin and Eliza Gellis, two important emerging scholars of Jewish rhetorics, these calls for further research are still very much in need of a response. There has been some attention to ethnic minorities in Israel, as illustrated by Anat Feldman's "In the Realms of Ethnicity, Religion, and Emigration: New Communities of Memory in Israel," which focuses on the memory activities of Libyan, Moroccan, and Tunisian communities. Katzir's work likewise recognizes the interconnection between medieval Sephardi Jewish and Muslim rhetorical interactions.[21] Yet this research reflects a mere tip of the iceberg. It is my hope that a watershed moment of consideration of a greater Mediterranean rhetorical tradition is on the horizon.[22]

While Sue Zaeske and Andrea Lieber have done significant work to begin to make women's contributions to Jewish rhetorical traditions visible, much more needs to be done both to include feminist approaches and to better understand the role of gender in Jewish rhetorics. Given the ubiquity of *kol-isha* as a constraining rule in observant communities, it is not surprising that women's voices have so far have been relatively absent from conversations about Jewish rhetorics. Yet as Zaeske and Lieber illustrate in their work on Esther and religious Jewish female bloggers, Jewish women's rhetorical strategies provide significant contributions to the ways we reconceive rhetors and rhetoric in the absence of recognized power. The intersections of gender and Jewish rhetorics are crying out for further research.[23]

While the world of Jewish observance and practice has begun to evolve to make space for LGBTQ+ individuals in Jewish communities, little scholarship has studied what this move has meant for Jewish rhetorical practices. Scholars such as Alexander Malanych and Gregg Drinkwater have begun this important work. Yet much remains to investigate concerning not only how LGBTQ+ individuals are reshaping Judaism but also how different Jewish communities engage with gender, marriage, and queer constructions of family. Moreover, the contemporary political moment warrants further investigation into the ways some feminist/intersectional activist groups shun Jewish participants because of their assumed subscription to Zionism or support of the state of Israel.[24]

Additionally, although growing awareness of Black Jews and other Jews of color is beginning to take hold in the world of Jewish and sociological studies (Parfitt, Bruder, Haynes), very little rhetorical scholarship attends specifically to the rhetorical needs and practices of these global communities. The presence of

African Jews in sub-Saharan Africa has received greater attention from a variety of scholars from disciplines outside rhetoric and composition, yet as Edith Bruder points out, often the very ways these groups assert and maintain both their identities and practices are accomplished through discursive, rhetorical means. While historians and Jewish communities alike emphasize the strong interconnections among Blacks and Jews during the U.S. civil rights movements, no one yet (to my knowledge) has rhetorically analyzed the leading role many Black Jews and Jews of color played in the contemporary Black Lives Matter movement. Michael Twitty's nonfiction account *The Cooking Gene* (which won the James Beard Award), Shais Rison's *Thoughts from a Unicorn*, and Yavilah McCoy's play *The Colors of Water* are just a few rich texts whose rhetorical consideration would deepen our intersectional understanding of the ways Jewish and African American rhetorical traditions intersect in the contemporary U.S. context. However, this constitutes just one of many important and much-needed approaches.

Additional rhetorical attention to constructions of race and religious identity would highlight the rhetorical practices of Ethiopian Jews both within and outside Israel, as well as other ethnic Jews outside the Ashkenormative purview. Perhaps the most important shift of all is to integrate this research into the curriculum at both the undergraduate and graduate levels.

Future research that seeks to foster generative engagement across religious and rhetorical traditions is also worthy of pursuit. In taking up scholarship along these lines, to-ness can serve as a valuable framework. To-ness provides a method for ethical engagement by allowing scholars who are working across religious and rhetorical traditions to acquire the knowledge and context needed to establish themselves as legitimate participants by demonstrating their familiarity with key concepts and relevant historical contexts, identifying their relationship to the material and the methods of study, and illustrating the multidirectional paths of influence in the interanimations they uncover. These types of to-ness-inspired relational interpretations and analyses are essential to research that attends to the ways rhetoric and religion are interanimated across diverse traditions and practices, for it is impossible to understand a specific set of ideas, beliefs, or practices without also creating a relationship with them and investigating where they come from, how they've been transmitted and reinterpreted, and also who or what they in turn continue to influence and shape. To that end, to-ness provides a multidirectional path for considering the way ideas and concepts travel across time, geography, and culture to highlight multiple paths of influence among religious and rhetorical traditions.

To-ness also offers both a historiographic method for study and documentation and an ethical stance for engagement, with both centered on the importance of creating and calling attention to relationship within and across religious and rhetorical traditions. To-ness likewise provides a method for connecting Hawhee and Olson's "pan-historiography" with LuMing Mao's call to engage in the art of "recontextualization," which pursues comparative work through juxtaposition rather than with recourse to an overarching principle (46). It thus enables scholars who seek to engage across religious and rhetorical traditions to move forward in historiographic projects within their particular area of expertise while also allowing scholars working in and among various rhetorical traditions to begin to speak with and talk back to one another. The way we research and teach these histories and historiographies must reflect the fact that these rhetorical paths are multidirectional. They must be deeply integrated and contextualized within cultural conversations and interactions that bring people from different traditions together, not with the goal of reaching consensus and flattening out conflict, but instead with the goal of learning from one another's experience in an ethical, nonappropriative way. To-ness offers an approach with which scholars working across different areas of religion and rhetoric can pursue these ends.

Entry Points: Approaches to Teaching Jewish Rhetorics

I have been teaching at the University of Kentucky, a land-grant, Research 1 university in the Southeast, since 2010. Since 2012, I have also directed the Jewish Studies Program, working to build additional course offerings and public programming; attract additional students to the minor; and educate both students and citizens of the Commonwealth of Kentucky about Jewish peoples, cultures, traditions, and histories. Not surprisingly, one of the ways I help communicate my research interests in Jewish rhetorics is through my teaching. In attempts to make the unknown or heretofore unencountered more familiar, I have taught a variety of courses at the intersections of Jewish studies and rhetoric, but I will discuss only one of them here. Rhetoric Between Athens and Jerusalem, an upper-division course that I have taught to a variety of different undergraduate populations, is meant to provide an introduction to comparative classical rhetoric. I began designing this course as our (then division) Department of Writing, Rhetoric, and Digital Studies was creating a major, and this course was intended to introduce classical rhetorical history and theory to those majors. Since the course is also writing intensive, it enrolls students from across the humanities, including English, philosophy, Jewish studies, and rhetoric. The course puts texts from the Greco-Roman tradition in direct conversation with Jewish rhetorical texts and calls students' attention to the ways these traditions differently conceive of argument, communication, persuasion, and even love.

In setting up the course in this way, my intention was to introduce students to the basic concepts of historiography, to complicate the way they conceive of and define rhetorical traditions, and to introduce them to Jewish rhetorical values and precepts, which were likely unfamiliar to them. Some of the first texts that I ask students to read are the first two chapters from Wayne Booth's *The Rhetoric of RHETORIC* for their careful consideration and condensed history of rhetoric. In addition to Booth, I assign Richard Graff and Michael Leff's "Revisionist Historiography and the Viability of the Rhetorical Tradition(s)," which introduces the concept of historiography and a narrative of how research has helped shape the field's trajectory. Our study questions for this first week include "What are the contexts in which you've heard the term 'rhetoric'? How do the methods described in the reading compare to the research methods of your home discipline? What is compelling and or confusing about the concept of historiography?" From there, we move to recent literature in the field that decenters the Greek tradition from being "the" rhetorical tradition, such as Carol Lipson and Roberta Binkley's *Ancient Non-Greek Rhetorics*, George Kennedy's "Rhetoric in Greece and Rome," and Sam Edelman's "Ancient Traditions, Modern Needs: An Introduction to Jewish Rhetoric." My guiding study questions: "What is similar and different in these rhetorical traditions? What are some of the pathways of interconnection or disconnect?" While space will not permit me to walk through the entire syllabus (available at rhetoric.fernheimer.org), I did want to explicate three key elements of my approach.

The first is that I put historiography and the creation of rhetorical traditions front and center so that students immediately begin to understand that traditions are consciously constructed and that canonization has important consequences for representation and exposure. In this way, I hope to introduce the concept of to-ness, even if I don't always call it that. By raising questions about the way cultural circumstances shape the types of traditions we invent, research, and teach, I hope to engage my students with the active role they are invited to play in reinventing rhetorical traditions or reconceptualizing traditions with which they are familiar. Many of my students come from various parts of the Kentucky Commonwealth, with different levels of both preparation for college and exposure to cultures beyond their own. Many are first-generation college students and have come from environments where exposure to Jewish people or culture is minimal; for some, I am the first Jewish person they have met. Their knowledge about Jewish culture, life, and tradition, if it exists at all, often comes to them filtered through the lens of what they call the "Old Testament" and often refracted through evangelical Christian interpretations or filtered through pop culture's truncated and caricatured representations of Jewish people. My goal is to expose them to the ways that Greek and Jewish rhetorical traditions interact and offer very different perspectives about communication, persuasion, argument, and who is entitled to participate in these acts. In so doing, I aim to complicate their understandings of both Jewish traditions and those more familiar to them.

The second thing I hope to do is expose students both to a variety of methods and the controversies surrounding those methods for engaging in comparative rhetorics. I ask them to read a series of exchanges by Scott Stroud and LuMing Mao to begin to think through what we might consider the ethical ways to engage in comparative projects. How should one approach or encounter a text that is not already familiar to them, from a culture that is equally unfamiliar? How do you know when you understand "enough" about that culture to begin to judge it on its own terms rather than through the terms of the cultures with which you are more deeply immersed and familiar? What choices do scholars have to make to gain access to a text? For example, is it better to encounter a text in translation than not to encounter or be exposed to it at all? Our discussions of methods necessitate the ethical impulse and ask us all to evaluate how one can ethically approach something that is "other" respectfully, informed not by an impulse to appropriate or usurp but rather by an openness to learn and better understand.

The third main thing I hope to do is expose students to the primary texts themselves in a comparative light and ethical way by introducing several key pairings. The first of these is a reading of Aristotle's *Rhetoric* paired with Everett Fox's translation of the Hebrew Deuteronomy. Fox's translation attempts to emulate as closely as possible the assonance and sounds of the Hebrew language in English, which is why it is one of my favorites. By putting Aristotle in direct conversation with the Hebrew Bible, my hope is that students begin to understand the very different ways these texts and the cultures that shaped them understood communicative acts. A second pairing is that of Plato's *Phaedrus* with Bloch and Bloch's translation of the Song of Songs, which asks students to consider the different ways Greek and Israelite cultures define love, its values, its virtues, and its relationship to knowledge. A favorite writing activity for this pairing, which when the course is taught in spring semester often coincides with Valentine's Day, is to write a "love letter" by following the inductive prescriptions set by Song of Songs. Students read their love letters aloud in class and evaluate one another's work based on how well they have emulated the values expressed in the poem. The final texts we investigate in class are Hebraic psalms, guided by Davida Charney's insightful analysis of Psalms 116 and 22, and JT Waldman's graphic narrative *Megillat Esther*, guided by Susan Zaeske's thoughtful article "Unveiling Esther as a Pragmatic Radical Rhetoric." In these final texts, we have the primary text along with rhetorical scholars' interpretations of these texts as rhetorical texts, and some of the more fascinating conversations often unfold around what it would mean to conduct everyday communication according to the precepts set forth in *Megillat Esther.* Since I ask students to read Waldman's visual interpretation, we also have an opportunity to discuss the way Waldman enacts Jewish rhetorical practices, like that of midrash, in the ways that he has illustrated the text. I like closing with this text because it also invites students to consider questions of gender and power in explicit ways.

NOTES

1. In Israel, the secular Tel Aviv suburb of Ramat Gan, which borders the *haredi* city B'nai B'rak, attempted to erect physical barriers between the two cities. Just today, April 29, 2020, New York mayor Bill de Blasio lashed out against *haredim* who flouted social distancing rules to attend a rabbi's funeral en masse. Instead of addressing this segment of the Jewish community specifically, however, his tweets conflated them with a mystical and monolithic community he referred to as "the Jewish Community," suggesting there was such a thing as a single, unified Jewish community (Stack).

2. See also Shmilovich and Hancock.

3. Historically, those who wished to persecute Jews—during the Inquisition; under Nazi rule; in contemporary culture, white supremacist groups—tend to approach Jewish identities with far more inclusive and capacious definitions (for example, having one Jewish grandparent) than those in the Jewish community tend to recognize (a Jewish mother, or father if one goes by Reform Judaism's rulings). According to Jewish law, also known as *halacha*, one is either born Jewish (to a recognized Jewish mother) or one converts in accordance with the tenets set by a particular Jewish community. The transformation in status is achieved through a process of education and inculcation into a community's beliefs and practices and confirmed by a *bet din*, a body of three religious judges.

4. In the introduction to *Jewish Rhetorics: History, Theory, Practice*, Michael Bernard-Donals and I introduce several "canons" of Jewish rhetoric, including to-ness. Though "canon" is borrowed from Greco-Roman tradition, these seven Jewish canons reflect the values and beliefs that gird the diversity of Jewish religious thought and practices, across significant time (more than four thousand years) and geographic space, of a diasporic people who live in communities across the globe with varying relationships to the majority cultures they encounter. In addition to to-ness, which emphasizes that Jewish rhetorics are based on logics of relationship and juxtaposition (either between individual and community or of insider to outsider), we also identified the canons of hearing (the relationship between speaker/audience), *hidush* (the relationship that yields innovation through textual exaction), multiplicity (the relationship[s] among multiple meanings), memory (the relationship of past to present and future), and

tzedek (the relationships that result in the pursuit of justice through ethical interactions). In a 2018 essay, my research team added collaboration, acknowledging the ways Jewish epistemologies rely on relationship with others to create knowledge, thus bringing the number of canons of Jewish rhetorical practice to seven, which occupies a mystical place in Jewish thought.

5. See also Fernheimer, *Stepping into Zion;* "Black Jewish Identity Conflict; "From Jew to Israelite."

6. See also Fernheimer, "*Talmidae Rhetoricae*," pp. 581–82, for a fuller discussion of Daube's essay and its significance for Jewish rhetorics.

7. For example, David Frank's 1981 essay, "*Shalom Achshav*'—Rituals of the Israeli Peace Movement" in *Communication Monographs*, focused on political movements in the contemporary nation-state of Israel, and David Stern's "Rhetoric and Midrash: The Case of the Mashal" focused on the midrashic form of *mashal* as a rhetorical tool and was published in *Prooftexts* that same year. Yehoshua Gitay also published his book *Prophecy and Persuasion: A Study of Isaiah 40–48* that same year, though with a biblical studies press. Arguably, his later articles on the same topic received broader readership through publication in *Prooftexts*.

8. For a more recent take on the project begun by Rabinowitz, see also Katzir's "Classical and Medieval Jewish Rhetoric."

9. Katz dates his participation to 1992–1994 in "Epistemology of the Kabbalah."

10. Ephraim Kanarfogel published *Jewish Education and Society in the High Middle Ages* in 1991, one of the first attempts to examine Rabbinic pedagogic strategies in the medieval period. In 1992, Marc Saperstein made available numerous Jewish sermons from this period with his collection *Jewish Preaching, 1200–1800: An Anthology*, published in the Yale Judaica series. Ivan Marcus's 1999 *Rituals of Childhood: Jewish Acculturation in Medieval Europe* deepened and expanded the work of Kanarfogel by tracking Jewish pedagogy for young boys in the same era.

11. See also Leon, *Book of the Honeycomb's Flow*; Ridolfo.

12. Note to Leff, Lipson, and Binkley (Gilyard and Nunley).

13. See Metzger and Katz; Lieber; Bernard-Donals; Handelman, "The Philosopher"; Fernheimer, "*Talmidae Rhetoricae*."

14. Additionally, he published *Dispute for the Sake of Heaven: Legal Pluralism in the Talmud*, which argues that there were pluralities of practice as well as argument in both the Bavli and the Yerushalmi Talmuds.

15. The monograph that grows from this research, *Rhetoric and the Dead Sea Scrolls*, was published in 2021 by Penn State University Press.

16. See Charney, "Performativity and Persuasion."

17. From 2001 to 2019, at least four courses in Jewish rhetorics were introduced at three Research-1 universities across the United States. From 2001 to 2010 at Old Dominion University, David Metzger taught three courses at the master's/doctoral

level, which introduced students to Jewish rhetorics. He transformed the course in classical rhetoric to become Hebraic and Hellenic Rhetorics, the course in modern rhetoric became Shoah and the Development of Modern Rhetoric, and he also taught a course called The Jewish Idea of Story. Influenced by Metzger's approach, in 2010 at the University of Kentucky, I introduced the course Rhetoric Between Athens and Jerusalem, an upper-division undergraduate course aimed initially at English and rhetoric majors to offer a comparative introduction to the history of classical rhetoric, which consciously paired texts from the Greco-Roman tradition with Jewish texts. I describe my strategy in the "Entry Points" section of this essay. That same year I also introduced another upper-division undergraduate course, Comics and Conflict in Israel/Palestine, which teaches about the rhetoric of Israel/Palestine through graphic narratives and rhetorical analysis. For more on this, see Fernheimer, "Comics and Conflict." In 2017, I introduced an honors first-year composition course titled Writing Jewish Kentucky, which introduces undergraduates to writing in the digital age and Kentucky's rich Jewish heritage through composition of and with the Jewish Kentucky Oral History Project (JKOHP), and in spring 2018, I introduced Composing Oral History: Jewish Kentucky, an upper-division writing course focused on archival research and construction in conjunction with the JKHOP. In 2019, Davida Charney introduced and taught her course Rhetoric in Ancient Israel at the University of Texas at Austin as an upper-division writing-intensive course.

18. See Frank, "The Rhetoric of Judaism"; Arnett; Bolduc; Fernheimer, "Confronting"; Kiewe, "Anti-Semitism."

19. Katzir is one of several scholars whose scholarly investigations begin to construct a rhetorical tradition for the broader Mediterranean. See also Guler; Diab; Baddar.

20. See chapter by Ridolfo and chapter by Metzger in Bernard-Donals and Fernheimer.

21. See Anat Feldman.

22. See also Diab; Guler; Baddar.

23. See also Gellis.

24. See Stockman.

WORKS CITED

Arnett, Ronald C. "An Immemorial Obligation: Countering the Eclipse of the Other." *Journal of Communication & Religion*, vol. 39, no. 2, 2016, pp. 7–21.

Baddar, Maha. "Toward a New Understanding of Audience in the Medieval Arabic Translation Movement: The Case of Al-Kindi's 'Statement on the Soul.'" *Rhetoric across Borders*, edited Anna Teresa Demo, Parlor Press, 2015, pp 59–70.

Bernard-Donals, Michael. "'By the Rivers of Babylon': Deterritorialization and the Jewish Rhetorical Stance." *College English*, vol. 72, no. 6, 2010, pp. 608–20.

Bernard-Donals, Michael, and Janice W. Fernheimer, editors. *Jewish Rhetorics: History, Theory, Practice*. Brandeis UP, 2014.

Bolduc, Michelle. "The New Rhetoric Project as a Response to Anti-Semitism: Chaïm Perelman's Reflections on Assimilation." *Journal of Communication & Religion*. vol. 39, no. 2, 2016, pp. 22–35.

Booth, Wayne C. *The Rhetoric of RHETORIC: The Quest for Effective Communication*. Blackwell, 2004.

Bruder, Edith. *The Black Jews of Africa: History, Religion, Identity*. Oxford UP, 2008.

Charney, Davida H. "Performativity and Persuasion in the Hebrew Book of Psalms: A Rhetorical Analysis of Psalms 22 and 116." *Rhetoric Society Quarterly*, vol. 40, no. 3, 2010, pp. 175–86.

—. *Persuading God: Rhetorical Studies of First-Person Psalms*. Sheffield Phoenix Press, 2015.

—. "Taking a Stance toward God: Rhetoric in the Book of Psalms." Bernard-Donals and Fernheimer, pp. 1–15.

Cnaan, Liphshiz. "Anti-Semitic Belgium Parade Features Costumes of Jews with Insect Bodies." *The Times of Israel*, 23 Feb. 2020, www.timesofisrael.com/anti-semitic-belgium-parade-features-costumes-of-jews-with-insect-bodies/.

Daube, David. "Rabbinic Methods of Interpretation and Hellenistic Rhetoric." *Hebrew Union College Annual*, vol. 22, 1949, pp. 239–64.

Diab, Rasha. *Shades of Sulh: The Rhetorics of Arab-Islamic Reconciliation*. U of Pittsburgh P, 2016.

Dolgopolski, Sergey. *What Is Talmud? The Art of Disagreement*. Fordham UP, 2009.

Drinkwater, Gregg. *Building Queer Judaism: Gay Synagogues and the Transformation of an American Religious Community, 1948–1990*. 2020. U of Colorado Boulder, PhD dissertation.

Edelman, Samuel M. "Ancient Traditions, Modern Needs: An Introduction to Jewish Rhetoric." *Journal of Communication & Religion*, vol. 26, no. 2, 2003, pp. 113–25.

Estrin, Daniel. "New Report Notes Rise in Coronavirus-Linked Anti-Semitic Hate Speech." *NPR*, 21 Apr. 2020, www.npr.org/sections/coronavirus-live-updates/2020/04/21/839748857/new-report-notes-rise-in-coronavirus-linked-anti-semitic-hate-speech.

Falk, Erika. "Jewish Laws of Speech: Toward Multicultural Rhetoric." *Howard Journal of Communication*, vol. 10, no. 1, 1999, pp. 15–28.

Feldman, Anat. "In the Realms of Ethnicity, Religion, and Emigration: New Communities of Memory in Israel" *Review of Religious Research*, vol. 57, no. 1, 2015, pp. 171–89.

Feldman, Ari. "Six Nights of Hanukkah, Seven Anti-Semitic Incidents in New York City." Forward, 27 Dec. 2019, forward.com/news/437346/anti-semitic-attacks-nyc-brooklyn/.

Fernheimer, Janice W. "Black Jewish Identity Conflict: A Divided Universal Audience and the Impact of Dissociative Disruption." *Rhetoric Society Quarterly*, vol. 39, no. 1, 2009, pp. 46–72.

—. "Comics and Conflict: Teaching about Israel/Palestine through Graphic Narrative." *Teaching the Arab-Israeli Conflict in the College Classroom*, edited by Rachel Harris, Wayne State UP, 2019. pp. 28–42.

—. "Confronting Kenneth Burke's Anti-Semitism." *Journal of Communication & Religion*, vol. 39, no. 2, 2016, pp. 36–53.

—. "From Jew to Israelite: Making Uncomfortable Communions and the New Rhetoric's Tools for Invention." *Argumentation and Advocacy*, vol. 44, no. 4, 2008, pp. 198–212.

—. *Stepping into Zion: Hatzaad Harishon, Black Jews, and the Remaking of Jewish Identity*. U of Alabama P, 2014.

—. "*Talmidae Rhetoricae*: Drashing Up Models and Methods for Jewish Rhetorical Studies." *Composing Jewish Rhetorics*, special issue of *College English*, vol. 72, no. 6, 2010, pp. 577–89.

Frank, David A. "Arguing with God, Talmudic Discourse, and the Jewish Countermodel: Implications for the Study of Argumentation." *Argumentation and Advocacy*, vol. 41, 2004, pp. 71–86.

—. "The Jewish Countermodel: Talmudic Argumentation, the New Rhetoric Project, and the Classical Tradition of Rhetoric." *Journal of Communication & Religion*, vol. 26, 2003, pp. 163–94.

—. "The Jewish Question in the New Rhetorics of Kenneth Burke and Chaïm Perelman." *Journal of Communication & Religion*, vol. 39, no. 2, 2016, pp. 54–65.

—. "The New Rhetoric, Judaism, and Post-Enlightenment Thought: The Cultural Origins of Perelmanian Philosophy." *Quarterly Journal of Speech*, vol. 83, 1997, pp. 311–31.

—. "The Rhetoric of Judaism and Anti-Judaism: Responses to Amos Kiewe's *Confronting Anti-Semitism: Seeking an End to Hateful Rhetoric*." *Journal of Communication & Religion*, vol. 39, no. 2, 2016, pp. 5–6.

—. "'Shalom Achshav': Rituals of the Israeli Peace Movement." *Communication Monographs*, vol. 48, no. 3, 1981, pp. 165–82.

—. "A Traumatic Reading of Twentieth-Century Rhetorical Theory: The Belgian Holocaust, Malines, Perelman, and de Man." *Quarterly Journal of Speech*, vol. 93, no. 3, 2007, pp. 308–43.

Gellis, Eliza. "'Hadassah, That Is Esther': Diasporic Rhetoric in the Book of Esther." *The Routledge Handbook of Comparative World Rhetorics*, edited by Keith Lloyd, Routledge, 2020, pp. 126–33.

Gilyard, Keith, and Vorris Nunley. *Rhetoric and Ethnicity*. Heinemann, 2004.

Gitay, Yehoshua. "Isaiah and His Audience." *Prooftexts*, vol. 3, no. 3, 1983, pp. 223–30.

—. *Prophecy and Persuasion: A Study of Isaiah 40–48*. Linguistica Biblica, 1981.

Graff, Richard, and Michael Leff. "Revisionist Historiography and Rhetorical Tradition(s)." *The Viability of the Rhetorical Tradition*, edited by Richard Graff et al., State U of New York P, 2005, pp. 11–30.

Greenbaum, Andrea, and Deborah Holdstein. *Judaic Perspectives in Rhetoric and Composition*. Hampton Press, 2008.

Guler, Elif. "An Overview of *Kut* and *Töre* as the Pillars of the Turkish Rhetorical Tradition." *The Routledge Handbook of Comparative World Rhetorics*, edited by Keith Lloyd, Routledge, 2020, pp. 106–15.

Hancock, Laura. "Some Ohio Coronavirus Protesters Using Anti-Semitic Symbolism." *Cleveland.com*, 21 Apr. 2020, www.cleveland.com/open/2020/04/some-ohio-coronavirus-protesters-using-anti-semitism-symbolism.html.

Handelman, Susan. "The Philosopher, the Rabbi, and the Rhetorician." *College English*, vol. 72, no. 6, 2010, pp. 590–607.

—. *The Slayers of Moses: The Emergence of Rabbinic Interpretation in Modern Literary Theory*. State U of New York P, 1982.

Hawhee, Debra, and Christa Olson. "Pan-historiography: The Challenge of Writing History across Time and Space." *Theorizing Histories of Rhetoric*, edited by Michelle Baliff, Southern Illinois UP, 2013, pp. 90–105.

Haynes, Bruce D. "People of God, Children of Ham: Making Black(s) Jews." *Journal of Modern Jewish Studies*, vol. 8, no. 2, 2009, pp. 237–54.

Hidary, Richard. "Classical Rhetorical Arrangement and Reasoning in the Talmud: The Case of Yerushalmi Berakhot 1:1." *AJS Review*, vol. 34, no. 1, 2010, pp. 33–64.

—. *Dispute for the Sake of Heaven: Legal Pluralism in the Talmud*. Brown UP, 2010.

—. *Rabbis and Classical Rhetoric: Sophistic Education and Oratory in the Talmud and Midrash*. Cambridge UP, 2019.

Kanarfogel, Ephraim. *Jewish Education and Society in the High Middle Ages*. Wayne State UP, 1992.

Katz, Steven B. "The Epistemology of the Kabbalah: Toward a Jewish Philosophy of Rhetoric." *Rhetoric Society Quarterly*, vol. 25, 1995, pp. 107–22.

—. "The Ethic of Expediency: Classical Rhetoric, Technology, and the Holocaust." *College English*, vol. 54, 1992, pp. 255–75.

Katzir, Brandon. "Against the Philosophers: Writing and Identity in Medieval Mediterranean Rhetoric." *Philosophy & Rhetoric*, vol. 52, no. 4, 2019, pp. 366–83.

—. "Classical and Medieval Jewish Rhetoric." *American Society for the History of Rhetoric*, ashr.org/teaching-resources/teaching-history-of-rhetoric/classical-and-medieval-jewish-rhetoric/. Accessed 23 Feb. 2022.

—. "Paths of Virtue: Legal Rhetorics in Judaism and Islam." *Rhetoric Society Quarterly*, vol. 48, no. 1, 2018, pp. 28–48.

—. "'The Truth of Reliable Tradition': Saadya Gaon, Arabic Rhetoric, and the Challenge to Rhetorical Historiography." *Rhetorica: A Journal of the History of Rhetoric*, vol. 35, no. 2, 2017, pp. 161–88.

Kennedy, George A. "Rhetoric in Greece and Rome." *Comparative Rhetoric: An Historical and Cross-Cultural Introduction*, Oxford UP, 1997, ch. 9.

Kiewe, Amos. "Anti-Semitism as Praxis: A Response Essay." *Journal of Communication & Religion*, vol. 39, no. 2, 2016, pp. 66–72.

—. *Confronting Anti-Semitism: Seeking an End to Hateful Rhetoric*. Troubador, 2011.

Koban, John E. "'Guard Your Tongue': Lashon Hara and the Rhetoric of Chafetz Chaim." *Journal of Communication & Religion*, vol. 40, no. 2, 2017, pp. 22–42.

Lesley, Arthur. "A Survey of Medieval Hebrew Rhetoric." *Approaches to Judaism in Medieval Times*, Brown UP, 1984, pp. 107–33.

Lieber, Andrea. "A Virtual Veibershul: Blogging and the Blurring of Public and Private among Orthodox Jewish Women." *College English*, vol. 72, no. 6, 2010, pp. 621–37.

Lipson, Carol S., and Roberta A. Binkley, editors. *Ancient Non-Greek Rhetorics*. Parlor Press, 2009.

—, editors. *Rhetoric Before and Beyond the Greeks*. State U of New York P, 2004.

Lynch, Paul, and Matthew Miller. "Twenty-Five Years of Faith in Writing: Religion and Composition, 1992–2017." *Present Tense: A Journal of Rhetoric in Society*, vol. 6, no. 2, 2017, www.presenttensejournal.org/volume-6/twenty-five-years-of-faith-in-writing-religion-and-composition-1992-2017/.

Malanych, Alexander. *The Burkean Closet: Theories of Identification and Queer Jewish Resistance*. 2014. U of Vermont, MA thesis.

Mao, LuMing. "Writing the Other into Histories of Rhetorics: The Art of Recontextualization." *Theorizing Histories of Rhetoric*, edited by Michelle Baliff, Southern Illinois UP, 2013, pp. 41–58.

Marcus, Ivan G. *Rituals of Childhood: Jewish Acculturation in Medieval Europe*. Yale UP, 1996.

McComiskey, Bruce. "Laws, Works, and the End of Days: Rhetorics of Identification, Distinction, and Persuasion in *Miqṣat Ma'aśeh ha Torah* (Dead Sea Scroll 4QMMT)." *Rhetoric Review*, vol. 29, 2010, pp. 221–38.

Messer Leon, Judah. *The Book of the Honeycomb's Flow | Sepher Nopheth Suphim*. Translated by Isaac Rabinowitz, Cornell UP, 1983.

Metzger, David, and Steven B. Katz. "The 'Place' of Rhetoric in Aggadic Midrash." *College English*, vol. 72, no. 6, 2010, pp. 638–53.

Moshin, Jamie, and Richard Benjamin Crosby. "Liminally White: Jews, Mormons, and Whiteness." *Communication, Culture & Critique*. vol. 11, no. 3, 2018, pp. 436–54.

Parfitt, Tudor. *Black Jews in Africa and the Americas*. Harvard UP, 2013.

Rabinowitz, Isaac. "Pre-modern Jewish Study of Rhetoric: An Introductory Bibliography." *Rhetorica: A Journal of the History of Rhetoric*, vol. 3, 1985, pp. 137–44.

Ridolfo, Jim. "Theory and Practice: Judah Messer Leon and Technologies of Rhetorical Delivery." Bernard-Donals and Fernheimer, pp. 46–57.

Rishon, Shais. *Thoughts from a Unicorn: 100% Black. 100% Jewish. 0% Safe*. Hyphen Publishing, 2012.

Rubenstein, Jeffrey L., editor *Creation and Composition: The Contribution of the Bavli Redactors (Stammaim) to the Aggada*. Mohr Siebeck, 2005.

Saperstein, Marc. *Jewish Preaching, 1200–1800: An Anthology*. Yale UP, 1989.

Schumann, Andrew. "Logical Cornerstones of Jewish Argumentation Theory." *Argumentation*, vol. 27, 2013, pp. 305–26.

Shmilovich, Tzipi. "Anti-Semitism Rears Its Head in U.S. Lockdown Protests." *Ynet News*, 3 May 2020, https://www.ynetnews.com/article/ryL1la72FI.

Slotkin, Alexander. "'The Woman Who Talks': A Qualitative Case Study in Feminist Jewish Rhetorics." *Rhetoric Review*, vol. 39, no. 4, 2021, pp. 457–70.

Stack, Liam. "De Blasio Breaks Up Rabbi's Funeral and Lashes Out over Virus Distancing." *New York Times*, 29 Apr. 2020, www.nytimes.com/2020/04/28/nyregion/hasidic-funeral-coronavirus-de-blasio.html.

Stern, David. "Rhetoric and Midrash: The Case of the Mashal." *Prooftexts*, vol. 1, no. 3 1981, pp. 261–91.

Stockman, Farah. "Women's March Roiled by Accusations of Anti-Semitism." *New York Times*, 23 Dec. 2018, www.nytimes.com/2018/12/23/us/womens-march-anti-semitism.html.

Tauber, Abraham. "Jewish Rhetoric." *Today's Speech*, vol. 17, no. 4, 1969, pp. 57–67.

Twitty, Michael W. *The Cooking Gene: A Journey through African American Culinary History in the Old South*. HarperCollins, 2017.

Waldman, JT. *Megillat Esther*. The Jewish Publication Society, 2005.

Zaeske, Susan. "Unveiling Esther as a Pragmatic Radical Rhetoric." *Philosophy & Rhetoric*, vol. 33, no. 3, 2000, pp. 193–220.

Zulick, Margaret. "The Active Force of Hearing: The Ancient Hebrew Language of Persuasion." *Rhetorica: A Journal of the History of Rhetoric*, vol. 10, no. 4, pp. 367–80.

—. "The Agon of Jeremiah: On the Dialogic Invention of Prophetic Ethos." *Quarterly Journal of Speech*, vol. 78, no. 2, pp. 125–48.

Interlude

PATRICIA ROBERTS-MILLER

My dissertation was about John Muir's (failed) attempt to stop the damming and flooding of the Hetch Hetchy Valley. Muir was raised in a very strict Disciples of Christ family—he memorized a chapter of the Bible every week or got beaten for not doing it. And it seemed to me that, especially when things got heated, he used a lot of scriptural rhetoric, such as comparing himself to Jesus throwing the merchants out of the Temple of Jerusalem, to John the Baptist, or to Isaiah. This was not a welcome observation at that point in time—Roderick Nash's (rather sloppy, I think) *Wilderness and the American Mind* was a bible, so to speak, and he (and others) repeatedly argued that Christianity was necessarily hostile to environmental protection. This was the early to mid-1980s, and there was a lot of work that assumed that philosophies or ideologies had necessary consequences (James Berlin's *Rhetoric and Reality* was popular in rhetoric at the time).

That argument seemed implausible to me for a lot of reasons, not the least of which was that Nash and others misunderstood crucial aspects of the history of American Christianity. The misunderstandings were sometimes very specific (such as that the seventeenth-century use of the word "aweful" is not at all what we now mean by "awful") and some broader (such as not understanding the notion of nature as "God's other book") and some much broader (such as the wild variation in ideologies among groups that are all called "Christian"), but all were consequential.

It also seemed to me unreasonable that a person could be raised within a particular tradition and abandon it completely—even I, poorly read in scripture as I was, knew that Muir interpreted his getting blinded as a "Saul on the road to Damascus" moment, his getting drenched by a waterfall as a baptism, and the Hetch Hetchy Valley as a sacred space. As it is with an individual, so it is with a culture. Even people who were thoroughly secular and hadn't been to church ever (or since they were little) talked about Muir as a voice crying in the wilderness. And people talked about themselves as a voice crying in the wilderness, with no idea where that phrase came from.

And, of course, it isn't just a phrase. It's a claim about the person's relationship to Truth. A voice crying in the wilderness is a prophet, directly connected to the Truth but ignored or reviled because that Truth is unwelcome. It's also a claim about public discourse—you shouldn't argue with a prophet, and a prophet has no reason to listen to their critics. That those critics disagree is proof enough that they are wrong. That's a strange way to think about public discourse in a democracy or, more precisely, is a way of thinking about public discourse that inhibits democratic deliberation. So, why in a democracy do we privilege an antidemocratic approach to public discourse?

The answer is that, as children of the Enlightenment, we both do and don't believe in the possibility of legitimate disagreement because we both do and don't believe in the power of reasoned persuasion. We like conversion narratives, and we especially like ones with moments of enlightenment—regardless of whether we're religious or not. Thus, a figure with its origin in religious rhetoric (the conversion narrative, for one) can turn up anywhere, from a literacy narrative to New Age self-help bestsellers.

Thinking of rhetorical strategies as crossing genres was difficult to do when I started because it was before the excellent work of people like Carolyn Miller who opened up our notion of genre. Rhetoric still had a tendency to categorize by some version of James Kinneavy's triad or the persuade/inform/express taxonomy. That taxonomy would make it seem that scientific rhetoric couldn't possibly be using a rhetorical strategy from religion—they're different categories. I'm oversimplifying of course, but my basic point is that there was a tendency to think about religious rhetoric as being the set of strategies used in texts we'd categorize as religious, rather than about how there isn't some bright line between, for instance, religious and political discourse. If you think there is a bright line, how do you explain a powerful text like David

Walker's *Appeal to the Coloured People of the World*, an antislavery jeremiad that is grounded in political theory, philosophy, and religion?

The notion of religious rhetoric as a separate category hadn't always been part of rhetorical studies. As more sources in rhetoric were published, such as the lectures of Hugh Blair, it was clear that religious rhetoric has long been part of a rhetorical education. In 1939, Kenneth Burke had brilliantly identified the religious bases of many of Adolf Hitler's rhetorical appeals in *Mein Kampf*—the "bastardization of religious forms of thought," as he said—so this understanding of political and religious rhetoric as intermingled was not an entirely new phenomenon.

That said, I think four major shifts in rhetorical studies in the 1990s led to major changes in thinking about religious rhetoric. The first was the pedagogical shift—that is, looking at how rhetoric was taught. The second was changing the focus from the Great Men rhetors to the often-marginalized rhetors making major political changes—such as abolitionists. They didn't experience rhetorical training or practice as though discourse were divided into religious versus other kinds. The third was the interest in cultural studies that meant works like James Darsey's *The Prophetic Tradition and Radical Rhetoric in America* (1997) could unapologetically talk about how a religious rhetorical strategy could be seen in gay rights rhetoric.

As brilliant as Burke's analysis of Hitler was, when he said "religious forms of thought," he meant Western Catholicism and some forms of Protestantism. The fourth shift was that, as people moved away from the Great (White) Men model of what is valuable to study, there was also a greater understanding that generalizations grounded in a very narrow notion of religion have a very narrow application. I think someone who made the slip that Burke did would now get corrected, and that's a good thing.

My area of specialization is sometimes called "pathologies of deliberation," that is, the beliefs, approaches, and practices that inhibit effective deliberation and head communities toward demagoguery. I often think about something a family friend once said. He said, "I've been involved in school politics, medical politics, church politics, and politics politics, and church politics is the worst. Everyone has God on their side." At times, at least in U.S. history, school politics and politics politics are treated by many as a subdivision of church politics. We're in one of those times.

I don't simply mean that specific issues in some area have religious implications (the teaching of evolution in school politics, birth control in medical politics, segregation in politics politics); rather, I'm concerned with the way we reason and disagree. In many sects, unshakable faith—refusal to consider counterevidence or listen to doubters—is considered an admirable sign of piety. An irrational and impractical course of action is, by many, considered an indicator of deep faith. It is also considered characteristic of the "prosperity gospel" and holy wars, approaches that make demagoguery the only available discourse. Of course, valuing fanaticism, the just world hypothesis (of which "prosperity gospel" is one instance), and demagoguery are not peculiar to religious discourse—Thucydides describes communities convulsed by a fanaticism that has nothing to do with religious beliefs; Callicles (in Plato's *Gorgias*) advocates a nonreligious version of the just world hypothesis; and wars (or politics) of extermination have been conducted by officially atheistic communities and governments. And, equally of course, not all sects value fanaticism, the just world hypothesis, or demagoguery. But what I think makes talking about how we argue so difficult is that so many people assume that donning the armor of God means deflecting the opinion of anyone who disagrees, evidence that is disconfirming, or doubts about our righteousness.

I am a person of faith, and I am not blaming religion. I am saying that being religious doesn't necessarily mean one is right, nor does it exempt us from the normal and desirable practices of deliberative democracy. As Burke showed, religion can be distorted in service of demagoguery, authoritarianism, and extermination. We have to be able to talk about that.

WORKS CITED

Berlin, James A. *Rhetoric and Reality: Writing Instruction in American Colleges, 1900–1985*. Southern Illinois UP, 1987.

Burke, Kenneth. "The Rhetoric of Hitler's Battle." *Southern Review*, vol. 5, 1939, pp. 1–21.

Darsey, James. *The Prophetic Tradition and Radical Rhetoric in America*. New York UP, 1997.

Nash, Roderick Frazier. *Wilderness and the American Mind*. 1967. 5th ed., Yale UP, 2014

Walker, David. *Appeal to the Coloured Citizens of the World*. 1829. Martino Publishing, 2015.

6. Rhetoric and Buddhism Unchained

KURT SPELLMEYER

The ancient Greeks first encountered Buddhism as a result of Alexander the Great's invasion of northwest India in the fourth century B.C.E. Among the Hellenized provinces that he left behind, one would become the fabled land of Gandhara, surrounding modern Kandahar in Afghanistan—sadly, once again invaded by the West only twenty years ago. But there, Greek philosophy and arts combined with Indian learning to create a synthesis of East and West such as the world had never seen. One key document of that period is *The Questions of Milinda*, which unfolds like a Platonic dialogue between the Indian Buddhist monk Nagasena and the Greek ruler Menander I, or "Milinda," in Pali, the language of early Buddhist texts. And given the distance between the two men and their respective societies, Nagasena's task was challenging indeed: to translate the teachings of the Buddha, whose name means "the Awakened One," into terms the Greek could appreciate, but without losing sight of the differences.

Tradition tells us Nagasena did his work so well that Menander became a Buddhist, but I have always thought that "convergence" rather than "conversion" best describes what took place. While the Greeks and Indians seemed worlds apart, their encounter in Gandhara gave both peoples something omitted or repressed by their own traditions. Greek logic and art left indelible marks on the Buddhist path, though the Indians initially looked with some distrust on dialectics and aesthetics. At the same time, Greeks in Asia eagerly embraced a way of being that their countrymen back home had forgotten after the pre-Socratics, one welcoming to paradox and forms of consciousness more alive, creative, and encompassing than Aristotelian rationality. It was a true fusion of horizons that left both civilizations changed, and such an event might still happen again. How the dharma—the Buddha's path or dispensation—in our time could be enlarged by rhetoric I will leave for another day, but here I want to argue that our discipline, though deeply rooted in the West, might emerge from the encounter more fully what it has already become—an agent of emancipation rather than the dutiful servant of hegemony. Postmodern and even posthumanist, inspired both by network theory and by ecological models of change, rhetoric could find in the dharma what some of us might least anticipate—an ally in the Gramscian war of positions now threatening to undo a century of social progress. And Buddhism, at the very least, might remind us that even when we have nothing left to draw on in our struggle, we have everything we need because nothing or "emptiness" (*shunyata*) can set us free from every constraint.

The History of a Non-Western Critical Tradition

At the outset then, I should explain that even though Buddhists in India shared with the Greeks a goal comparable to *eudaimonia*, human flourishing, they understood the path to that goal quite differently. When Socrates in the *Symposium* praises the ascent to wisdom, he describes a dialectical process that gradually transports the thinker out of the realm of sensation and into the dimension of unchanging Ideas, or Forms (*eidoi*). Once we have entered this timeless dimension, we will attain wisdom (*sophia*) by becoming one with a universal Mind (*nous*), metaphorically described in another dialogue, the *Phaedrus*, as a "place beyond heaven" (*huperouranios topos*) (*Phdr.* 247c ff).

Like Socrates, the Buddha believed in the pursuit of wisdom (Pali *panna*), but he questioned the reliability of discursive thought as the means to that end. Drawing instead on the ancient Indian shamanic tradition, he recommended the embodied practice (*bhavana*, praxis or cultivation) of seated meditation, which involves two complementary elements: mental stabilization (*samatha*) and the analytical inspection of reality (*vipassana*). The goal of *samatha* is the attainment of *samapatti*, non-dualistic awareness, and only in this selfless condition can we observe things as they really are without the distortions produced by language, culture, and the psychological defense mechanisms that modern people call "projections" and that later Buddhists termed *vijñapti*. When we become adept at this embodied, critical phenomenology, we will see that the self has no independent core comparable to an eternal soul. Rather, the self is what we today would recognize as an emergent property of the complex system to which it belongs—basically, the universe—which the Buddha also understood to be impermanent, constantly changing, ultimately without a core, and self-creating out of nothing (Sanskrit *swayambhu*).

Much of this should sound familiar to readers conversant with the work of Jacques Derrida, Michel Foucault, Gilles Deleuze and Félix Guattari, Judith Butler, Donna Haraway, and Bruno Latour, or with that of rhetoricians who have drawn on their ideas. And these same thinkers might also agree with Buddhists about the existential benefits that follow from a turn away from the *cogito*—the assumption that consciousness begins with the "I." Once we experience the nonexistence of the self (P. *anatta*), we cease to suffer from a sense of helplessness and can even find joy in what we do because we have broken with the mental tic of grasping (*upadana*) at outcomes as though as individuals we can control events, when those events actually arise from interdependent causes and conditions (*pratītyasamutpāda*). Contemporary rhetoricians might agree as well that in exchange for whatever we lose after we give up the fiction of the self, we get more than amply repaid with a new sense of solidarity that extends, the Buddha said, beyond humankind to embrace every variety of "sentient being"—a category that includes nonhuman animals as well as any artificial minds rising to the level of self-awareness. Long before Bruno Latour elevated network theory, Buddhists used the metaphor of the "net of jewels" to describe our interrelatedness, convinced that liberation (Sk. *vimutti*) can only be a liberation for and with others.

Of course, the tenets of non-self and interdependence would suggest that even the Buddha's own teachings have been shaped by specific causes and conditions, a point to which he would readily assent. And among those "causes and conditions" were the social and political developments of his time. While legend has it that the Buddha was born to a royal family, he was probably the son of a tribal chieftain who played a leading role in the parliament of a small state, the Shakya Republic, one of seven or eight democratic polities on the northeastern periphery of the subcontinent. The *suttas*, or Buddhist scriptures, record that on one occasion, the Shakya parliament asked the Buddha himself to deliver a teaching at the dedication of the newly rebuilt hall. Within the Buddha's lifetime, however, the Shakya state and its democratic neighbors were subdued and absorbed by several large military powers, and one of them, Kosala, waged a successful genocidal war against the Buddha's family and compatriots. One way to understand Buddhism's role, first in India and then in ancient China, is to see it as a 2,500-year struggle to preserve a culture of democracy. And in the course of that history, the dharma developed a uniquely egalitarian phenomenology, epistemology, and aesthetics. As we shall see, this commitment to an egalitarian culture profoundly influenced Buddhist thinking about language, communication, and learning.

A second factor that shaped the dharma is economic rather than political and social. Although we today might associate Buddhism with remote mountain temples in China or Tibet, Buddhism's rise in India actually coincided with the rapid growth of cities, increasing trade, the formation of a market economy, specialization, stratification, and the fortunes of an upwardly mobile "middle class"—from which Buddhism eventually drew the great majority of its supporters. At first, in the Shakya Republic, the Buddha's followers belonged primarily to the independent landholders known as *gahapati*, who, like Athens' free citizens, could participate in parliamentary deliberations. But later, as Buddhism spread across northeastern India, it drew heavily from the ranks of merchants, skilled tradespeople, government officials, and other professionals. Often migrating to the city from the rural hinterlands, they embraced Buddhism because it offered them the chance to reinvent themselves and to reinvent, as well, social relationships in ways that were not divinely ordained, as the older theistic traditions held, but genuinely open to experimentation.[1] It is no accident that the heroes of one great Buddhist literary monument, the *Divyavadana*—roughly comparable to the *Canterbury Tales*—are traders crossing deserts or sailing stormy seas to faraway ports. And Buddhism's mercantile adventurousness went hand in hand with cultural curiosity. Its cosmopolitanism made it receptive to immigrants arriving from everywhere, and the dharma followed those same routes in the opposite direction, spreading peacefully to central Asia, China and Tibet, Japan and Korea, Sri Lanka, and as far south as Malaysia and Indonesia.

But in India itself, this openness—social, political, and economic—put Buddhism increasingly at odds with cultural conservatives, especially those in the north-central region known as Kuru, the brahminist heartland of what we could describe as the Veda-belt, with reference to the Vedas, ancient, pre-Buddhist scriptures that prescribe a caste hierarchy as well as the subordination of women. Against brahminist intellectuals, Buddhists engaged in a struggle for hearts and minds on the subcontinent, sometimes flourishing and sometimes in retreat, often on the receiving end of state-sanctioned violence comparable to pogroms in Europe or Jim Crow laws in the United States.[2] Historians sympathetic to the brahminist cause claim that Buddhism had grown too reliant on royal patronage and too preoccupied with metaphysical concerns, neglecting the needs of ordinary folk, when, in fact, Buddhists consistently played an oppositional role, defending the disfavored, underprivileged, and marginalized. Unfortunately, Buddhism slowly lost ground, and a Muslim invasion in the thirteenth century dealt a final, fatal blow, destroying its preeminent universities, still vibrant centers of learning. Yet even as its fortunes declined in India, a diasporic Buddhism took root and expanded throughout East Asia, where it survives today.

A Buddhist Rhetoric?

Any discussion of Buddhist rhetoric has to take account of this history because Buddhist thinking about language responded to exigencies quite different from those facing Western rhetoric, which was almost always employed in the service of various hegemonies (the Athenian and Roman ruling classes, the medieval Catholic Church, European colonialism, Western patriarchy, and so on). Moreover, the modern West's reception of Buddhism has been shaped not only by our five centuries of global conquest and colonization but by a reflexive Eurocentrism and by a consumer capitalism that has reduced Buddhism to "inspirational" aphorisms and corporate-sponsored courses on mindfulness designed to combat workplace stress.

The term "Buddhist rhetoric" might abet this process of cultural appropriation. Over the course of several drafts, that phrase persisted as my title, but gradually I came to appreciate how deeply problematic a choice it would be. "Rhetoric," I finally understood, describes a rich but still parochial way of representing our linguistic interactions, and I now believe that we should recognize Buddhism as a "parallel universe," one resisting the limits imposed by our traditional idea of the "rhetorical." But the persistence of difference should not obscure important areas of convergence with post-traditional rhetoric. In theory and practice, Buddhism might make common cause with rhetoricians now working to reconstruct the field by detaching it from the "chains" of my title—from its origins in a patriarchal, slaveholding society obsessed with competition and control, as well as from that society's Enlightenment successor. Any list of these rhetoricians would include Thomas Rickert, Diane Davis, Scot Barnett, Casey Boyle, and others, not themselves Buddhist, so far as I know, but like-minded in their commitment to a pluralistic anti-ontology that attributes the multiplicity of our ways with words not to a deficit of knowledge but to the growth of our understanding.

That Buddhism should have an affinity with contemporary rhetoric might seem improbable at first because nothing like rhetoric can be found in that religion's early days. On the subject of language, the Buddha himself had a great deal to say, especially about the ethics of "right speech" (P. *samma vaca*), the principle enjoining his followers to avoid any uses of words that might cause injury.[3] Yet India's greatest Buddhist university, Nalanda Mahavihara, founded in the fifth century C.E. and destroyed by Muslim Turk invaders eight centuries after that, offered a graduated curriculum that began with five subjects that played much the same role as the medieval Western trivium of grammar, logic, and rhetoric: *sabdavidyā* (grammar and lexico-graphy), *silpasthanavidyā* (arts), *chikitsavidyā* (medicine), *hetuvidyā* (logic), and *adhyat-mavidyā* (philosophy) (Kumar 159–91). We see grammar here and something like etymology, but notably absent from the list is a discipline approximating rhetoric. Buddhist thinkers understood that we need words to communicate, and for this reason, dialectic and debate played a central role in the education of Nalanda students, just as they still do in Buddhist education. Even now, monks and nuns, and lay teachers as well, are expected to write effectively, read widely, and study throughout their lives.[4]

And, given how much they have to learn, their study can never end. Indeed, the Chinese Buddhist master Huineng described it as infinite.[5]

Each of Buddhism's different "schools"—the Theravada, the Mahayana, and the Vajrayana of Tibet—developed its own canon that may include anywhere from 80 volumes to more than 120, most of them ostensibly transcriptions of the Buddha's speech, though modern scholarship has called that claim into doubt. But even beyond the canon proper, already many times the Bible's length, the commentaries and collected works of Buddhism's version of the Jewish "*hakhamim*" or Christian "Fathers of the Church"—the *sutras*, *sastras*, *tantras*, and so on—are so numerous that no one can say with certainty just how many there are. Tibetan Buddhists even believe that some of the great sages of the past have left behind hidden teachings, called *terma*, along with secret instructions, passed down orally, for public revelation when the time is right. Buddhist thinking about language, then, has assumed the forms of ethics, grammar, semantics, semiotics, and hermeneutics, but when it comes to the discipline of rhetoric, in its founding formulation as the study of the "means of persuasion," things get more complex. Both Indian and Chinese intellectuals developed disciplines we can readily designate as "rhetoric," but Buddhism's relation to them remained for some time ambivalent and even polemical. Of early Buddhism, we could say that it adopted a rhetoric of anti-rhetoricity.

One way to explain the absence of an explicitly "rhetorical" tradition in the early Buddhist culturesphere is to look more critically at how its key term "persuasion" has operated in the West, where, I would propose, it has often involved the opposite of the "fusion of horizons" celebrated by phenomenology. At least in its Aristotelian form, it more closely approximates the assimilation of the "weaker" horizon by the "stronger" one under the sign of a Reason or Logic imagined as a universal law. We could even say that in persuasion we find the paradigm of social relations that transformed the Athenian city-state into a warlike imperial power, feared and resented by its rivals. Even in its more generous Burkean form, persuasion still requires something like agreement or identity, a common "sub-stance" that seems to me appropriative in a subtler way.

By contrast, in the case of Buddhism, dissuasion—the encouragement of disbelief—has typically enjoyed pride of place in its thinking about language, whereas all agreement is understood to be impermanent, conditional, and incomplete. Indeed, the dharma's allegiance to dissuasion is so thoroughgoing that even the teachings of the Buddha himself, as recorded in those many canonical texts, are commonly considered to be true only relative to their context of utterance and as merely conventional expressions of the inexpressible. As the

Buddha announces in the *Lankavatara Sutra*, "Words are not the ultimate truth, nor is what they express the ultimate truth. . . . Words arise and cease and shift, with their occurrence depending on changing causes and conditions" (119). But words are not simply too blunt an instrument to convey the truth about the way things are; rather, they actively distort our perceptions by inducing us to trust in the reality of all kinds of things that don't exist at all—"flowers in the sky" and "the rabbit's horns" are the common Buddhist metaphors for them—whereas we generally ignore countless things that ought to matter, among these the prevalence of suffering everywhere we turn.

But the trouble with language doesn't end there. As Buddhist thinkers have recognized from the beginning, words embody a specific karma or history that they carry forward over time—a history, more often than not, of false consciousness, since most people, from the Buddhist point of view, spend their lives in the pursuit of power, wealth, approval, sensory pleasure, or, at a bare minimum, the furtive circumvention of suffering by shunting it off on others. We shape language to suit our needs, but our "needs" have often arisen from our greed, anger, and self-delusion, which Buddhism calls the "three poisons." These we rarely notice, or want to, because our language reinforces the illusion of an "I," a subjectivity or quasi-permanent self separate from everything else. Words bribe us, to put it crudely, into colluding with the status quo by promising to deliver whatever it takes to make us seem more substantial to ourselves.

In this suspicion of language, Buddhism and contemporary rhetoric seem to have converged. The Buddhist view of words as bearers of a history that escapes or exceeds our intentions is one that most of us today would accept, thanks to rhetoric's fifty-year-long detour through poststructuralism, critical theory, and feminism after Judith Butler's explorations of performativity. But the dharma might offer rhetoric something more than a premodern version of postmodernity. It's certainly true that Buddhist intellectuals consistently rejected any effort to invest language with a foundational status as the "word of God" or some equivalent, insisting that it was mutable like everything else and subject to forces, including politics and sheer accident, which undermined any claim to its unmediated correspondence with reality. But from the existence of a fissure between reality and representation, Buddhists have concluded not simply that representation is constrained in the ways described by Lévi-Strauss, Derrida, and Latour but that the fissure—the emptiness—is reality itself and ultimately unrepresentable.[6] From this it does not follow, however, that representation is futile but rather that all representation is expedient and that its inevitable failure is the source of an indestructible and inexhaustible agency. Out of "nothing," we can recreate ourselves and our worlds.

Emptiness, Hierarchy, and Resistance from Below

If Aristotle legitimized the privilege of the Athenian elite by linking their mastery to the order of nature, the brahminists laid claim to a religious purity based on their hereditary access to a transcendent, universal Self, the Atman. In the brahminist imaginary, society could be understood as a *shikhara*, or temple tower, stacking up smaller and smaller plateaus until it reached the divine Atman, like a flame or flower crowning the very top. One step below the Atman were the brahmin, the highest caste, and after them were the various castes on down to the *chandala*, or untouchables, so polluted that their shadows could contaminate a brahmin accidently passing by. Few hegemonies have displayed a comparable will to power—relentless, comprehensive, and particularly cruel.

Like the Athenian elites for whom Aristotle wrote his *Rhetorica*, those in India spoke in the voice of authority, but there, that authority was sacred. For example, the ancient *Rigveda*, a scripture thought to be more than three thousand years old, recounts the founding of the universe with the sacrifice of the Purusha, or cosmic man:

> When they divided Purusha, in how many different portions did they arrange him? What became of his mouth, what of his two arms? What were his two thighs and his two feet called?
>
> His mouth became the brahman; his two arms were made into the rajanya [warriors]; his two thighs the vaishyas; from his two feet the shudra was born. (*Rigveda* 10:90; de Bary 16–17)

Scholars still heatedly debate whether these passages actually appeared in the earliest versions of the Vedas or whether brahminists inserted them at a later date. But just as some Christians in the modern West refer to the Bible uncritically as the revealed "word of God," so did brahminist intellectuals develop theories of language to support the Vedas' status as revelation, attributing gradations of wealth and prestige to a person's karmic evolution over many lifetimes. And based on the belief that *prana*, the energy of the universe, would descend into the reciter of the Vedas and the syllables of certain other sacred texts, brahminists devised a linguistic vitalism that reinforced their claim to possess a uniquely "evolved" consciousness. A widely held assumption even today on the subcontinent is that in Sanskrit, the language of the Vedas and the gods, sound and meaning are perfectly aligned.

Because Buddhism rejected not only the divinity of language and the relevance of the gods but the logic of caste as well, the dharma posed a mortal threat.

The brahmins—originally large landholders—saw their power erode rapidly with the rise of an educated, urban merchant class, predominantly Buddhist, in the northeast state of Magadha. Though brahminism finally secured an iron grip over the whole subcontinent, so precarious was its hold at the time of Buddhism's ascendency that it could ill afford to allow the city dwellers to create their own, egalitarian reality. And so, a persistent motif in Indian thought has long been the brahminist attempt to close the space of possibility between words and things, while Buddhists struggled to keep it open in the face of increasingly formidable odds.

In China, Buddhism's home after it disappeared from India, the elite justified their privilege differently, employing a language of merit that claimed Confucius as its inspiration. A commoner by birth, Confucius spent his life as an itinerant philosopher in the service of various aristocratic clans often at war with one another. Confucius taught that personal ambition lay at the core of this violence, and he insisted that humanity could flourish only if everyone privileged the common good, a proposition that sounds vaguely socialist, but one that had the opposite of a leveling effect. Like India under brahminist control, China's Middle Kingdom had a steep hierarchy, imagined not as a temple tower but as a single, all-embracing family, with the emperor as father to everyone. Below him, we find the aristocrats (*shi*), and below them the peasant farmers (*nong*), artisans (*gong*), and merchants (*shang*). Within this structure, anyone could rise—as high even as to the imperial court—but only by assiduous self-cultivation of a special kind: everybody had to internalize the spirit of harmony, *hé* or *héxié*, modeled by Confucian teachings.

Precisely because China's rulers keenly understood the social disruption that could arise from the slippage between words and things, they took measures to lock up the lexicon:

> Tsze-lu said, "The ruler of Wei has been waiting for you, in order with you to administer the government. What will you consider the first thing to be done?"
>
> The Master replied, "What is necessary is to rectify names." "So! indeed!" said Tsze-lu. "You are wide of the mark! Why must there be such rectification?"
>
> The Master said, "How uncultivated you are, Yu! A superior man, in regard to what he does not know, shows a cautious reserve.
>
> "If names be not correct, language is not in accordance with the truth of things. If language be not in accordance with the truth of things, affairs cannot be carried on to success.

> "Therefore a superior man considers it necessary that the names he uses may be spoken appropriately, and also that what he speaks may be carried out appropriately. What the superior man requires is just that in his words there may be nothing incorrect." (*Analects* 13.3, trans. Legge)

Social harmony depends, in other words, on calling everything by its "proper name," an appealing notion even for us—think of Orwell's "Politics and the English Language." Or, rather, the notion seems appealing until we ask about the sources of our linguistic patrimony and about who benefits by choosing a word like "patrimony" to describe what we might also call our "mother tongue." But the rectification of names involves the suppression of just such questioning.

Confucius wants his followers to take on faith the timeless wisdom embodied in the monuments of Chinese civilization: Confucius's own works as well as the Five Classics—the *Book of Documents*, the *Book of Odes*, the *Book of Rites*, the *Book of Changes*, and the *Spring and Autumn Annals*. The task of the *junze*, or superior man, was to absorb the Five Classics so thoroughly that his every thought and word would conform to them. Like most forms of harmony ideology, including brahminism, Confucian tradition looked back to an originary moment, though not, as in the Vedic Purusha myth, one that happened at the beginning of the world. Instead, Confucius turned to the time of the legendary Three Emperors, who ruled during something like Greece's mythic Golden Age through the persuasiveness of their virtue alone—the dawning moment of Chinese rhetoric. And this rhetorical effectiveness they acquired through their ability to internalize and manifest the order of the universe itself.

Let me pause here for a moment to sum up, before I turn to the contestatory role that the dharma played in both societies. Like our classical rhetoric, its equivalents in ancient India and China might be viewed as ideological apparatuses designed to legitimize the elite by ascribing to them a moral excellence reflected in their flawless use of language. All three traditions privileged language as the principal lever over human behavior, tout court, and for each, the control of language enabled the suppression of the social differences responsible for words' polysemy, polyvalence, and promiscuity. Of course, words can have no meaning without these very qualities since only their imprecision makes it possible for us to communicate at all. Clearly, people differ in countless ways, and so they always will, but they need to assume, when they begin to converse, the existence of a prior consonance that they actually create in the back-and-forth of speaking. Like clothes, we have to cut our words a little too big if we want them to fit everyone. When you think of "virtue," for example, you might recall the time when you decided not to sleep with your best friend's lover. But someone else might think of virtue as hiking for three months along the Appalachian Trail. Only the built-in slippage of words allows the one word to do double duty here. For this reason, the project represented by the Confucian rectification of names had to remain a Sisyphean task, as would any exhaustive catalogue of "the means of persuasion" in Athens. And the same would hold true for any effort to prevent words not found in the holy Vedas from creeping into daily life and even sacred ritual. And so it was to these very qualities—polysemy, polyvalence, and promiscuity—that counter-hegemonic Buddhism turned in its centuries-long struggles with the brahmins and the mandarins, employing what we might call, after Paulo Freire, a "pedagogy of the oppressed." But Buddhist thinkers also understood that if they fought back against hegemony only on the terrain of words, they would have already conceded too much. Buddhist thinkers took one additional step by showing that experience, sensation, and cognition were themselves arbitrary, politically fraught, and susceptible to change—in other words, groundlessly rhetorical.

From Anti-Rhetoric to Hyper-Rhetoric

The dilemma facing Buddhism in India, and then later in China, was much like the one facing us in the twenty-first century. How do we defend what Carl Popper called an "open society" against absolutists who represent that openness as a moral vacuum, a cultural failure, or a crime against God's laws? Since most authoritarian societies lay claim to a fully realized truth, they have a tactical advantage over those who understand culture as a process or project that will naturally change the more we learn. In both India and China, Buddhist thinkers could have tried to counter their opponents by advancing a fixed value system of their own, based not on the Vedas or the Chinese "mandate of heaven" but on the Buddha's insights at the moment of his enlightenment, especially his teachings on nonviolence and the primacy of compassion. Indeed, this is the strategy that Buddhism employed for its first five or six centuries. But Buddhist thinkers after that period found themselves wrong-footed by the pace of social change that they themselves had helped to create, along with a resurgent brahminism. And so they had to reconceive Buddhist teaching in a radically different way—as fundamentally "empty," groundless or contingent. This new movement, which described itself as the Mahayana, or Great Way, required a new attitude toward language as well. Abandoning its old anti-rhetorical stance, Buddhism now became hyper-rhetorical, openly proclaiming the contingent nature of sensation and cognition.

Consider these lines from chapter 6 of the *Diamond Sutra*, a central text for the Mahayana. They describe an extended conversation between the Buddha and a disciple, the monk Subhuti:

> [Buddha:] "All that has a form is illusive and unreal. When you see that all forms are illusive and unreal, then you will begin to perceive your true Buddha nature."
>
> "When [I, the Buddha, explain] these things using such concepts and ideas, people should remember the unreality of all such concepts and ideas. They should recall that in teaching spiritual truths the Buddha always uses these concepts and ideas in the way that a raft is used to cross a river. Once the river has been crossed over, the raft is of no more use, and should be discarded. These arbitrary concepts and ideas about spiritual things need to be explained to us as we seek to attain Enlightenment. However, ultimately these arbitrary conceptions can be discarded. Think Subhuti, isn't it even more obvious that we should also give up our conceptions of non-existent things?" (trans. Johnson)

I should explain that the sutra was composed by one or more anonymous monks hundreds of years after the Buddha's death. For them to put their words into the Buddha's mouth is radical enough, but they go even further by placing *sous rapture*—"under erasure," as deconstructionists say—the entire soteriology they inherited. While preserving the traditional lexicon, which included items like "enlightenment," "purification," "*arhat*" (awakened person), and so on, they also proclaimed these same terms to be fundamentally groundless but possessing, all the same, a pragmatic or rhetorical usefulness that could lead the Buddha's followers to awakening. Here, the term "awakening" has come to signify an existential and phenomenological transformation that reveals groundlessness itself to be the path to liberation. For a better understanding of how radically the passage above departs from, say, conventional Christian religious discourse, consider how most Western Christians would view the following: a newly discovered gospel in which Jesus declares that none of his teachings are ultimately true and that he has simply offered them to assist those still on the road to salvation. Then Jesus would go on to explain that salvation itself was just an empty word.

The authors of the *Diamond Sutra* understand that we, as symbolic beings, cannot dispense with language and ideas, but the sutra also cautions that any formulation of the truth claiming for itself the status of "the ultimate" or "the complete" becomes an obstacle to further encounters with a larger horizon—a horizon beyond "being" as well as "nonbeing"—that always lies outside the boundaries of the known. The Buddha's famous metaphor of his teaching as a raft could be accepted at face value to mean that the dharma finally takes us *there*—to the "other shore" of enlightenment—as the early Pali sutras say. But later in the dharma's development, the encounter with groundlessness led Buddhists to see awakening in a different light, not as a final condition but a process that has no end point. One raft, we might say, takes us to the next. And beyond any single "other shore" lies another one in a multiverse imagined by later sutras as containing infinite "Buddha worlds"—infinitely various ways of constructing our experience, some liberating, others imprisoning. No longer accepted as definitive descriptions of a fixed reality beyond words, the Buddha's teachings now point instead to the malleability of "reality," and by insisting on its groundlessness and contingency, they call our attention to the excluded, the overlooked, and the repressed. These hold the key to our awakening because only they can enlarge our current ways of seeing, and for this reason, they hold the key, as well, to more humane forms of social life.

Had Buddhism developed something like a distinctive field called "rhetoric," it would have certainly have had its doubts about one of the discipline's founding principles: the assumption that social life cannot survive without the commonplace—without shared tropes or figures of speech that make two or more interlocutors mutually intelligible. Instead, Buddhism would insist that the emphasis on the commonplace suppresses the divergent truths that hegemony has made unintelligible. As a result, undistorted communication would need to begin with the *un*common—what remains difficult to express and even to absorb. In the words of Wansong Xingxiu, a thirteenth-century Chinese Ch'an (Jp. "Zen") monk, "A roundabout explanation is easy to understand—it imparts with one hand. A direct expression is hard to understand—it opens up in all directions." We might expect that the direct explanation would be the most accessible, whereas its roundabout counterpart would be "difficult." But Wansong insists that just the opposite is true. "I urge you not to use clear speech," he writes, "for if speech is clear, getting out [of its assumptions becomes] all the more difficult" (*Book of Serenity* 255). Plain speech, in other words, allows us to remain inattentive, well within the orbit of our accustomed mental habits. It "opens up in all directions" because it shows us only what we expect. But unclear speech, Master Wansong maintains, forces us to reconstruct our ideas about how things really are—a discovery made independently in the West by twentieth-century critical theory.

Because they accepted Wansong's advice, Zen teachers worked hard to create all kinds of barriers that would present their students with new opportunities to transform their experience, as in this Zen story:

> A monk asked [Zen master] Jianfeng, "It is written that the enlightened ones of the ten directions [the points of the compass as well as up and down] are all on one road that leads to nirvana. But where is that road?"
>
> Jianfeng drew a line in the air with his staff and said, "It is right here."
>
> The monk later asked [Master] Yunmen the same question. Yunmen said, "The fan [in my hand] leaps up to the thirty-three heavens and hits the emperor of the gods [Indra] on the nose. When the carp of the eastern sea is hit with the stick, it rains buckets. Do you understand? Do you understand?" (*Book of Serenity* 255)

It's not surprising that a Buddhist monk would ask his teacher how to find the "one road" leading to nirvana, or enlightenment. But the teacher's opaque response leaves the monk nowhere to plant his feet. The preposterous anecdote of a fan rising into the realm of the gods makes no more sense than the reference to a mysterious fish that produces rain. And after the monk hears that answer, if he doesn't give up and leave the temple for good, he will return to his meditation mat, where he will enter a state of emptiness (Ch. *wu-hsin*, Jp. *mu-shin*) while his active unconscious (Sk. *tathagatagarbha*, Ch. *rulaizang*) processes the account. Once the processing is complete, he will have undergone the gestalt switch that allows him to discover something new—and that is the koan's real "answer." But even without sitting on a mat hour after hour, we can get the point: hermeneutic confusion generates a liberating reorientation. That reorientation will involve something like the fusion of lifeworld horizons described by Western phenomenology, except that the world on the other side of the process will be genuinely sui generis. This is precisely the process that Aristotle tried to forestall with his emphasis on the commonplace, not only because it threatens to expose mastery as an illusion, but also because it allows for proscribed realities to enter in.

But the pedagogy of the *un*-commonplace will require us to rethink the nature of meaning itself, which does not arise, as we have typically believed, from a correspondence between your experience and mine. Correspondence, indeed, is only repetition, and repetition adds nothing to the information we already have. No matter how many times we play the same note on a guitar or piano, we cannot be said to make music until we introduce some variation, and only from the counterpoint of variation and sameness does meaning arise as well. And counterpoint we might understand as a representation of the encounter with someone or something new. Meaning, then, follows from the shared construction of an experience that has no fixed or essential characteristics without our active participation. This insight lies at the heart of what is arguably the crowning achievement of the Buddhist Mahayana, the thousand-page *Flower Ornament Sutra*, which shows us, step by small step, how we build up our infinitely expandable mental picture of reality through a constant oscillation between repetition and variation, correspondence and dissonance. "All living beings," in the sutra's words, "with minds and thoughts each different, / create [the] various worlds" (*Flower Ornament* 968). While we need the correspondences, moments when your mental picture matches mine, dissonance puts our pictures into motion. And even though it's only natural for us to fear the loss of continuity, the authors of the sutra want us to understand that only discontinuity makes it possible for us to discover the limitations of our perspective and the existence, as the sutra says, of uncountable horizons beyond the ones we occupy right now.

If the *Flower Ornament* is correct, its account would help to explain why so much of our formal education seems meaningless or, worse, boring, doled out in increments calibrated to minimize the students' sense of discontinuity. Although I don't have hard evidence, I would guess that people become physicists or physicians, geographers or historians, precisely because their fields introduced to them something that challenged their sense order and mastery and that presented them with the chance to engage in the active reconstruction of reality. As we in language studies recognize, poetic discourse uniquely dramatizes relations of this kind between discontinuity and meaning, but all communication depends on the same dynamic. Because the West has so long denied the radical rhetoricity of our nonlinguistic experience, we have confined this insight to poetry and the arts generally, even though it underlies every way of encountering the world.

The task of the teacher, then, is actually to make learning difficult, not easy, and to multiply the opportunities for confusion, misunderstanding, disagreement, and misreading, while at the same time helping students exercise their ability to create a multiverse out of nothing—a feat in the West reserved only for God—and then to notice, along the way, just how exciting it is to be alive without foundations. And I would add that we already know this truth instinctively. How many of us, after all, would enjoy sitting down to read twenty-five or thirty student papers advancing more or less the same argument in more or less the same way? What most of us want, I feel confident, is twenty-five or thirty arguments exploring different ways of thinking that rely on different evidence or, at least, the same evidence used differently. Yet it seems to me that we would be hard pressed to explain the pleasure—the thrill—produced by the situation I have just sketched out if we rely exclusively on the mainstream of Western thinking about meaning, language, and learning, with the exception, as I have said, of the poststructuralist and posthumanist thinkers. It was the poststructuralists in particular, those disciples of Nietzsche, who opened up our civilization just enough to let a little emptiness come in. But a Buddhist rhetoric would sit uneasily beside its Nietzschean counterpart in one important way, because when God disappears, as he did in India at the time of the dharma's inception, what took his place was not the *Übermensch*, a Zarathustra from his mountains looking down on a sheeplike humanity. In place of the god-term, Buddhism redirects our reverence to all "sentient beings." As for rhetoric, its purpose, finally, is neither persuading nor dissuading but dissolving the illusion of our separateness.

Entry Points: A Buddhist Rhetoric and Pedagogy

If we believe that our ability to communicate, act in concert, or merely refrain from murdering one another depends on our like-mindedness, then Buddhism's "pluralistic anti-ontology" might sound like a one-way ticket to hell. But behind those assumptions we can find another one associated with the history of authoritarian states: we need to protect social coherence from the ongoing threat of complete disintegration. And irrespective of their politics or their disciplines, many teachers understand order's preservation as their primary task. For example, those of us in rhetorical studies and related fields might feel deeply threatened by "disorganized" arguments, but we seldom ask ourselves why. I would suggest that these arguments symbolize for us social relationships breaking apart or broken already. Not only does our response expose our forebodings about collapse, but it also concretizes "order" as a quality imagined to be waiting in some Platonic heaven. Yet if the universe, as many Buddhists think, is indeed a self-organizing system, then teachers and other knowledge workers would do well to reconsider their willingness to assume the policeman's role. What if order will always emerge from the constellation of possibilities before us at the moment, like the pattern in a Persian rug that we don't see until we step back and it suddenly appears? Or like the formation of ice crystals on the window in midwinter? In a self-organizing universe, recurrent patterns will arise naturally from random chance, a phenomenon long recognized by scientists who study complexity—but also familiar, at least implicitly, to every writer laboring through draft after draft until, finally, the argument comes together, revealing a coherence no one could foresee or control at the outset of the process. The trouble is that when we try to explain what we've done, we often revert to our culture's common sense, and so we might say, "I finally knocked my chapter into shape," when actually nothing of the kind took place. Instead, a pattern finally emerged, and we participated in its emergence.

And in that case, what the writer needs most is *mu shin*—an empty or patiently receptive mind—rather than mastery because the difficulty always facing us is not that our words and ideas go wild, kicking down the walls and fences, but that our assumptions discourage us from taking part in a process of self-organization unfolding right before our eyes. Far from imposing order, as we might think, we actually allow it to manifest itself by getting out of our own way. Of course, some people will object that any order we discover exists only in our own mental processing rather than in the words on the page, but the Buddhist principle of interdependence would suggest that the gestalt contributes to the moment of emergence and that if we were to alter anything—including our own participation—the outcome would deviate in some way. And although we might imagine receptivity as a quality unrelated to dissuasion, if not actively opposed to it, the two are intimately linked. Only by relinquishing our beliefs can we permit ourselves the spaciousness that Zen master Shunryu Suzuki calls "beginners' mind," a condition of "not knowing" in which we attentively observe the self-organizing moment as it comes and goes (Suzuki 21–22). Indeed, another Zen master, Boshan, describes this spacious attentiveness as "the Great Doubt" in his book by the same name (Boshan 15–18, 39–40). The potential energy generated by this transitional state of prolonged uncertainty we in the West have perceived as a loss, a lack, or a personal failure, and indeed, it often feels that way to us. Especially when such moments impinge on the beliefs that we care most about, they have been stigmatized as a "crisis of conscience," "a loss of faith," and even "a dark night of the soul," when actually this emptiness, and nothing else, contains the possibility from which new insight will arrive.

The purpose of reading and writing, then, is not to impart knowledge but to renew our precious ignorance, without which we become unintelligent. From experience, we all know how hard it is to breathe life into the crushing prose of a memo from a dean or some other functionary, since it might tell us something we need to know but never strays beyond the already-known, our pedestrian ways of seeing. But when we read any new and difficult text—something we've done all our lives—we experience an interval of *mu shin*, or empty mind, as we gradually undergo a reconstellation of our ideas, assumptions, and emotions, a process that can feel terrifying, thrilling, or a bit of both. The duration of that interval will depend on how deeply challenging we happen to find the newly emergent coherence. And until the reconstellation takes place, the text and its claims will feel separate from us; but then, at its completion, the distance disappears.

With that change, the text no longer qualifies as something we "believe" or "disbelieve" because both responses presuppose a universal content far removed from our particular situation. The existence of such a content would imply that everyone should understand the text in the exactly same way regardless of conditions on the ground, when, in fact, all of us have to undergo the process of reconstellation differently. Texts, then, operate like metaphors, and metaphors, we should remind ourselves, add meaning by taking meaning away. They designate, but do so disjunctively, in ways that destabilize and open up both sides of the equivalence, the so-called tenor and vehicle. To say, for example, "My love is a rose" is to set aside our conventional understandings about love, positing not simply that it is indeed a rose but that it possesses and also lacks unspecified rose-like properties. And what holds true for texts holds true for words, whose meaning, according to Buddhist thought, also relies on disjunctive denotation. The word "tree," for example, can be applied to maples, birches, oaks, and sycamores but also to family trees, idea trees, and to the wooden devices we insert in our shoes to help them keep their shape when we're not wearing them. "Tree" can have that flexibility because it implicitly excludes the set "all things that are not trees." Words, then, create a "hole" of alterity that we are always free to fill in with our experience. And so, when we've undergone many times the process of reconstellation, we will inhabit our ideas in a new way, not as beliefs but as opportunities, and without the existential desperation that Buddhists call "grasping." No longer a destination or a resting place, ideas become a vehicle for going somewhere new.

To see ideas as available for use without the need for belief or disbelief is to understand them as empty in the Buddhist sense. Of course, they have content insofar as they exist within webs of intertextuality, systems of pure differences that invest them with meanings defined by their relationships with other ideas. But their emptiness allows them to be transposed to new positions that can create new knowledge and opportunities for action in the world. Ordinarily, we avoid these transpositions because they put at risk conventional proprieties, but once we no longer feel obliged to protect social cohesion by staving off "disorder," we can allow new meanings to emerge from the process of reconstellation. Connecting Wall Street's casino economy to Puritan attitudes toward pleasure, or Cubism to social mobility—moves like these once belonged exclusively to the Western artistic avant-garde, granted special license by the otherworldliness of the Kantian aesthetic—but Buddhism has employed them tactically for the purpose of our liberation from *samsara*, the mental habits that imprison us in collective unhappiness. It's significant that this Sanskrit word *samsara* suggests cycling around and around—repeating the same mental habits without knowing how to extricate ourselves. But through practices like Zen koan training and Tibetan Great Seal meditation, Buddhists use Burkean "perspectives by incongruity" to break out of the vicious circles that the dominant have created to rope us in.

A rhetoric of dissuasion, then, goes hand in hand with a pedagogy of the un-commonplace that relies on heuristics calculated to create contradiction, estrangement, discontinuity, and defamiliarization. It's no accident that the literature of Zen includes countless scenes like the one where a future master puts his sandals on his head, walking backward out the door, while his grief-stricken teacher sits sobbing. In another vignette, a senior monk has an enlightenment experience when his teacher, just after slapping his face, asks why he doesn't bow. In still another koan, a master tells his monks to bury a dead fox found outside the monastery walls with honors befitting a high priest. Quite appropriately, teachers of writing today cannot exercise the same carte blanche that Zen masters of the Tang dynasty employed in their attempts to help their students open up, but even without risking a lawsuit, we can certainly ask our students to transgress the boundaries separating, say, economics from environmental science, or the ethnography of fast food from political theory, or gender studies from the arts. By teaching students how to transgress the limitations imposed on knowledge by a university system long implicated in hegemonies of various kinds, we are helping them to recognize and resist forms of domination not so far removed from the ones perfected by the brahminists in India and China's Confucian masters. Like authoritarians long ago, our elites today maintain their authority by convincing us that they embody the order of nature itself, often under the sign of "science" or "the economy," and they warn that deviation puts us all at risk of catastrophic disorder—starting with semicolons and paragraphs but expanding until it brings about civilizational collapse.

Buddhist thinking turns this logic on its head. Yes, authoritarians often succeed in convincing us that beliefs are what unite or divide us. But complex societies operate in an information ecology where knowledge changes all the time, and its valences also keep changing as it circulates from one context to the next, each with its own local "reality." In this ecology, the most zealous atheist can work quite comfortably alongside the most committed fundamentalist as long as their beliefs have no relevance in that context—say, stocking shelves at the grocery store, looking for bacteria in a petri dish, or calculating the interest on a loan. And even in a context where beliefs enter in, most people know how to create a field of indifference to protect themselves as they shift contexts throughout the day. The ease of their transit would probably leave most authoritarians feeling aggrieved about the "loss of moral values," but Buddhist tradition would suggest that what we don't know is our real common ground, instead of what we know. Indeed, we spend most of our waking hours there—between ideas, not in them. And the West could use more theories of language that explain how this can even be possible.

It's fitting that this discussion should end with a paragraph about beginnings. For those unfamiliar with Buddhism and the other traditions represented here, the editors of this collection have asked all of the authors to provide what they describe as "points of entry." As you might expect if you've read this far, Buddhist teaching would suggest that every point allows us entry because the center, being nowhere, is everywhere. In the words of the Indian sage Virupa,

> It is empty from the beginning, like space
> The emptiness of the mind is unborn. . . .
> Like space, it is all pervasive . . .
> It has always been empty and selfless
> From the very beginning. (Namgyal 321)

This is why one of the monuments of Buddhist thought, the Perfection of Wisdom teaching, exists in sutras of various length: 300 lines, 500, 700, 2,500, 8,000, 18,000, and 25,000, each conveying the same message. Long and short, large and small, are, after all, entirely relative, and so, how much we need to read depends on our readiness to understand that reality always exceeds the descriptive power of anybody's words. Still, a good place for beginners to start might be with Peter Harvey's *An Introduction to Buddhism*. Then, I would recommend a much more demanding book, *Buddhism in the Shadow of Brahminism*. Other sources I recommend are Shunryu Suzuki's classic *Zen Mind, Beginner's Mind* and two books on Zen (Ch. Chan or Ch'an) by Peter Hershock, *Chan Buddhism* and *Liberating Intimacy: Enlightenment and Social Virtuosity in Ch'an Buddhism*. Another book I greatly admire is Chogyam Trungpa's masterpiece *Cutting through Spiritual Materialism*, as well as Traleg Kyabgon's *Mind at Ease: Self-Liberation through Mahamudra Meditation*.

NOTES

1. See Chakravarti, *The Social Dimensions of Early Buddhism*; Gombrich, *How Buddhism Began: The Conditioned Genesis of the Early Teachings*; and Schumann, *The Historical Buddha*.

2. Here the most important scholar is Johannes Bronkhorst, *Greater Magadha*, *Buddhism in the Shadow of Brahminism*, and *How the Brahmins Won*. See also Verardi, *Hardships and Downfall of Buddhism in India*.

3. See, for example, *Magga-vibhanga Sutta. Samyutta Nikaya* 45.8.

4. See Bronkhort, *Buddhist Teaching in India*; Kumar; Dutt; Joshi; and Mookerji.

5. The Chinese text of the "Four Great Vows," attributed to Huineng, the first non-Indian (that is, Chinese) "Patriarch" or "Great Ancestor" of Zen, is as follows: "I vow to save all sentient beings everywhere. / I vow to cut off all the passions everywhere. /

I vow to study all the Buddhist teachings everywhere. / I vow to achieve the unsurpassed Buddha Way" (*Platform Sutra* 143, trans. Yampolsky).

6. See, for example, Lévi-Strauss 395–96; Derrida 144–64; Latour 12–16.

WORKS CITED

The Book of Serenity. Translated by Thomas Cleary, Shambhala, 1988.

Boshan. *Great Doubt: Practicing Zen in the World*. Translated by Jeff Shore, Wisdom, 2016.

Bronkhorst, Johannes. *Buddhism in the Shadow of Brahminism*. Brill, 2011.

—. *Buddhist Teaching in India*. Wisdom, 2009.

—. *Greater Magadha: Studies in the Cultures of Early India*. Brill, 2007.

—. *How the Brahmins Won: From Alexander to the Guptas*. Brill, 2016.

Chakravarti, Uma. *The Social Dimensions of Early Buddhism*. Munshiram Manoharlal, 2015.

Confucius. *The Analects (Lun Yu)*. Translated by James Legge, 1893. *Cambridge Chinese Classics*, www.camcc.org/_media/reading-group/lunyu/lunyu-en.pdf. Accessed 1 July 2019.

de Bary, Theodore. *Sources of Indian Tradition*. Columbia UP, 1958.

Derrida, Jacques. *Of Grammatology*. Translated by Gayatri Chakravorty Spivak, Johns Hopkins UP, 1974.

The Diamond Sutra: A New Translation. Translated by Alex Johnson, diamond-sutra.com/. Accessed 22 Sept. 2019.

Dutt, Sukumar. *Buddhist Monks and Monasteries of India: Their History and Contribution to Indian Culture*. Allen and Unwin, 1962.

The Flower Ornament Scripture: A Translation of the Avatamsaka Sutra. Translated by Thomas Cleary, Shambhala, 1993.

Gombrich, Richard F. *How Buddhism Began: The Conditioned Genesis of the Early Teachings*. Munshiram Manoharlal, 1996.

Joshi, Lal Mani. *Studies in the Buddhistic Culture of India during the Seventh and Eighth Centuries a.d.* Motilal Banarsidass, 1977.

Kumar, Pintu. *Buddhist Learning in South Asia: Education, Religion, and Culture at the Ancient Sri Nalanda Mahavihara*. Lexington Books, 2018.

The Lankavatara Sutra: A Zen Text. Translated by Red Pine, Counterpoint, 2012.

Latour, Bruno. *Down to Earth: Politics in the New Climatic Regime*. Translated by Catherine Porter, Polity, 2018.

Lévi-Strauss, Claude. *Tristes Tropiques*. Translated by John Weightman and Doreen Weightman, Penguin, 2012.

Magga-vibhanga Sutta. Samyutta Nikaya 45.8. Translated by Thanissaro Bhikkhu. *Access to Insight*, www.accesstoinsight.org/tipitaka/sn/sn45/sn45.008.than.html. Accessed 12 Sept. 2019.

Mookerji, Radha Kumud. *Ancient Indian Education: Brahmanical and Buddhist.* 2nd ed., Motilal Banarsidass, 1998.

Namgyal, Dakpo Tashi Namgyal. *Mahamudra—the Moonlight—Quintessence of Mind and Meditation.* Translated by Lobsang P. Lhalungpa, Shambhala, 2006.

The Platform Sutra of the Sixth Patriarch. Translated by Philip B. Yampolsky, Columbia UP, 1967.

Schumann, H. W. *The Historical Buddha.* Translated by M. O'C. Walshe, Motilal Banarsidass, 2016.

Suzuki, Shunryu. Zen Mind, *Beginner's Mind.* Weatherhill, 1970.

Verardi, Giovanni. *Hardships and Downfall of Buddhism in India.* Monohar, 2011.

Interlude

ELIZABETH VANDER LEI

In 1999, I was starting my second year as an untenured faculty member in the English Department at Calvin College (now Calvin University) when I first read Beth Daniell's *College Composition and Communication* article "Narratives of Literacy: Connecting Composition to Culture." I was captured by Beth's description of the effect of Paulo Freire's Catholicism on his pedagogy, and this paragraph has stuck with me so long that I know it almost by heart:

> What Freire offers North America is not a method of teaching literacy we can carry from the Third World to the First, but an attitude of profound love for the human beings we teach. Being treated as if one is worthy, as if one's life is important, as if what one has to say is significant and deserving of attention, as if one is—yes—a fellow child of God, allows some people, even the most silenced, to "come to voice," to use bell hooks' term, and, in so doing, to see the world and themselves differently. Freire taps into that striving, in his students, in his teachers, in his readers, for something beyond ourselves, offering a spiritual perspective on the teaching of literacy: Not a grand narrative where we get to be heroes of an economic revolution but a grander narrative that calls us to be laborers in the vineyard, a narrative that is problematic indeed in a culture that values the separation of public and spiritual life. (402)

In one way or another, most of my scholarship has been working out the implications of Beth's argument for a writer "being treated as if one is worthy, as if one's life is important, as if what one has to say is significant and deserving of attention," particularly for students of faith in a first-year writing classroom. Beth's description of what students need is a goal that I can believe in strongly enough to put my shoulder behind it. And Beth's goal makes manifest the inadequacies of approaches to working with students that are rooted in politeness or tolerance or even kindness. None of these virtues can approach the transformative experience that Beth describes and that I hope students experience in writing classrooms. Equally obvious from Beth's description is the incommensurability of the student experience she describes and currently popular transactional and instrumental views of education, views that narrow students' expectations to an exchange of tuition dollars, not just for academic credit but for *useful* academic credit, as in academic credit that will improve their vocational prospects.

In my teaching and scholarship, I have had in mind a writing classroom with a goal that is more formative than transactional (though transactional enough, perhaps, to engage students initially), a classroom where students are engaged enough to believe what they are saying and courageous enough to say what they believe. And, along with Freire and Beth Daniell, I believe that to create such transformational classrooms, people must care about one another enough to honor everyone, even those who hold commitments and espouse ideas that others might not share and might even disagree with. Of course, reality regularly disappoints such ideals, but I have found sturdy support for them in a theoretical framework of hospitality.

In their book *Hospitality and Authoring*, Richard and Janis Haswell define hospitality as "a human practice that recognizes the innate dignity and promise of the guest, the stranger, the foreigner, the Other" (23). Haswell and Haswell describe some of the ways that hospitality can be diverted to other types of human interaction (commercialism, colonialism, charity, for example), but because hospitality requires something from everyone and offers everyone an opportunity to be changed, it counters transactional or instrumental views of education in which something (knowledge, skill, a credential) is given and received in an exchange that has been sanitized to minimize the risk of anyone being altered by the experience.

Perhaps I resonate with the concept of hospitality because throughout my career so many people have taught me the value of hospitality. For example, Haswell and Haswell emphasize the importance of an "ethos of dignity" in a Christian mode of hospitality and "extreme respect" in a nomadic mode of hospitality (18–19). I learned the value of the dignity of rhetors in graduate school when Keith Miller invited me into the study of rhetoric and religion. It was his careful scholarship on civil rights rhetors like Martin Luther King Jr. and Malcolm X that taught me to respect the rhetorical heft of religious faith. And working with Keith left me with a nagging question: If religious faith could shape the powerful messages of these civil rights leaders, how might religious faith shape what students write in their first-year writing classes?

In 2000, I gave a paper at the Council of Writing Program Administrators conference for writing program administrators working at religious institutions. I felt self-conscious delivering that paper because for the first time, I found myself relying on my religious convictions, though I was careful to keep the focus on Calvin College, not on me. Pat Bizzell was in the audience; afterward, she introduced herself and suggested lunch. Over sandwiches, we talked about my paper; she asked questions and suggested lines of inquiry. Pat's encouragement set me on a scholarly trajectory I'm still on today. Her warm engagement with my ideas demonstrated the value of reciprocity, another key feature of hospitality that distinguishes hospitality from charity, a "one-sided beneficence" (Haswell and Haswell 19). Having experienced Pat's hospitality, I am reminded that no small part of hospitality is not needing to have it all my way—at the root of hospitality is a desire to listen to one's guests and to expect to learn something from them. This is a lesson I learned even more thoroughly when bonnie kyburz and I coedited a collection of essays titled *Negotiating Religious Faith in the Writing Classroom* (2005), a process that depended on patient listening, careful explanations, and a few impassioned arguments.

That same year, Tom Amorose, Beth Daniell, Anne Gere, David Jolliffe, and I founded Rhetoric and Christian Tradition, a symposium of scholars interested in the connections between religious faith and rhetoric. Our first meeting on September 12, 2002, demonstrated the value of another key feature of a hospitable writing classroom: vulnerability—the willingness to open one's home, so to speak, to others. Our conversation opened with Beth and Tom describing the emotional weight of having traveled through airports the day before, on the one-year anniversary of 9/11. An hour into our discussion, my spouse called to say that months-delayed adoption paperwork had cleared: our daughter, Josie, waiting in a foster home in South Korea, was ready to come home. In those two days of meetings, our personal lives and our sometimes-raw emotions interrupted and enriched our scholarly conversations. For reasons none of us are likely to be able to explain fully—the context of 9/11? the long-awaited phone call?—we were able to be vulnerable with one another, and we left that meeting bound together not only by a scholarly agenda but, more importantly, by friendship.

The vulnerability that hospitality requires may be its trickiest element to evoke in the writing classroom. As both a teacher and a scholar, I am well aware that it is easier to make impassioned calls for vulnerability in the classroom than it is to build the trust and sense of security that vulnerability requires. If hospitality depends on vulnerability, vulnerability depends on what Haswell and Haswell describe as respect for the "innate dignity" of all parties, which can sometimes feel like one is being taken seriously. In "When the First Voice You Hear Is Not Your Own," Jacqueline Jones Royster uses the metaphor of a bad house guest to exemplify what not being taken seriously—what disrespecting "cross-cultural misconduct"—feels like (32). She notes, "we all deserve to be taken seriously, which means that critical inquiry and discovery are absolutely necessary" (33).

In my essay "'Ain't We Got Fun?' Teaching Writing in a Violent World" (2014), I propose that we take students of faith seriously enough to listen to the ways that religious faiths understand themselves. In particular, I look to contemporary Christian theologians Stanley Hauerwas and Miroslov Volf for a richer understanding of the interpretive communities that Christian students are a part of and the first principles shared by and contested within those communities. Implicit in that approach is a challenge to us to be vulnerable enough to look to scholars who have expertise in religious faith for guidance and to accept that religious faith is more complex than we might have otherwise imagined. If we are unable to be vulnerable in this way, we risk engaging with religious faith in transactional or instrumental ways—dipping into a complex field of study and practice as a tourist or a voyeur rather than as a truly hospitable guest.

Composition scholars are familiar with voyeuristic scholarship; as scholars we seek to avoid an inhospitable "trespass vision" of others and their ideas, one that is rooted more in "intellect and imagination," as Royster describes, than it is in lived experience or even "the serious study of the subject matter" (34). But what kind of hospitality do composition scholars offer students of faith? In "Where the Wild Things Are: Christian Students in the Figured Worlds of Composition Research" (2015), I returned to a question that had tugged at me since I first read a draft of Juanita Smart's essay "Frankenstein or Jesus Christ? When the Voice of Faith Creates a Monster for the Composition Teacher": How have composition scholars (myself included) represented students of faith in our research? A linguistic analysis of composition scholarship about Christian students indicates that our arguments for acceptance are undercut by geographic metaphors of exclusion that position students of faith outside the civilized (and civilizing) territory of the writing classroom. Discovering that I had monstered Christian students in my own scholarship, disheartening as it was, highlighted for me the value of hospitality as a theoretical framework with which to challenge what Royster describes as a "magnetic force field" of institutional pressures and discourse patterns.

Given the opportunities offered by hospitality as a theoretical framework and the challenges that I outline above, how might we commit ourselves to the possibilities that hospitality offers us as writing teachers? Pat Bizzell points out a way forward for writing teachers in her article "Faith-Based Worldviews as a Challenge to the Believing Game." Perhaps we start with our students, just as they are. That may mean we begin with their transactional expectations for what the university offers them and then offer them something more. We might begin by trying to understand what they have been committed to and which of those commitments they may be reevaluating. In short, we start by learning what matters to our students and trying, in good faith, to make that matter to us, too, if only because they matter. What we teach students matters, but what we teach will matter to our students only if they, in their whole selves, matter to us first.

How do we move forward as scholars? We still have much to learn about our students. What questions are they interested in asking? What silences do they choose to maintain? What is their trajectory of development? We also have much to learn about the limits of vulnerability. For both students and teachers, much is at stake in the questions we're willing to ask, the answers we're willing to consider. Under what circumstances do we open our door to strangers? When is it the better part of wisdom to keep it shut? And we have much to learn from other scholars who are engaging similar research questions in areas such as critical disability studies and colonialism.

Perhaps most importantly, we can re-engage with Royster's compelling description of the work that is (still) before us and re-commit ourselves to taking people seriously enough to believe in them and with them, at least for a while. And, when we can't believe with them, to respond in ways that honor them and their place in the community. If we could offer such hospitality, we might "tap into that striving . . . for something beyond ourselves," whatever that something may be.

WORKS CITED

Bizzell, Patricia. "Faith-Based Worldviews as a Challenge to the Believing Game." *Journal of the Assembly for Expanded Perspectives on Learning*, vol. 14, Winter 2008–2009, pp. 29–35.

Daniell, Beth. "Narratives of Literacy: Connecting Composition to Culture." *College Composition and Communication*, vol. 50, no. 3, 1999, pp. 393–410.

Haswell, Richard, and Janis Haswell. *Hospitality and Authoring: An Essay for the English Profession*. UP of Colorado, 2015.

Royster, Jacqueline Jones. "When the First Voice You Hear Is Not Your Own." *College Composition and Communication*, vol. 47, no. 1, 1996, pp. 29–40.

Smart, Juanita M. "Frankenstein or Jesus Christ? When the Voice of Faith Creates a Monster for the Composition Teacher." *Negotiating Religious Faith in the Composition Classroom, edited by* Elizabeth Vander Lei and bonnie kyburz, Heinemann Boynton/Cook, 2005, pp. 11–23.

Vander Lei, Elizabeth. "'Ain't We Got Fun?' Teaching Writing in a Violent World." *Renovating Rhetoric in Christian Tradition*, pp. 89–104.

—. "Where the Wild Things Are: Christian Students in the Figured Worlds of Composition Research." *Mapping Christian Rhetorics: Connecting Conversations, Charting New Territories*, edited by Michael-John DePalma and Jeffrey M. Ringer, Routledge, 2014, pp. 65–84.

Vander Lei, Elizabeth, and bonnie kyburz, editors. *Negotiating Religious Faith in the Composition Classroom*. Heinemann Boynton/Cook, 2005.

7. Engaging with Arab(ic)-Islamic Religious Rhetorics

Why it Matters to Rhetorical Studies

RASHA DIAB

> We were exposed to an even stranger kind of rhetoric, the rhetoric of the Middle Eastern world.
>
> —Edward P. J. Corbett

> [I]t should not simply be taken for granted that *al-balāgha*, in contrast to *al-khatāba*, would somehow constitute a "native" and completely unique system of "rhetoric" that is peculiar to Muslims and free of foreign influences.
>
> —Philip Halldén

> Broader definitions of rhetoric are useful in comparative rhetoric because they force scholars outside disciplinary assumptions and habits of reading and force engagement with alterity.
>
> —Sue Hum and Arabella Lyon

Philip Halldén—theology and religious studies scholar—poignantly asked in 2005, "What is Arab Islamic rhetoric?" Halldén quotes Corbett, who acknowledges the distinctiveness of non-Western rhetorics and states, "We were exposed to an even stranger kind of rhetoric, the rhetoric of the Middle Eastern world" (19). Rightly, Halldén notes that little is known about such rhetorics despite ample evidence and the longevity of Arab(ic)-Islamic rhetorical practices and study. Burgeoning work on cultural rhetorics in the past five decades made abundantly clear the gap in studies of non-Western rhetorical traditions and the dearth of work done on non-Judaic and non-Christian religious rhetorics. At the intersection of both gaps, Arab(ic)-Islamic rhetorics' richness, complexity, and invisibility are inconspicuous. Therefore, many who are bewildered by "the stranger kind of rhetoric" ask, "What is Arab Islamic rhetoric?" And, the answer is complex.

The combination of Arab/Arabic and Islamic limits and broadens the scope of rhetorical exploration. Assumed homogeneity of the Middle East (and even the Far East and West) eclipses a diverse religious and linguistic landscape in the Middle East and elsewhere. Islamic brackets us historically from the rise of Islām in the early seventh century to the present and directs our gaze to the Muslim populace, which comprises different sects (e.g., Sunnī, Shi'ī). Contra stereotypical representation, there are many religious groups in the Middle East. These include—besides polytheist, atheist, Christian, and Jewish peoples—the Bahā'ī, Druze, Yazīdī, and Zoroastrian traditions. *Arab* includes non-Muslims and limits us to the study of an ethnic group that speaks Arabic in North Africa (from Mauritania on the Atlantic coast of Africa to the Red Sea on the east coast) and much of the Middle East. This ethnic group is bound not just linguistically but also culturally, historically, geographically, and politically. *Arabic* is used by non-Arabs as well. This includes bi/multilingual Kurds who live in Syria and Iraq. *Arab(ic)-Islamic*, therefore, can expand the landscape to include, for example, Iranian rhetoricians/rhetors who enriched Arab(ic)-Islamic civilization. These include Ibn al-Muqaffa' (linguist and rhetorician), *'Abd al-Ḥamīd al-Kātib* (chancery writer), and Zamakhsharī (Qur'ānic exegete). And, if we loosen the connection between the Arabic language and narrow ethnic identification, we branch out to include a complex web of identifications. Such identifications would cover peoples of varied ethnic and racial groups that identify with/contribute to Arabic language/culture and Islām as confession/culture. This includes non-Muslim Arab (e.g., Christian Arabs) and Muslim Arab communities in the diaspora and Muslims in the world (e.g., Far East and West). Shedding light on *Arab(ic)* and *Islamic* charts a vast and complex rhetorical landscape and piques interest in the reasons for its invisibility.[1] The main goal of this chapter is to shed light on reasons for, and the epistemic gaps caused by, such invisibility, and the main payoff is to revisit terms that can render the details of the tapestry of rhetoric and religious rhetoric more visible.

Epistemic Gaps

Arab(ic)-Islamic rhetoric's invisibility is accentuated by two interrelated phenomena. First, the call for (and the response to) this edited collection is authorized by a lack/lag in the study of religious rhetoric and especially non-Christian religious rhetorics. Second, there is a mismatch between the expansive geographical region where Arab(ic)-Islamic rhetoric thrives; the millions of peoples who communicate with/through these rhetorical traditions; the durability, growth, and abundant evidence of varied rhetorical practices and areas of study as demonstrated below; and the dearth of rhetorical scholarship on

Arab(ic)-Islamic rhetoric. Concomitantly, the (in)conspicuous influence of religion on these varied rhetorical practices and studies is also invisible.

The rise of Islām in the seventh century neither happened in a religious vacuum, nor did Muslims live in isolation. The rise of Islām was preceded and followed by centuries of religious discourse, which can be defined broadly to include discourse *of*, *to*, and *about* God in (non)religious domains and toward (non)religious ends (e.g., Pernot; Souders). The rise of Islām coincided with a proliferation of new rhetorical exigences and changed the political, cultural, and educational scene in the Middle Ages and beyond. In short, the tapestry of religious rhetorics is misshapen by continued disregard of the unique context of Islām, commonalities of religious rhetoric and experience, and (dis)similar rhetorical exigences for Muslims around the world. Therefore, a fuller appreciation of the rich tapestry of religious rhetorics is enhanced by a nuanced understanding of how religious exigences and functions emerge and work in tandem/tension with one another in/out of religious spheres.

The invisibility of Arab(ic)-Islamic rhetoric points to a consequential epistemic gap. In a world beleaguered with religious tensions within/across different faith traditions, we need to resist the selective study of the nature and (mis/ab) uses of religious rhetoric, while also recognizing the political economy of such selective investments. In a transnational world that prides itself on shrinking time and space, we need to recognize the toll of epistemic gaps and the increasing significance of shrinking epistemic gaps. In what follows, I attend to this epistemic gap, address reasons for and responses to Arab(ic)-Islamic rhetoric's invisibility, and identify areas of Arab(ic)-Islamic religious rhetoric to further explore.

Minding the Gaps: Explaining the Continued Invisibility of Arab(ic)-Islamic Rhetoric

A search on/for Arab(ic)-Islamic rhetoric typically and eventually leads to (a) medieval translations of and commentaries on Aristotle by Muslim scholars and philosophers (e.g., Baddar, "Arabs," "From Athens"; Borrowman; Ezzaher; Fakhry, "Al-Farabi") and (b) poetics (e.g., Black; Bonebakker). Sometimes, surprisingly—or not—Halldén's "What Is Arab Islamic Rhetoric?," which is about homilies and the art of preaching, comes up. Each one of the aforementioned areas belongs to a different line or strand of rhetorical development. The first relates to philosophic rhetoric, or the study of the validity of rhetorical discourse. The second relates to rhetorical/literary criticism, or the theory of literary discourse and the study of form, devices, and tropes. The third belongs to oratory, or the study of public address in different social/political domains. In a preliminary search, each of these three lines of rhetorical development pops up for a reason, yet the invisibility of Arab(ic)-Islamic rhetorics endures, as evidenced by a casual look at (history of) rhetoric books. The epistemic consequence is clear: few in the discipline can name a rhetor, a rhetorician, a book, or a rhetorical term, for example, related to Arab(ic)-Islamic rhetoric.

Understandably, each one of these three areas centers on one strand of rhetorical development. Rhetoric, then, becomes the shorthand reference to that strand. Though convenient for focusing attention, this has a trade-off: when/if unannounced, this usage can at least result in a definitional problem. If a strand of rhetorical development is attended to and used to define and focus rhetoric (i.e., as poetics, philosophic rhetoric, or preaching), then rhetoric's parameters are set too narrowly, hiding religious context and exigences and, therefore, obscuring other strands (e.g., epistolary rhetoric). Equally important, even when put together, these three lines of rhetorical development only partially represent the longevity, complexity, and versatility of Arab(ic)-Islamic rhetorics, as the rest of the chapter demonstrates. The points raised here indicate a consequential definitional problem: What do we attend to and define as rhetoric? If we attend to how and why rhetoric is defined, can we render Arab(ic)-Islamic rhetorics more visible?

Because rhetoric's narrow and capacious definitions are impactful, cultural rhetoric scholars warn against disciplinary and historiographic practices that deflect attention away from local exigences and advocate for "[b]roader definitions of rhetoric . . . [that] force scholars outside disciplinary assumptions and habits of reading and force engagement with alterity" (Hum and Lyon 154). Heeding their counsel, in the first part of the chapter, I address the selective attention to philosophic rhetoric and poetics and the consequences of using one term denoting rhetoric in other rhetorical traditions out of context. Addressing these methodological concerns directs attention to the Arab(ic)-Islamic rhetorical landscape, exigences, and practices, which are addressed in the second part of the chapter. Because of the vastness of this rhetorical landscape, only two lines of rhetorical development are described in broad strokes.

Selective (In)Attention to Philosophic Rhetoric and Poetics

Considering the continued invisibility of Arab(ic)-Islamic religious rhetoric, it is important to reflect on the nature, reasons, and effects of what pops up in preliminary searches. Arab(ic)-Islamic poetics and philosophic rhetoric loom large in any preliminary research, yet they are, paradoxically, under the radar of rhetoric studies. This paradox warrants attention because it dovetails with the invisibility of Arab(ic)-Islamic religious rhetorics. To address this paradox, I draw on revisionist historiography and cultural rhetorics.

PHILOSOPHIC RHETORIC

There are numerous reasons for the selective attention to Arab(ic)-Islamic philosophic rhetoric. In the Greco-Roman tradition, philosophic rhetoric is mainly concerned with the validity of argument and philosophic concerns about persuasion, truth, and fairness. Plato's *Gorgias* and *Phaedrus* and Aristotle's *Rhetoric* are representative works (e.g., Kennedy). In contradistinction to technical and sophistic rhetoric, philosophic rhetoric reigns and is centered, though not without contestations, in the Greco-Roman tradition. Concomitantly, it pops up in a preliminary search for Arab(ic)-Islamic rhetoric.

When Arab(ic)-Islamic philosophic rhetoric is studied by scholars trained in the Western tradition, the object of study, typically, is Arab/Muslim scholars' translation of Plato and Aristotle. Arab(ic)-Islamic philosophic rhetoric includes al-Farābī (born circa 870 C.E.); the well-known philosopher is commonly known as the second master after Aristotle.

al-Farābī's engagement with Aristotle is recognized because it seems familiar and proximate. al-Farābī is read as *just* translating or commenting on (read: explaining) Aristotle. Therefore, his work is deemed derivative and meritorious because it preserves Aristotle. al-Farābī's logico-rhetorical theory (Baddar) is often (mis)recognized as "an important chapter in the history of Aristotelian logic in early medieval Islam,"[2] as the "Islamized" version of rhetoric, or as the means of reintroducing Aristotle to medieval Europe (e.g., Borrowman). Does this help us know Arab(ic)-Islamic philosophic rhetoric? Scholars of a revisionist history of rhetoric and cultural rhetorics help us answer this question.

History of rhetoric scholars attend to the rhetoricity of historical accounts and the far-reaching consequences of historiographic assumptions. To illustrate, Carole Blair explains "(1) that historiographic stances in histories of rhetoric contain embedded, but typically unacknowledged, presuppositions about history and/or rhetoric; and (2) that historians' assumption of these stances has culminated in partial historical accounts that mask their own partiality" (403). Among assumptions about the (dis)continuity of rhetorical traditions is the assumption of influence, which manifests as "influence study." Influence study is a historiographic term that refers to the study and account of a rhetorical figure's (e.g., Aristotle) formative impact. The resultant "influence narrative" centers the figure and "present[s] classical rhetoric as the single coherent and systematic view, the single origin from which all later rhetorics derive, or as the prototype against which all later theories must be judged" (409). Consequently, it crops out the agency, exigences, and purposes of those who are *just* influenced. And "their rhetorics [are] reduced to versions of, and thus monuments to, classical rhetoric. Any theoretical *difference* that they may have with ancient sources is sacrificed to the desire to maintain a linear, influential tradition. But these differences are the potential source of theoretical significance and insight"(409). Blair's concern is valid. Epistemic and political assumptions, if not desires, underwrite iterations of influence studies. Iterations of influence studies can be seen even in calls for studies of Arab(ic)-Islamic rhetorics.

Consider this call for more comparative rhetoric studies: "The impact of classical rhetoric across cultures and through time is still in need of study. It is known, for example, that classical rhetoric was influential, and in some cases even preserved by the Byzantine Empire and the Arab world, yet relatively little is known about these phenomena" (Enos and Blakeslee 30). This call centers classical Western philosophic rhetoric. It recognizes the Arab world *only* as a receptacle and preserver of classical rhetoric and a tool to document its reach.

Inherently, influence studies center and render visible what is deemed a "single origin" (Blair 409). As such, influence study (and the resultant narrative) (a) dictates the research agenda, (b) marks what is current (read: valuable), and (c) renders Arab(ic)-Islamic philosophic rhetoric invisible; it deflects attention away from the religious and cultural exigences that prompted seeking, translating, and writing commentaries on philosophic work including Aristotle's *Organon*. In short, to quote Blair's criticism, influence studies sacrifice "differences[, which] are the potential source of theoretical significance and insight" of Arab(ic)-Islamic rhetorics.

DECENTERING INFLUENCE STUDIES, CENTERING LOCAL EXIGENCES

Decentering influence to underscore local exigences—one of cultural rhetorics' methodological commitments—is crucial to identifying the Arab(ic)-Islamic rhetorical landscape wherein Arab(ic)-Islamic philosophic rhetoric emerges. Centering local exigences helps scholars attend to the religious context and exigences rendered invisible in/by an influence narrative. A case in point is Maha Baddar's medieval and cultural rhetoric scholarship, which confirms that "the works selected for translation went far beyond Greek texts, routinely including languages such as Persian, and Indian" and shows "that the translations had practical and ideological purposes to fulfill, not simply archival ones" ("Arabs," 13). Similarly, Peter Adamson highlights practical and ideological purposes of the translation movement. Adamson explains, in his study of al-Kindī (800–870 C.E.), that Muslim intellectuals resorted to Greek texts as resources for defending and better understanding their own religion. Underscoring the rhetoricity of medieval translations and commentaries, Baddar "challenge[s] colonial attitudes toward the Translation Movement [that assumed it was] exclusively imitative and preservative of Greek heritage" ("Arabs," 13). She continues: "We know that the translation of philosophical works did not take place in vacuum, but that it served the needs of dedicated thinkers who were genuinely interested in using and modifying the knowledge produced in different places [like Persia and India] and time periods to resolve theological, political, and social problems that arose in their culture" (30–31). These included "the practical needs and the ability to engage dialectically with people of different religious dispositions, whether within Islam itself, or members of different faiths, especially Christians" (14). Baddar's explanation makes the rhetoricity and dialogic nature of these translations and commentaries evident. Consequently, decentering influence and recentering local context make religious exigences and rhetorical challenges loom large and demand specialized expertise in Arab(ic) and Islamic culture (Alomari).

POETICS

It is hard to (dis)miss the endurance of and pride in Arab(ic)-Islamic poetics—prescriptive inquiry into the principles of literary discourse—and poetic expression before and after the rise of Islām. Poetry is known as the register or canon of the Arabs (*al-shi 'r dīwān al-'Arab*). Literary criticism flourished as an area of study and practice, and numerous Arab(ic) scholars are well known for their contributions to the study of tropes and nuances of Arabic style. But in the West, their work is overshadowed by the disciplinary separation of the "sister-arts" of rhetorical and literary criticism.

When/if poetics are reduced to compendia of literary devices and tropes, inquiry into literary rhetoric becomes an exercise in the appreciation of "the internal rhetoric, the artistic features, of great artists," a pursuit assumed to decenter context, exigence, and dynamic rhetorical interaction between rhetor and audience. Kennedy pejoratively terms this rhetorical phenomenon *letteraturizzazione* (*Classical Rhetoric* 119), or "the tendency of rhetoric to shift focus from persuasion to narration, from civic to personal contexts, and from speech to literature, including poetry" (3). Kennedy's description of the shift centers persuasion, civics, and speech; all seem to hearken to particular modalities of rhetorical discourse in the West. Kennedy's description of the shift partially explains the decentering of literary rhetoric in history of rhetoric books, the presence of disciplinary silos, and the corresponding invisibility of studies of Arab(ic)-Islamic poetics.

The study of Arabic poetics is classified under the umbrellas of *naqd adabī* (literary criticism) and *balāghah* and is mainly sponsored by Arabic, Middle Eastern, and religious studies. In its most expansive meaning, *balāghah* covers meaning, expression, and ornamentation. Despite their relevance, *naqd adabī* and *balāghah* are invisible to rhetoric studies for two reasons: (a) the aforementioned separation of literary criticism from rhetorical criticism and "classical" rhetoric from cultural rhetorics and (b) assumptions about rhetoric and *balāghah*. Because of its centrality, the second point is expanded upon in the next section. Unbeknownst to many, the development of literary criticism in the Arab(ic)-Islamic tradition and composing compendia of tropes and linguistic devices intersect with the need to interpret al-Qur'ān. Often unstated, *balāghah*, which covers meaning, expression, and ornamentation, has expansive and contractive definitions. The end effect is that Arab(ic)-Islamic poetics and its relation to religious discourse is under the radar of rhetoric studies. In the coming section, therefore, I demonstrate *how* assumptions about rhetoric and *balāghah* eclipse this area of study.

BEYOND A ONE-TO-ONE CORRESPONDENCE: THE PROBLEM OF CENTERING *BALĀGHAH*

Comparative and cultural rhetoric scholars warn against "longing for a one-to-one correspondence" (Hum and Lyon 156) or assuming that rhetoric in other traditions, religious and otherwise, can be identified using one term only. Similarly, Arab(ic)-Islamic rhetoric cannot be assumed chartable using one term. As an antidote, comparative rhetoricians recommend "[f]inding appropriate culture-specific definitions [and terms]" (156). This is consistent with Halldén's accurate explanation that the invisibility of Arab(ic)-Islamic rhetoric is partially due to the centering of the word *balāghah* and *'ilm* or *fann al-balāghah* (rhetoric and the episteme or art of rhetoric). Both terms are poor indicators of the wide-ranging lines of literary and rhetorical development that accompanied the rise of Islām and their continuity beyond the classical period.

To make this point clear, Halldén distinguishes between two Arabic terms that can be translated as "rhetoric."[3] These are *balāghah* and *khaṭābah*:

> In the dictionaries, two different words are generally given as translations in Arabic for the word rhetoric: *al-balāgha* and *al-khatāba*. As metarhetorical concepts, these terms are prefixed by *'ilm* (episteme/scientia) or *fann* (techne/ars). . . . In most studies explicitly concerned with Arab Islamic rhetoric, *al-balāgha* tends to be in focus. One can

> safely say that *al-balāgha* has received far more scholarly attention than *al-khatāba*. (Halldén 20)

Originally, *balāghah*, and relatedly *fann* or *'ilm al-balāghah*, had the expansive meaning of the systemic use and study of discourse, which would cover religious rhetoric. This expansive meaning is inherently rhetorical. To illustrate, *al-balāghah*'s trilateral root (b lgh) connotes reaching in the sense of (1) reaching the audience and (2) attaining excellence in expression (ibn al-Athīr 94; Bonebakker 75). Worth noting, *al-balāghah* comprises three areas of rhetorical knowledge, namely, *'ilm al-ma 'ānī*, *'ilm al-bīyān*, and *'ilm al-badī'*—or the sciences of meaning, clarity of expression, and ornamentation, respectively. As such, *balāghah* centers the art of eloquent communication, broadly defined. For example, in the capacious definition of ibn al-Muqaffa'—eminent eighth-century (died circa 756–759) Persian thinker, translator, chancery secretary, writer, and littérateur—*balāghah* covers both poetry and prose, letters and oratory, matters of meaning and matters of style:

> When asked about the meaning of *balāghah*, ibn al-Muqaffa' explained that it is a comprehensive term that comprises varied iterations of eloquent expression that manifest in silence, in listening, in reference [*ishārah*] to others' speech, in speech, in provision of evidence or refutation. It can manifest as initiated discourse or response; as poetry, rhymed prose, or oratory; or as epistle . . . (qtd. in Alī 12–13)

Unfortunately, the expansive definition of *al-balāghah* of early medieval scholars and writers didn't last; the history of the term's uptake tends to be more contractive than its original usage implies. Shedding light on this contractive uptake of *balāghah*, Al-Musawi explains that "it was style as craft, or *elocutio*, that drew the foremost attention" (30). Put differently, there is a tendency to focus on the second and third areas of *balāghah*, namely, *'ilm al-bīyān* and *'ilm al-badī'*—or studies of clear expression and ornamentation, respectively (e.g., Jenssen; Halldén). This tendency is a by-product of disciplinary, intellectual, and political shifts that are beyond the scope of this chapter. But what is worth clarifying at this juncture is that according to Jenssen, for example, *bīyān* and *badī'* are studied under the umbrella of (intellectual history of) language studies, whereas *'ilm al-ma 'ānī*, which early medieval scholars emphasized greatly, seems more pertinent to the study of logic and theology. In the Arab world, these areas of study (i.e., *bīyān* and *badī'*), when introduced together, are emphasized as part of *balāghah*'s investment in literary criticism, which has an aesthetic bent.

Rarely are the history and scope of *balāghah* explicitly addressed. Reduced as such, *balāghah*, which is assumed to be the term denoting rhetoric, doesn't match how rhetoric is defined to center on persuasion, civics, and speech, as noted earlier, and seems distant from rhetorical studies.

Accordingly, this centering of *balāghah* has, as Halldén rightly notes, far-reaching consequences. The contraction of *balāghah* to denote mainly *bīyān* and *badī'* also eclipses areas of religious rhetorical practice and study like (a) exegesis, which can be considered closer to *'ilm al-ma 'ānī*, (b) disputation (Belhaj), and (c) epistolary and documentary practices (Diab, "Epistolary Rhetoric"; Serjeant), which were relied on to manage (political) affairs of the Muslim community. Equally important, (d) *balāghah*'s contraction contributes to the invisibility of the oratorical art, which is deemed "foreign" and more akin to philosophy. The centering and contraction of *balāghah*, a selective focus on philosophic rhetoric and poetics, and the narrative of influence as manifest in the study of translations and commentaries render invisible numerous rhetorical practices and an expansive landscape of Arab(ic)-Islamic religious rhetoric. I turn next to several areas of rhetorical practice and study that grew exponentially after the rise of Islām.

Nascent Rhetorical Exigences

Recognizing alterity with humility and critical reflection is key to re-visioning a rhetorical landscape eclipsed by what Royster refers to as "Western dominance in interpretive authority" (149). So, this section centers local rhetorical exigences (*aghrāḍ balāghīyah*) as entry points for research. These exigences point to a complex and rich rhetorical landscape. In the process, I point to rhetorical functions, terms, practices, and traditions.

The rise of Islām resulted in intra/inter-communal rhetorical exigences and varied rhetorical practices. These exigences and practices created a rich rhetorical landscape, which comprises discourse that is explicitly religious and discourse that exceeds "God-talk" and might not seem to be affected by religion. The first type comprises discourse that centers the sacred and is a discourse *of*, *about*, and *to* God (e.g., Pernot). Evidently, the rhetorical goals of the nascent community of Muslims included learning and providing meaningful interpretations of al-Qur'ān, articulating eloquently Islām's message, spreading the word of Allah, and eulogizing and praying to Allah. Here are four illustrations:

- Zooming in on the discourse *of* Allah allows us to explore both al-Qur'ān and exegesis, a rich and complex area of rhetorical knowledge, which is briefly addressed below.

- Zooming in on the discourse *about* Allah and Islām allows us to survey innumerable panegyric orations (*khuṭbạh*), poems, and stories (in al-Qur'ān) as well as scholarship on theological or exegetical disputation (*munāẓara*) (e.g., Belhaj).[4]
- Zooming in on the discourse *to* Allah allows us to examine the rhetorical exigences of prayer and a supplicant's persuasive appeals. Because prayer is culturally specific in terms of dictum, decorum, and rite, scholars can study not just *how* prayer is persuasive, performative, and constitutive but also *what* prayer meant/means in Islām.
- Zooming out, we can probe how religious rhetoric is also evident in panegyric rhetoric that is not just *about* Allah but also about the ideal Muslim. In some panegyric poetry, Prophet Muḥammad or other religious figures are representative of the ideal Muslim or Islām in practice.[5]

Additionally, the emerging religious community needed to invest in unifying and building a community of/for believers. A capacious definition of religious rhetoric can help us see other rhetorical exigences and functions.

Defined capaciously, "religious rhetoric can be extended to apply to all areas in which religion's language of transcendence seeps into symbolic action, even when religion itself does not explicitly appear" (Souders). For example, legal discourse on rights complements *ḥuqūq Allāh* (the rights of God) with *ḥuqūq al-'ibād* (the rights of people). *Ḥuqūq al-'ibād* manifest in legal-political instruments including peace agreements (Bassiouni; Diab, "Legal-Political Rhetoric," "Peacemaking") that seek to affirm rights and resolve conflicts. Among the aforementioned enduring rhetorical exigences and practices, interpretation and preaching continue to be pressing and demanding. I now briefly turn to shed light on both as two prominent illustrations of Arab(ic)-Islamic religious rhetoric. Needless to say, though I focus on their medieval history, both are dynamic and current rhetorical arts with conspicuous historical, theoretical, and practical dimensions.

*Exegesis (*Tafsīr*)*

The need to interpret the meaning of al-Qur'ān and appeals to systematize this process called for increased interest in *tafsīr*. This need intensified after Prophet Muḥammad's death and is relevant to rhetorical studies for varied reasons: the discourse of God is rhetorical; rhetoric was evidently used to interpret and communicate, debate, and defend (methods of) interpretation; and rhetoric studies were further developed and systematized in the process. Scholars agree that theologians' interest in rhetoric and philology grew because they pored over the meaning and inimitability (*i'jāz*) of al-Qur'ān.[6] *Tafsīr* eventually developed to be part of Qur'ānic studies (*'ulūm al-Qur'ān*), which also include the study of al-Qur'ān's revelation and compilation.

Prophet Muḥammad interpreted verses and references when needed for the mainly Arab population who knew well Arabic vocabulary, syntax, and rhetoric (al-Dhahabī; Saeed). However, as different peoples entered Islām, the need for interpretation increased and changed. Muslims needed commentary to decode the meaning, context, and significance of verses (*ayāt*) and chapters (*sūrahs*) of al-Qur'ān. Prophet Muḥammad's companions (*al-Ṣaḥābah*) and followers (*al-Tabi'īn*) valued his explication and invested in its preservation. But soon, the preservation/transmission of these interpretations, as well as vetting the emerging modalities of interpretation, became pressing.

Debates about *tafsīr* ensued. Predictably, a move toward systematization followed. Scholars called for reliable and consistent interpretation. Duteously, religious scholars sought to interpret al-Qur'ān and labored at exegesis and studied its genesis, goals, development, sources, methods, and schools (e.g., Alhelwah; al-Dhahabī; Saeed). This was also their rhetorical response to (a) the emergence of religio-political groups (e.g., Sunnī, Shi'ī, Khārijī) with distinct legal, theological, philosophical, and mystical exegetical perspectives (Saeed 194–208) and (b) charges that al-Qur'ān had "grammatical and stylistic mistakes" (Alhelwah 179).[7] The objective was to ensure that al-Qur'ān is read meaningfully and consistently with the goals (*maqāṣid*) of Islām and reasons for revelation (*asbāb al-nizūl*). It is within this context that the science of interpretation, or *'ilm al-tafsīr*, emerged and was systematized.

Because of the relevance of their work to rhetoric, I'll identify some linguistic and rhetorical methods used for *tafsīr* without pretension of full representation. These methods blend textual and contextual interpretation. Among other things, methods of interpretation draw on lexicology, intertextuality, genre (e.g., narration), *naẓm* (composition/arrangement), *majāz* (figurative language), and reasons of descent (*asbāb al-nuzūl*), which is a form of contextual analysis (e.g., Alhelwah; al-Dhahabī).[8] The complexity and rhetorical nature of this work can be illustrated by work on and debates resolved by *majāz*.

Scholars studied and wrote handbooks on eloquence and *majāz*, which encompasses a wide range of figures of style and speech. The work of Ibn Qutaybah and al-Jurjānī stands out. Abū Muḥammad 'Abd Allāh Ibn Muslim Ibn Qutaybah (828–889; renowned judge, linguist, philologist, theologian, and writer) wrote *Ta'wīl Mushkil al-Qur'ān* (Interpreting Challenging Qur'ānic Passages).

It comprises sixteen chapters that clarify facets of linguistic and rhetorical expression that can help in correctly interpreting al-Qur'ān. Refuting claims of its fallibility, Ibn Qutaybah's work elucidates how "ignorance of the ways of expression in the Arabic language, especially as used in the Qur'an" causes misunderstanding (180). As an antidote, the book's sixteen chapters provide linguistic and rhetorical analyses of al-Qur'ān that offer a corrective interpretation. In chapters 2–6 (24–102), he demonstrates how those with expertise in the Arabic language are better equipped to interpret what is misread as semantic, stylistic, or grammatical mistakes. He complements these chapters with chapter 7 (103–34), in which he explicates the nature and function of figurative language (*majāz*). The chapters that follow explicate the purposive use and implicature of literary devices in al-Qur'ān—metaphor (*isti'ārah*) in chapter 8 (135–84), inversion (*al-maqlūb*) in chapter 9 (185–209), omission and abridgment (*ḥathf* and *'ikhtiṣār*) in chapter 10 (210–31), and repetition (*tikrār*) in chapter 11 (222–55).

Another noted figure is 'Abu Bakr Abd al-Qāhir al-Jurjānī (died 1078 or 1081). His work stands out as both a further development of and a departure from other studies at the time. al-Jurjānī wrote two books: *Dalā'il al-I'jāz* (Proof of the Inimitability [of al-Qur'ān]) and *Asrār al-Balāghah* (The Secrets of *Balāghah*, or Eloquence). In *Dalā'il al-I'jāz*, he builds on and extends previous work on *i'jāz* and is "concerned with the question of what makes one discourse more eloquent. To answer this question, he offers his theory of *naẓm* (arrangement), which states that eloquence is found not in utterances alone nor in ideas alone, but in the combination of words in discourse according to the rules of syntax" (Alhelwah 213).

At the time, this was a departure from the established focus on the utterance (*lafẓ*) or expression: "Previous theories of rhetoric . . . located the secret of eloquence in the euphony of individual words or in oral delivery and correct articulation" (Alhelwah 213). Instead, al-Jurjānī explicates using ample evidence that rhetorical excellence results from arrangement (i.e., *naẓm*) and the interrelationships (*ta'līq*) of the different constituents of speech (Alhelwah; Rammuny). "He argued that eloquence is manifest in the choice of correct and proper words for expressing those [intended] ideas" (Alhelwah 217). Not surprisingly, in his work, al-Jurjānī addresses the nature and implicature of rhetorical phenomena like word-order variation (e.g., fronting, or *taqdīm*), omission (*hadhf*) and qualification (*qaṣr*), conjunction and disjunction (*al-faṣal wa al-waṣl*), and metaphorical language (*majāz*). al-Jurjānī's work sought to strengthen the process of interpreting al-Qur'ān and proving its inimitability, but his contribution also led to systematizing and deepening the study of rhetoric more broadly. "The first four topics [i.e., word variation, omission, conjunction and disjunction, qualification] were enlarged and systemized by later authors under the branch of *'ilm al-ma'ānī* (grammatical semantics)" (Alhelwah 222). al-Jurjānī is a pioneer, and his work instigated further research that eventually led to the "emergence of grammatical semantics and major branches of Arabic rhetoric, namely, *'ilm al-ma'ānī* (the science of meaning, or semantics) and *'ilm al-bayān* (the science of clarity, or expressiveness)" (Alhelwah 197).

The contribution of *tafsīr* to the study of rhetoric cannot be exaggerated. In the Arab(ic)-Islamic rhetorical tradition, *tafsīr* is unique. Its emergence and systematization are reflective of and responsive to a complex rhetorical situation wherein exegetes found themselves confronted with a community of Muslims with different cultural and linguistic backgrounds, a proliferation of interpretive methods, and claims about al-Qur'ān's fallibility and imitability. Moreover, *tafsīr*'s history, path, and development contribute to the history of rhetoric broadly. Not only did *tafsīr* further the interpretation and accessibility of al-Qur'ān (i.e., the discourse of God), but *tafsīr* also energized the study of poetics, which entails a form of (in)direct training in reading (non)religious texts.

Though *tafsīr* seems to be just a scholarly affair, its effect ripples within and beyond academic circles. Since preachers, who have a weekly platform in the Friday *khuṭbah*, base their work on its interpretive insight, *tafsīr* does impact millions of people. Millions of Muslims participate in the weekly Friday congregation, and they are affected by, if not trained in, its form of public discourse. Consequently, it is not hard to imagine the impact of the Friday *khuṭbah* on Arab(ic)-Islamic popular discourse, which I address in the following section.

Khuṭbah *and* Fann al-Khaṭābah

Khaṭābah refers to public address. *Khaṭābah*'s most observable iteration in the Arab(ic)-Islamic tradition is the Friday *khuṭbah*. In the seventh century, the emerging religious community needed to share and shape religious knowledge as well as build a community. This nascent community had a pre-Islamic oratorical tradition to draw on. Arabs prided themselves on rhetorical and linguistic excellence and artistic prose, which included oratory. This is well documented by contemporary and medieval scholars (e.g., Ṣafwat). The major types of *khuṭbah* include political and military speeches, soothsayers' utterances (*saj' al-kuhān*), marriage ceremonials (*taḥmīd al-nikāḥ*), and speeches of counsel (*wa'ẓ*) (e.g., Qutbuddin; Serjeant).

Unsurprisingly, there is ample evidence of the continuity of this tradition after Islām (e.g., al-Ḥufī; Qutbuddin; Serjeant), both in Mecca, where early Muslims were persecuted, and in Medina, where they emigrated. Orations were regularly used after emigration to Medina in 622 C.E. (i.e., ten years after revelation) and comprised religious orations, which include ritual speeches (e.g., speeches following feast [*'īd*] prayers), pious counsel, and religio-political speeches (e.g., Qutbuddin; Serjeant).

Because orations exemplify eloquence and respond to many recurring exigences, medieval and contemporary scholars invested in compiling, analyzing, and explaining orations. The well-known eighth-century Iraqi intellectual, litterateur, and rhetorician Abū'Uthmān 'Amr ibn Baḥr al-Jāḥiẓ (circa 776–868/869) wrote about the pre- and post-rise of Islām oratory in Arabia, identified women and men orators, and analyzed well-known orations in *Kitāb al-Bayān wa al-Tabyīn* (A Book on Eloquence and Exposition).[9] Similarly, renowned tenth-century Shī'ah scholar al-Sharīf al-Rāḍī compiled the orations of 'Alī ibn abī Ṭālib—the fourth and most prolific orator of the Rightly Guided Caliphs—in his anthology titled *Nahj al-Balāghah* (The Way of Eloquence) in 1009. His compilation preserved 241 sermons (plus 79 letters and over 480 wise sayings). The tradition of compiling oratorical exemplars continued after the Middle Ages.

As to contemporary anthologies, Ṣafwat's two-volume anthology titled *Jamharat Khuṭṭab al-'Arab fi al-'Isūr al-'Arabīyah al-Zāhirah* (A Compilation of the Arabs' Orations during the Prosperous Periods) stands out as a treasure trove of speeches that predate Islām (vol. 1, pp. 1–50) and speeches from the early Islamic period. The anthology includes the speeches of Prophet Muḥammad (570–632 C.E.), his Rightly Guided Successors, or Caliphs (*al-Khulafā' al-Rāshidūn*), like Abū Bakr (573–634) and 'Alī (599–661), and many other orators like al-Ḥassan al-Baṣrī (642–728), well-known preacher, theologian, exegete, and judge.

Prophet Muḥammad gave numerous speeches, which were preserved and compiled throughout the centuries. Ṣafwat compiles twelve in *Jamharat Khuṭṭab al-'Arab.*[10] Most speeches are characterized by their brevity. Many are well known and often memorized. Ṣafwat begins the section on Prophet Muḥammad's speeches (pp. 51–60) with his first in Mecca. In it, Prophet Muḥammad asserts that there is one God. He also declares that he is the messenger of Allah, that he is sent to the Arabs in particular and to all peoples in general, and that people die as they sleep and are risen as they wake up. Then Prophet Muḥammad affirms that all deeds are reckoned with and that there is a hell and a heaven. The section also includes Prophet Muḥammad's first Friday homily, which is much longer (56–57), and his "Farewell Speech" (*khutṭbat al-wadā'*), which synthesizes his teachings. To illustrate, the speech underscores rights and accountability to Allah and others. For example, the equality of all people across racial, tribal, and economic standing is emphasized, and the rights of women are asserted. Prophet Muḥammad advises against exploitation as manifest in usury and addresses social ills (e.g., adultery, oppression, humiliation of people). To this day, the "Farewell Speech" is often quoted to counsel and remind people of core tenets of Islām in the weekly Friday *khuṭbah* and on other occasions.

Relatedly, Cherif Bassiouni, prominent professor of law, compiled speeches (and other types of legal-political documents) in *Al-Wathā'iq Al-Dawlīyah al-Ma'nīyah bi-Ḥuqūq Al-'Insān* (International Instruments on Human Rights). Though the two-volume book is on international instruments, texts in the section devoted to Islamic instruments relate to the study of Arab(ic)-Islamic orations. For example, in his address to Muslims (A.H. 11/631 C.E.), Abū Bakr (the second Rightly Guided Caliph) affirms the right to hold political leadership accountable and the right to equality before the law.

In addition to anthologies, there are also handbooks and studies of oratory. Ibn al- 'Aṭṭār al-Dimashqī's (died A.H. 724/1324 C.E.) *Kitab Adab al-Khaṭīb* (A Handbook for the Preacher) focuses on the excellences or etiquette of the preacher of Friday *khuṭbah*. In the book, Ibn al-'Aṭṭār addresses personal and oratorical skills and excellences of the preacher (e.g., rules and regulations of *khuṭbah*), self-presentation and dress, and how to begin a *khuṭbah*. The tradition of studying oratory continues and is exemplified by al-Ḥufī and Qutbuddin's explication of the art: types, parts, styles, and functions of orations.

This rich history of *khaṭabah* is almost blocked out of view by the assumption that there is only one word that denotes rhetorical study and practice. Transcending the current, narrow uptake of *balāghah* points to *khaṭabah* and contributes to rhetorical studies in numerous ways. Not to be dismissed as another term for public oration, *khuṭbah* is a culturally grounded form of congregation. To illustrate, the Friday *khuṭbah*, which punctuates the life of Muslims, is part of worship and an ongoing act of remembrance (*dhikr*).[11] This is a religious practice that cannot be separated from core doctrinal tenets of Islām. With increased interest in *khuṭbah*, there was also a complementary interest in the Muslim orator (*khaṭīb*) and their training. Accordingly, *khuṭbah*'s cultural specificity extends religious rhetorical studies.

Concluding Remarks

This chapter has taken a three-pronged approach. It identifies reasons for the invisibility of Arab(ic)-Islamic religious rhetorics; sheds light on Arab(ic)-Islamic religious rhetorical exigences, studies, and practices; and demonstrates its longevity, richness, interconnectedness, and versatility. This chapter invites scholars of rhetoric to further research the rich terrain of Arab(ic)-Islamic religious rhetorics.

When religious rhetoric is defined narrowly, the need for studies in interpretation and oratory, two of the most obvious areas of religious rhetoric, seems clear. When defined capaciously to include "symbolic action, even when religion itself does not explicitly appear" (Souders), the dearth in other rhetorical areas becomes more visible. In addition to legal and peacemaking rhetorics, which were touched on earlier, there is a need for studies that highlight the interrelated histories of philology and rhetoric, and how both coincided with Qur'ānic rhetoric becoming *the* inimitable exemplar. These studies will set a high bar for the linguistic and rhetorical competences of the educated person. There is also a need for studies that complement the aforementioned study of commentaries on Aristotle with the study of the intersection of Islamic philosophy, speculative theology (*kalām*), and increased interest in theological disputation, which so far has been studied by scholars of religion and philosophy. Additionally, belletristic rhetoric (*adāb*) and institutional rhetoric (e.g., Alhelwah 88–91; Diab, "Epistolary Rhetoric") grew and defined the literati and chancery writer as well versed in worldly areas of knowledge (e.g., geography, governance systems) and invested in religious knowledge—including Qur'ān, Ḥadith, and jurisprudence (*fiqh*). The invisibility of these areas of rhetorical study and practice contorts our perception of not just Arab(ic)-Islamic rhetoric but also religious rhetoric and rhetoric in the Middle Ages and beyond.

Entry Points

There is a wealth of information awaiting our exploration in the study of epistolary rhetoric, legal-political rhetoric, hermeneutics, and belletristic rhetoric. I'll just address two entry points that brim with potential, namely, commentaries on Aristotle and *khaṭabah*. In what follows, I return to these two areas to chart in broad strokes a path toward the study/teaching of these two traditions.

The translation and commentary tradition. Many are introduced to Aristotle's *Rhetoric*. So, an introduction to the commentary tradition might be an accessible and generative entry point to the study of Arab(ic)-Islamic rhetoric. Not only are there translated primary sources, but there are also secondary sources. They are valuable because they underline pitfalls of such a study and provide generative frames of reference. This work sheds light on the religious, intellectual, and cultural milieu that fostered cultural encounter and the patronage system that led to the establishment of centers for learning. For example, Hārūn al-Rashīd and his son al-Ma'mūn were patrons of knowledge, and the House of Wisdom (Bayt al-Hikmah) in Bagdad comprised a library, an academy, and a center for translation. At Bayt al-Hikmah, Aristotle's work was translated from Greek and

Syriac into Arabic. These translations in turn played a great role in the creation of a culture of knowledge. Aristotle's rhetoric was commented on, studied, and critiqued in an environment of conflictive and generative debates concerning potential tensions between reason and belief as well as tension among philosophy, rhetoric, and religion (e.g., Baddar; Ezzaher; Fakhry, *History of Islamic Philosophy*). As to translated primary sources, there is accessible research on the work of renowned philosophers. Some of the most well known are Avicenna (980–1037 C.E.), Averroës (1126–1198 C.E.), al-Kindi (circa 800–870 C.E.), and al-Fārābī (878–circa 950 C.E.). Ezzaher, a rhetoric scholar, provides an Arabic-English translation of al-Fārābī's short commentary on Aristotle's *Rhetoric*. Butterworth, a scholar of medieval Arabic and Islamic political philosophy, provides an Arabic-English translation of Averroës's short commentary on Aristotle's *Rhetoric*. To see the rhetoricity and contribution of these commentaries, there is a need to complement the study of the commentary with principles of historiography. Baddar's work aligns well with insights from revisionist historiography and comparative and cultural rhetoric. These insights include attending to the nature and impact of influence studies as well as attending to local exigences, terms, context, and purpose, something I tried to model in this chapter.

The khaṭabah tradition. Khaṭabah and Friday *khuṭbah* offer another generative area of study because of the availability of both accessible translations of primary sources as well as scholarship in this area. Three pieces referred to earlier can together help introduce *khaṭabah*'s pre-Islamic origins, its major types and functions, its form and structure, and some of the linguistic and rhetorical expectations of the orator. A good starting point can be Halldén's "What Is Arab Islamic Rhetoric?," which is packed with corrective information about *khaṭabah* and its invisibility as well as a survey of Arabic sources on rhetoric. Though this piece might be hard to follow, it demonstrates the abundance of work on Arabic rhetoric and its surprising invisibility.

Qutbuddin's scholarship abounds with useful historical background, translated exemplars, and visual organizers that help introduce the general types and formal features of *khuṭbah*. For example, in "Khuṭba," she introduces the term *khuṭba* and the Arabic literary landscape, identifies key sources, and surveys pre-Islamic and early Islamic religious *khuṭṭab*. Similarly, Serjeant's "Early Arabic Prose," which also situates *khuṭbah* in relation to an investment in communicative excellence and in prose, surveys different types of prose including orations before and after Islām. Equally important, Qutbuddin points to sources that anthologized orations to model and/or offer guidance to the orator. Qutbuddin also provides a typology (e.g., political and religious) of early Arabic orations, which she complements with a list of subtypes. For example, she identifies several subtypes of religious speeches including those dedicated to pious counsel, ritual sermons, religious ceremonial/occasional speeches, and legislative speeches (191). Moreover, she identifies characteristic structural and stylistic features (205). Finally, she provides the original Arabic and her translation of some of the most famous *khuṭṭab* (223). Her translation includes orations for Prophet Muḥammad; Fāṭimah, his daughter; and Zaynab, who is Fāṭimah's daughter and Prophet Muḥammad's granddaughter.

NOTES

1. I point to the complexity of *Arab(ic)-Islamic* with no pretension to debate the distinction or utility of expansive versus contractive definitions of Arab(ic)-Islamic, which is probably a beneficial pursuit after a critical mass of scholars of Arab(ic)-Islamic rhetoric emerges.

2. This sentence is excerpted from the back cover of Lameer's book: "*Al-Farabi and Aristotelian Syllogistics* deals with an important chapter in the history of Aristotelian logic in early medieval Islam and offers a unique and comprehensive analysis of the writings of the outstanding Muslim philosopher Abu Nasr al-Farabi (died 950/51)."

3. Halldén's article focused only on the art of preaching and homilies, but the same logic can be extended to other rhetorical arts. Therefore, more terms (e.g., debate, or *munāẓara*) should be added to further illustrate the risk of assuming that the use of *balāghah* results only in a nuanced or fuller understanding of the array of rhetorical practices and studies.

4. Scholars study how to effectively dispute claims about the divine, defend al-Qur'ān's inimitability (*i'jāz*), and advocate for ways to effectively interpret al-Qur'ān (e.g., Alhelwah; Widigdo). Learning to debate was not just a response to opposition or charges (e.g., al-Qur'ān being fake) but also a response to an ethical-rhetorical Qur'ānic mandate to argue fairly and responsibly (e.g., chapter 16, verse 125).

5. For more on panegyric poetry about Prophet Muḥammad, which spans various historical periods, see Stetkevych.

6. The inimitability of al-Qur'ān refers to, among other things, how al-Qur'ān is stylistically unique both in the sense of being unprecedented and unmatchable, as well as including information that is not available to Prophet Muḥammad (see Alhelwah 86).

7. Methods used to interpret, which are beyond the scope of the chapter, vary. To illustrate, exegesis can be based on (a) received tradition (*al-tafsīr bi al-ma'thūr* or *al-manqūl*), which draws on interpretation received from Prophet Muḥammad, his Companions, and their Successors, and (b) speculative or reason-based interpretation (i.e., *al-tafsīr bi al-ra'y*) (e.g., al-Dhahabī; Saeed), which draws on wide-ranging areas of knowledge like philology and lexicology, *balāghah*, theology, and jurisprudence, as well as historical and sociopolitical circumstances of revelation. Exegesis can also be

based on intra-Qur'ānic (i.e., using al-Qur'ān itself to interpret verses and chapters) interpretation.

8. Despite the conspicuous rhetorical nature of these methods, they are invisible to rhetorical studies because this work is mainly done by religious scholars. Interestingly, some philologists who sought to interpret al-Qur'ān were criticized because interpretation is the prerogative of religious scholars. For example, Abu 'Ubaydah Ma'mar ibn al-Muthanna (scholar and philologist) wrote a book called *Majāz al-Qur'ān* (The Figurative Language of al-Qur'ān). At the time, his use of *majāz* was broader than what the term implies, for it meant "all expressions that were vague or unusual and needed a philological, lexicographical, or syntactical explanation" (Alhelwah 139). Abu 'Ubaydah's work is seen as an early attempt to theorize the figurative language of al-Qur'ān, but he was criticized by his contemporary al-Aṣma'ī "for interpreting the Qur'an based on his own linguistic opinions. Most of them [religious scholars] believed that interpreting the Qur'an should be left for the religious scholars who were more qualified than philologists for this task" (140).

9. The title is also translated as "Book of Eloquence and Oratory," "Eloquence of Expression and Clarity of Expression," and "Book on Clear Communication."

10. al-Khaṭīb compiles 574 speeches—some are published elsewhere as "sayings" (*aḥādīth*; singular *ḥadīth*)—in his anthology titled *Khuṭṭab al-Rasūl.*

11. *Dhikr* can be translated as remembrance or recollection. It is not just a cognitive act. Rather, it is a fundamental aspect of a prayerful, present disposition, which can be explained as a disposition of alignment with Allah. One of its manifestations would be praying individually or with a congregation.

WORKS CITED

Abdel Haleem, M. A. S. "Grammatical Shift for Rhetorical Purposes: *Iltifāt* and Related Features in the Qur'ān." *Bulletin of the School of Oriental and African Studies*, vol. 55, no. 3, 1992, pp. 407–32.

Adamson, Peter. *al-Kindi*. Oxford UP, 2006.

Alhelwah, Khalid. *The Emergence and Development of Arabic Rhetorical Theory, 500 C.E.–1400 C.E.* 1998. The Ohio State U, PhD dissertation.

Alī, Mohammad Kurd. Introduction. *Rasā'il al-Bulaghā'* [Epistles of the Masters of Eloquence]. Dār al-Kutub al-'Arabīyah al-Kubrá, 1913, pp. 6–16, www.wdl.org/en/item/12974/view/1/3/.

Alomari, Wael Omar. "The Impact of Religious Motivation in the Emergence of Arabic Rhetoric: A Reading in the Era of Composition to Independent Authorship." *Journal of King Abdulaziz University*, vol. 27, no. 1, 2019, pp. 207–25.

Baddar, Maha. "The Arabs Did Not 'Just' Translate Aristotle: Al-Farabi's Logico-Rhetorical Theory." *The Responsibilities of Rhetoric*, edited by M. Smith and B. Warnick, Waveland Press, 2010, pp. 230–42.

—. *From Athens (via Alexandria) to Baghdad: Hybridity as Epistemology in the Work of al-Kindi, al-Farabi, and in the Rhetorical Legacy of the Medieval Arabic Translation Movement*. 2010. U of Arizona, PhD dissertation.

Bassiouni, Cherif. "al-Wathā'iq Al-Islāmīyah [Islamic Instruments]." *Al-Wathā'iq Al-Dawlīyah al-Ma'nīyah bi-Ḥuqūq Al-'Insān* [International Instruments on Human Rights]. Vol. 2, Dār al-Shurūq, 2006, pp. 23–44.

Belhaj, Abdessamad. "Ādāb Al-Baḥth Wa-al-Munāẓara: The Neglected Art of Disputation in Later Medieval Islam." *Arabic Sciences and Philosophy*, vol. 26, no. 2, 2016, pp. 291–307.

Blair, Carole. "Contested Histories of Rhetoric: The Politics of Preservation, Progress, and Change." *Quarterly Journal of Speech*, vol. 78, no. 4, 1992, pp. 403–28.

Black, Deborah L. "The Imaginative Syllogism in Arabic Philosophy: A Medieval Contribution to the Philosophical Study of Metaphor." *Mediaeval Studies*, vol. 51, 1989, pp. 242–67.

Bonebakker, Seeger Adrianus. "Aspects of the History of Literary Rhetoric and Poetics in Arabic Literature." *Viator*, vol. 1, 1971, pp. 75–96.

Borrowman, Shane. "The Islamization of Rhetoric: Ibn Rushd and the Reintroduction of Aristotle into Medieval Europe." *Rhetoric Review*, vol. 27, no. 4, 2008, pp. 341–60.

Butterworth, Charles E., translator. *Averroes's Three Short Commentaries on Aristotle's "Topics," "Rhetoric," and "Poetics."* State U of New York P, 1977.

Corbett, Edward P. J., *Classical Rhetoric for the Modern Student*. 3rd ed., Oxford UP, 1990.

al-Dhahabī, Muḥammad Ḥussaīn. *'Ilm Al-Tafsīr* [The Science of Interpretation]. Dār Al-Ma'ārif, n.d.

Diab, Rasha. "Epistolary Rhetoric." *The Routledge Handbook of Comparative World Rhetorics*, edited by Keith Lloyd, Routledge, 2020, pp. 144–54.

—. "Legal-Political Rhetoric, Human Rights, and the Constitution of Medina." *Rhetorica: A Journal of the History of Rhetoric*, vol. 36, no. 3, 2018, pp. 219–43.

—. "Peacemaking and the Chancery in Medieval Cairo: Revisiting Medieval Arabic Rhetoric." *Rhetoric Across Borders*, edited by Anne Demo, Parlor Press, 2015, pp. 121–33.

Enos, Richard Leo, and Ann M. Blakeslee. "The Classical Period." *The Present State of Scholarship in Historical and Contemporary Rhetoric*, edited by Winifred Bryan Horner, U of Missouri P, 1990, pp. 9–44.

Ezzaher, Lahcen E. "Alfarabi's *Book of Rhetoric*: An Arabic-English Translation of Alfarabi's Commentary on Aristotle's *Rhetoric*." *Rhetorica: A Journal of the History of Rhetoric*, vol. 26, no. 4, 2008, pp. 347–91.

Fakhry, Majid. "Al-Farabi and the Reconciliation of Plato and Aristotle." *Journal of the History of Ideas*, vol. 26, no. 4, 1965, pp. 469–78.

—. *A History of Islamic Philosophy*. Columbia UP, 1983.

Halldén, Philip. "What Is Arab Islamic Rhetoric? Rethinking the History of Muslim Oratory Art and Homiletics." *International Journal of Middle East Studies*, vol. 37, no. 1, 2005, pp. 19–38.

al-Ḥufī, Aḥmad Muḥammad. *Fann al-Khaṭābah* [The Art of Oratory]. Al-Haī'ah al-Masrīyah lil-Ta'līf wa lil-Nashr, 1964.

Hum, Sue, and Lyon, Arabella. "Recent Advances in Comparative Rhetoric." *The Sage Handbook of Rhetorical Studies*, edited by Andrea Lunsford et al., Sage, 2008, pp. 153–63.

Ibn al-Athīr, Ḍiyā'al-Dīn Naṣr Allāh ibn Muḥammad. *Al-Mathal al-Sā'ir fī Adab al-Kātib wa al-Shā'ir* [Contemporary Exemplars: On the Arts of the Writer and Poet]. Edited by Aḥmad al-Ḥufī and Badawī Ṭabanah, vol. 1, 1st ed., Nahḍat Maṣr, 1959.

Ibn Qutaybah, Abū Muḥammad 'Abd Allāh Ibn Muslim. *Ta'wīl Mushkil al-Qur'ān* [Interpreting Challenging Qur'ānic Passages], edited by Al-Sayīd Aḥmad Ṣaqr, al-Maktabah al-'Ilmīyah, 1973, archive.org/stream/FP14945/14945#page/n18/mode/2up.

al-Jāḥiẓ, Abū'Uthmān 'Amr ibn Baḥr. *Kitāb al-Bayān wa al-Tabyīn* [The Book on Eloquence and Exposition]. Al-Maṭba'ah al-'Ilmīyah, 1895.

Jenssen, Herbjrn. *The Subtleties and Secrets of the Arabic Language: Preliminary Investigations into Al-Qazwīnī's* Talkhīṣ Al-Miftāḥ. Vol. 2, Centre for Middle Eastern and Islamic Studies, U of Norway, 1998.

al-Jurjānī, 'Abd al-Qāhir. *Asrār al-Balāgha* [The Mysteries of Eloquence]. Edited by Hellmut Ritter, Istanbul Government Press, 1954.

—. *Dalā'il al-I 'jāz* [Proof of the Inimitability of al-Qur'ān]. Maktabaht Muḥammad 'Alī Ṣubaīḥ wa Awlāduhu, 1960.

Kennedy, George. *Classical Rhetoric and Its Christian and Secular Tradition from Ancient to Modern Times*. 2nd ed., U of North Carolina P, 1999.

al-Khaṭīb, Muḥammad Khalīl. *Khuṭṭab al-Rasūl* [The Speeches of the Prophet]. Dār al-Faḍīlah, 1983.

Lameer, Joep. *Al-Fārābī and Aristotelian Syllogistics: Greek Theory and Islamic Practice*. Brill, 1994.

Al-Musawi, Muhsin J. "Arabic Rhetoric." *Encyclopedia of Rhetoric*, edited by Thomas O. Sloane, Oxford UP, 2001, pp. 29–33.

Pernot, Laurent. "The Rhetoric of Religion." *New Chapters in the History of Rhetoric*, edited by Laurent Pernot, Brill, 2009, pp. 325–46.

Qutbuddin, Tahera. "*Khutba*: The Evolution of Early Arabic Oration." *Classical Arabic Humanities in Their Own Terms: Festschrift for Wolfhart Heinrichs*, edited by Beatrice Gruendler and Michael Cooperson, Brill, 2008, pp. 176–273.

Rammuny, Raji M. "Al-Jurjani: A Pioneer of Grammatical and Linguistic Studies." *Historiographia Linguistica*, vol. 12, no. 3, 1985, pp. 351–71.

Royster, Jacqueline Jones. "Disciplinary Landscaping, or Contemporary Challenges in the History of Rhetoric." *Philosophy and Rhetoric*, vol. 36, no. 2, 2003, pp. 148–67.

Saeed, Abdullah. *The Qur'an: An Introduction*. Routledge, 2008.

Ṣafwat, Ahmad Zakī, editor. *Jamharat Khuṭṭab al-'Arab fī al-'Isūr al-'Arabīyah al-Zāhirah* [A Compilation of the Arabs' Orations during the Prosperous Periods]. Vol. 1, Al-Maktabah Al-'Ilmīyah, 1937.

Serjeant, Robert Bertram. "Early Arabic Prose." *The Cambridge History of Arabic Literature: Arabic Literature to the End of the Umayyad Period*, edited by Alfred Felix Landon Beeston et al., Cambridge UP, 1983, pp. 114–53.

al-Sharīf al-Rāḍī. *Nahj Al-Balāghah* [The Way of Eloquence], edited by Ṣubḥī Ṣāliḥ, Dār al-Kitāb al-Maṣrī, 1837.

Souders, Michael. "Religious Rhetoric." *Oxford Bibliographies in Communication*. Edited by Patricia Moy, Oxford UP, 2013.

Stetkevych, Suzanne Pinckney. *The Mantle Odes: Arabic Praise Poems to the Prophet Muhammad*. Indiana UP, 2010.

Widigdo, Mohammad Syifa Amin. "Aristotelian Dialectic, Medieval *Jadal*, and Medieval Scholastic Disputation." *American Journal of Islamic Social Sciences*, vol. 35, no. 4, 2018, pp. 1–24.

Interlude

ROBERT P. YAGELSKI

I first encountered Zen when my college roommate shared with me his copy of *Zen Flesh, Zen Bones*, a classic text he was reading for a course on Eastern philosophy. As college students seeking their way in a world of newfound ideas are wont to do, he and I spent hours talking about that book and others like it, drawn to its seemingly irreverent yet incisive take on the puzzling questions about meaning and truth that we believed we were exploring. I had been raised in a conservative Catholic home and spent the first twelve years of my educational career in Catholic schools—first a parish grade school and then a Jesuit high school. By the time I enrolled in college at age eighteen, I was wrestling with my faith and questions about meaning and purpose. I was ripe for exposure to new ways of thinking, but my upbringing and early education had given me no reference point for what I encountered in *Zen Flesh, Zen Bones*, which simply didn't make much sense to me at the time. Yet something in that text spoke to me. I wouldn't return to it for nearly two decades, but the book settled into my consciousness.

When I began practicing Zen many years later, I was still confronting questions of faith and meaning, though time and experience had profoundly reshaped those questions. By then, I was a scholar, engaged in what seemed to me a different kind of inquiry about questions that I thought had little to do with the problems of faith and meaning: What is writing? What role does it play in our lives, in society? How can we teach writing effectively? How *should* we teach writing? Over time, however, the practice of Zen helped me see that the search for meaning and the study of writing were not really different sets of concerns. They were part of the same nagging impulse to try to understand human life and to work out how to live with others on this earth we share. I came to see my scholarship as part of a bigger project of learning to live better together. And eventually those two journeys—my search for meaning and my scholarly inquiries into writing—began to converge.

This was no revelation, of course. My colleagues and friends in the field all seemed to be engaged in their own versions of that same project in some way—so too, the scholars who influenced my thinking about writing and teaching: bell hooks, David Orr, Barbara Couture, Thomas Kent, Peter Elbow. And Paulo Freire. Especially Freire. The more I revisited his work, the more I caught glimpses of the intellectual and the spiritual converging in the service of something bigger. If you read his accounts of his work with disenfranchised peasants in Brazil and Chile and elsewhere, and if you trace his intellectual influences (Gramsci and Marx, for example), you begin to see that Freire fashioned his theories of education out of the clay of his own life experiences and his Catholic education. Those theories, which have influenced so many educators, are driven by a vision of a just and equitable society. His problem-posing method of critical pedagogy is about realizing that vision. Freire's pedagogy is as much about living better together as it is about literacy learning.

For me, the convergence of the spiritual and the intellectual was in large measure a function of the way in which my practice of Zen exposed some of the blind spots in my own education, formal and otherwise, and slowly I came to see both the limitations and the affordances of the Western worldview with which I was imbued. One of those blind spots, appropriately enough, is the false dichotomy between the spiritual and the intellectual. I experienced that binary as an obstacle in my Zen practice even as I was wrestling with it as an intellectual problem in my scholarly work. Eventually, these two seemingly distinct experiences led me to profoundly rethink how I understood writing. To put it somewhat differently, confronting the contradictions that so bewildered me when I first encountered Zen as a college student helped me come to appreciate the value of the *experience* of writing, which in turn became the focus of my scholarly work.

Ultimately, I suppose, I am talking about ways of knowing. Initially, Zen seemed removed from the intellectual world I inhabited as a trained academic (and the rigorous Jesuit education I had enjoyed as a high school student). I wish neither to oversimplify nor to romanticize the matter. Despite the convergences I have tried to describe between my spiritual and intellectual journeys, there are significant differences in how we come to know the world (and ourselves as beings in that world) within these frameworks. But the contradictions I experienced became generative, in large part because Zen shook up my way of knowing—and being. I'm not sure I would have found my way into my current scholarly inquiries if I had not taken up Zen practice. Nor would I have engaged Zen as I did without the experience of my Catholic education and the crisis of faith I had as a younger man.

These circuitous journeys have converged in a way that has opened up what I hope are promising avenues of inquiry into writing and being together on this earth. For me, the value of the experience of writing, as I have tried to describe it in my scholarship, is not separate from the pressing need to find ways to live better together.

This, at least, is the story I need to tell. Like any story, it is a construction, a way to make sense of what has happened. Both Zen and academe teach us to be skeptical of such stories. Yet, as I write this in late 2020, the frightening developments all around us make the story feel even more necessary.

As the spring semester of 2020 ended, amidst the worldwide COVID-19 pandemic, the uncertainty about what might happen next was almost overwhelming, and my colleagues and I in the writing program I direct sometimes struggled to adapt. One colleague, who teaches international students, shared with me something one of her students had written in an end-of-semester reflection as both she and her students tried to make sense of what was happening. In her own reflection on the experience of teaching during the pandemic-induced shutdown, she wrote about how her student, who was from Malaysia but who could not return home because of travel restrictions implemented to slow the spread of the virus, thanked her for what he had experienced in her class. Stuck alone in an apartment in an American city, the student described to her how he watched beautiful pink flowers outside his window bud, bloom, and wither, which he took as a metaphor for the life he was experiencing in quarantine by himself in a foreign country. The writing class, he told my colleague, was the only synchronous class he had during this time, and though it was online, it became for him a crucial human connection, a sign of life amidst thousands of untimely deaths. According to my colleague, this unprecedented experience of teaching during a horrifying pandemic helped her appreciate the need for humility to accept constant change and for a willingness to adapt her pedagogy to serve the changing needs of her students.

This, to my mind, is what it means to describe writing—and teaching—as a practice of living. In these moments, the professional and the spiritual converge, and there is no distinction between them. Just as there is no distinction between my colleague and her student from Malaysia, between our students and ourselves, between you and me.

WORKS CITED

Reps, Paul, and Nyogen Senzaki, compilers. *Zen Flesh, Zen Bones: A Collection of Zen and Pre-Zen Writings.* 1957. Tuttle Publishing, 1998.

8. Race at the Intersection of Rhetoric and Religion

ANDRE E. JOHNSON

In her groundbreaking essay "Between Abundance and Marginalization: The Imperative of Racial Rhetorical Criticism," Lisa Flores argues that "race is foundational to the work of rhetorical criticism and that any criticism void of this consideration is incomplete, partial, if not irresponsible" (6). About this, she writes,

> If rhetorical scholars are to attend to all matter of discourse, whether understood as questions of impact, influence, or circulation, or questions of argument and audience, or questions of affect and materiality, we cannot ignore race. Rhetorical meanings, as they circulate on and around bodies, are already raced. Bodies that speak and listen, that exhort and cajole, that desire and hate are already raced. (7)

To address this need in rhetorical studies, Flores calls on critics not only to adopt a racial rhetorical criticism, but she argues as well that this is an imperative we must heed: "This work must be done if we, as rhetorical scholars, believe that race is a rhetorical matter. The range of interests, approaches, and topics included in the growing body of racial rhetorical criticism demonstrates the continuing relevance of racial matters and the persistent need for rhetorical attention" (15–16).

Heeding the call of Flores, scholars have made the proverbial "rhetorical turn" as it relates to rhetorical criticism and race. For instance, in 2017, *Rhetoric Review* devoted an issue to rhetoric and race titled *Rhetoric, Race, and Resentment: Whiteness and the New Days of Rage*. In the issue, the editors wanted to move beyond "our understandings of what racism is," or racism's manifestations, to "explore questions about how rhetoric has been used, with intentionality and skill, to disrupt a sense of 'order and rightness,' even when *these are in direct opposition to a public discourse that states otherwise*" (Carstarphen and Welch 255). They reasoned that since rhetoric and race were commingled in the "structures of power and privilege, it is important that rhetoricians peer deeply, even uncomfortably, into the ways that discursive, semiotic, and symbolic skill are being used to maintain those power structures at all costs" (255).

In 2018, *Communication and Critical/Cultural Studies* devoted an issue that also examined the intersection of rhetoric and race. Inspired by a 2018 panel at the Rhetoric Society of America conference that "revolved around Flores's article," the issue was to continue the "hard and ongoing work of naming, disrupting, and divesting from disciplinary and institutionalized whiteness" (Houdek, "Imperative" 293). The bold plan of this special issue was to "mark a broader commitment to center race and race scholarship, and particularly black and nonwhite scholars' work, within future issues of this and other journals, on review boards, and more" (293).

As editor Matthew Houdek noted, he and the other contributors hoped that the essays in this issue would "help continue to confront the discipline's racial inequalities, inequities, and forms of silencing, gatekeeping, and oppression" ("Imperative" 293). Also, they wanted to "advance the conversation regarding the ethics, practices, and politics of cultivating a robust platform for staging intersectional racial rhetorical criticism beyond the logics of mere inclusion" (293). They further wanted to "motivate a divestment from whiteness and a reinvestment in a discipline that is grounded in accountability, care, and responsibility around the issues and interventions raised by the contributing authors, among others" (293).

Even before the publication of Flores's article and her call for rhetoric scholars to attend to race in rhetorical criticism, I realized that in my work, I had already heeded that call. In 2015, I edited a special issue of the *Journal of Contemporary Rhetoric* dedicated to understanding the relation of rhetoric to race. Similar to Houdek's aim, what I wanted to do with the collection of essays in that issue was to "offer new insights that would begin to frame future communication studies on race, racism, and racialized discourses" (Johnson, "Understanding" 64). Moreover, I was interested in essays that would "contribute to our current knowledge of the rhetorics of race while revealing their historical and cultural significance through detailed case studies of discourse across a wide range of contemporary contexts" (64). We hoped that by doing this, we would "demonstrate ways racial knowledge and power becomes possible through rhetorical inquiry" (64).

Other rhetorical scholars, especially in the field of communication, are taking up Flores's call. For example, Matthew Houdek's essay on racialized violence and the burning of Black churches ("Racial Sedimentation"), Michelle Kelsey Kearl's examination of rhetorics of race and disability ("Stolen"), Mollie K. Murphy and Tina M. Harris's work on the "White Savior" narrative in the film *The Help* ("White Innocence"), and Rishi Chebrolu's rhetorical analysis of Dylann Roof's manifesto ("Racial Lens") contribute to our understanding of how race works and functions rhetorically. In this chapter, however, following the lead of other rhetoric scholars who have asked us to attend more to race in our studies and not to marginalize the scholarship that is already published, I invite scholars of rhetoric and religion to start examining how race functions in our religious discourses. I do this because if, as Houdek notes, "the whiteness of rhetorical studies is outrageous" and the "time has come to confront it" ("Imperative" 292–93), it is also time to confront the fact that research in rhetoric and religion and, indeed, religious communication itself is catastrophically white.

This became apparent to me when Christopher A. House and I edited a special issue of the *Journal of Communication and Religion* (*JCR*)—the flagship journal in the religious communication field—in 2018. Titling the issue *Communication, Religion, and Race in America: 50 Years Later and Where Do We Go from Here?*, we aimed to address the shortage of race scholarship in the field of religious communication, but more specifically in the journal itself (House and Johnson). A search of past issues of the *JCR* using the keywords "race" and "communication" or "racism" and "communication" turned up disappointing results. Even when we searched for "race" or "racism" alone, the results were the same.

Therefore, in this chapter, I call on us to understand how we use rhetoric as a method and to explore how rhetorical approaches to religion can contribute to a deeper and more meaningful conception of both religion and race. I use the term "rhetoric" here to refer to language and other forms of symbolic activity that motivate or guide people in matters of belief. I see rhetoric as what communicators invite their audiences to do. I argue that scholars must begin to address rhetoric, race, and religion from both a historical and a contemporary perspective and to examine explicit and implicit warrants in religious discourse that help us theorize ways in which religion(s) and race operate.

To highlight this call and concern, I attempt to do two things. First, I share some of my own journey and discovery in the field of religious communication as a scholar of prophetic rhetoric. Prophetic rhetoric is "discourse grounded in the sacred, rooted in a community experience that offers a critique of existing communities and traditions by charging and challenging society to live up to the ideals they espoused while offering celebration, encouragement, and hope for a brighter future" (Johnson, "Prophetic Persona" 270–71). It is a rhetoric "characterized by a steadfast refusal to adapt itself to the perspectives of its audience" and a rhetoric that dedicates itself to the rights of individuals (Darsey 5–6). Located on the margins of society, it intends to lift the people to an ethical conception of whatever the people deem as sacred by adopting, at times, a controversial style of speaking (Johnson and Stone 11; Johnson, "'To Make the World'" 18).

I argue that while the field has grown since the work of James Darsey, a missing component in it, as well as in religious communication itself, is an understanding of how race functions within religious discourses. I contend that this lack of understanding in the literature is tied to the way many scholars understand prophetic rhetoric. In short, many have followed Darsey in framing the prophetic tradition in a Eurocentric fashion—a tradition birthed in freedom and democracy and where race has no space or place.

Second, I argue that, within the African American prophetic tradition, prophesying carries a race critique because the tradition's birth and context are profoundly different from a Euro-American heritage. This tradition was not birthed in freedom and democracy but birthed from slavery and shaped in Jim-and-Jane-Crow America. It has been the primary vehicle that has comforted and given voice to many African Americans. Through struggle and sacrifice, this tradition has expressed Black people's call for unity and cooperation, as well as the community's anger and frustrations. It has been both hopeful and pessimistic. It has celebrated the beauty and myth of American exceptionalism and its unique place in the world, while at the same time damning it to hell for not living up to the ideals America espouses. It is a tradition that celebrates the Creator or the Divine's hand in history—offering "hallelujahs" for deliverance from slavery and Jim and Jane Crow, while at the same time asking, "Where in the hell is God?" during tough and trying times. It is a tradition that develops a theological outlook quite different at times from orthodoxy—one that finds God again very close, but so far away (Johnson, "To Make the World").

As Flores and others have done, I too invite rhetorical scholars to attend to race in the field of religious communication and, more specifically, rhetoric and religion. One way, I argue, of doing this is to examine the African American prophetic tradition. In so doing, scholars will begin not only to unpack how those rhetors spoke against a tradition and system that still devalues them and their contributions but also to gain a better and more holistic understanding of how rhetoric and religion function.

The Study of Prophetic Rhetoric

My interest in the academic study of prophetic rhetoric started while I was a PhD student. I had decided to study prophetic rhetoric and selected my figure, Bishop Henry McNeal Turner of the African Methodist Episcopal (AME) Church. Then the 2008 presidential campaign brought my study to the forefront. During the Democratic primary, clips from Barack Obama's former pastor Rev. Dr. Jeremiah Wright surfaced. In them, audiences heard Pastor Wright condemn the United

States' government and critique the foreign policy of the Bush administration. From the many comments in the media by politicians, pundits, and pollsters, one thing stood out to me. Many people who offered comments simply did not understand the elements of the African American prophetic tradition. Even people in my own department were "concerned" over Wright's "comments." For me and others, however, who knew about this prophetic tradition, Wright's words were of no concern at all.

While my academic interest in prophetic rhetoric may have started while I was in my PhD program, my interest in prophetic discourse—speaking truth to power—reached back farther. I also serve as a pastor of a Black church. What this means is that I come from and out of a tradition that produced prophetic rhetors—Allen, Stewart, Turner, Wells, Du Bois, Terrell, King, Hamer, X, and Davis—throughout American history. Not to see them studied as exemplars of prophetic rhetoric, or their rhetoric seriously examined within the larger frame of religious discourse, was disconcerting. As I continued to research the field, I was shocked to discover just how white it was.

For instance, when James Darsey published his foundational work, *The Prophetic Tradition and Radical Rhetoric in America* in 1997, many in the field of communication—especially those who studied religious rhetoric—held the work in high regard. Steven Browne wrote that Darsey's book was a "richly textured, sometimes dazzling, always provocative study of the prophetic tradition in American culture" (459). James Andrews went even further. He called the book "important" and wondered whether anyone who "purports to study public address in America—from a historical or contemporary standpoint—can ignore it" (518). Those who read the book will see an "intricate and compelling argument laid out, evidence convincingly assembled, and theory-based criticism skillfully enacted by a scholar who can blend wit, erudition, and passion" (518). Darsey continued to receive praise for the book, winning the prestigious Marie Hochmuth Nichols Award for scholarship in rhetoric and public address as well as the Diamond Anniversary Book Award and the Winans-Wichelns Award from the National Communication Association (Woodyard 27).

This is not to say, however, that others did not notice the whiteness of Darsey's work, but the remarks came from historians and not from communication or rhetorical scholars. For example, Robert H. Craig in his review of the book celebrated Darsey's "historical study of American rhetoric" as "an intriguing, well-written, and fascinating treatment of an unexplored dimension of American life," while at the same time criticizing Darsey for limiting the prophetic and radical tradition to "Euro-American males." Craig astutely notes, "if one of the defining characteristics of the biblical prophets is their ceaseless demand for divine justice, then to limit the American radical rhetorical tradition to Euro-American males does an injustice to the radicality of the very biblical tradition that gives rise to the prophetic voice" (635). Craig wondered about "public witness individuals such as Mother Jones, Ida B. Wells, Frederick Douglass, and César Chavez, among a host of others, to ask to what degree their inclusion might expand our understanding of a distinctive tradition otherwise so carefully delineated by James Darsey" (635).

In his critique of Darsey's work, Edward Countryman questioned how Darsey could sum up the entirety of the mid-nineteenth century with one figure—Wendell Phillips—and leave "Douglass, King, and many other figures of real power out of the picture." Similarly, Mark Pittenger, in his review of the book, wondered how Darsey could leave Martin Luther King Jr., other civil rights leaders, and even Cornel West out of the tradition (180).

According to many rhetorical and communication scholars, Darsey had produced a crucial work that provided the foundation to all who would follow. Indeed, the publication of *The Prophetic Tradition and Radical Rhetoric in America* led many rhetorical scholars to deem prophecy worthy of study. However, it also did something else. It provided the framework and foundation for future studies in prophetic rhetoric, and much of this work, as Anthony Stone and I have argued elsewhere, "negates the contributions of African-American scholars and those who study African-American prophetic rhetoric" (11). It is this "lack of attention by scholars," we contend, that "lead[s] many to understand prophetic rhetoric only from a white (male) European framework that understands the people as the New Israel and grounded in the ideals of freedom, individualism, and 'called people of God'" (11). Furthermore, we surmise that it is this "oversight that impedes scholars from seeing that the African-American version of prophetic rhetoric is profoundly different" (11).

An example of this is Kristen Lynn Majocha's "Prophetic Rhetoric: A Gap between the Field of Study and the Real World." In this "brief survey" of the scholarship on prophetic rhetoric, she argues that her essay will "exhaustively uncover how 'prophetic rhetoric' has been discussed in the current literature." Though she does mention Cornel West and Michael Eric Dyson as contributing to the study of prophetic rhetoric—only by calling specific figures "prophetic"—her essay is heavily influenced by Darsey. Moreover, Majocha contends that we do not know "how to uncover prophetic rhetoric" or "how to test for prophetic rhetoric" (14).

Darsey's influence is not only present in Majocha's survey, however. Since 1997, according to a search for "prophetic rhetoric" in Communication & Mass Media Complete, much of what we know about prophetic discourse draws heavily from Darsey. Examples include Amos Kiewe's "Theodore Herzl's *The*

Jewish State: Prophetic Rhetoric in the Service of Political Objectives," David M. Timmerman's "Christian Pacifism and the Prophetic Voice: Dietrich Bonhoeffer's Peace Address," Richard Benjamin Crosby's "'Which Is the Wisest Course?' Political Power and Prophetic Agency in Nineteenth-Century Mormon Rhetoric," Michael Souders's "The Prophetic Imagination and the Rhetoric of 'Freedom' in the Prosperity Gospel," and Leland Spencer's "Bishop Leontine Turpeau Current Kelly: Toward an Ironic Prophetic Rhetoric." I believe this is what Houdek gets at when he speaks of this as a "structural problem" ("Imperative" 293). We can only cite whom and what we know, and if that is already embedded in whiteness, we will continue to replicate that. I knew even in my time as a graduate student that I wanted to do something more with prophetic rhetoric than to reproduce whiteness. Surely, Black people adopted prophetic personas, and they had to differ from what the canon was teaching me. Therefore, I set out on a quest to find and name that tradition.

The African American Prophetic Tradition

Works from the early 2000s pointed to this tradition. Eddie S. Glaude's *Exodus! Religion, Race, and Nation in Early Nineteenth-Century Black America*, Chanta M. Haywood's *Prophesying Daughters: Black Women Preachers and the Word, 1823–1913*, David L. Chappell's *A Stone of Hope: Prophetic Religion and the Death of Jim Crow*, Edward J. Blum's *W. E. B. Du Bois: American Prophet*, George Shulman's *American Prophecy: Race and Redemption in American Political Culture*, and Richard S. Newman's *Freedom's Prophet: Bishop Richard Allen, the AME Church, and the Black Founding Fathers* all drew from prophecy as an essential thread, but none of these works explicitly examined the prophetic rhetoric of African Americans or the African American prophetic tradition.

Drawing from the work of Robert Terrill on Malcolm X ("Protest"; *Malcolm X*), critics studying prophetic rhetoric tend to situate the discourse within two primary traditions—apocalyptic and the jeremiad. The most studied within the African American tradition is the jeremiad. Scholars such as Wilson Jeremiah Moses in *Black Messiahs and Uncle Toms: Social and Literary Manipulations of a Religious Myth* and David Howard-Pitney in *The African American Jeremiad: Appeals for Justice in America* focus on the multiple ways that Blacks used the jeremiad to appeal to their audiences. What I discovered, however, is that the Black tradition of prophetic rhetoric does not exclusively reside in either the apocalyptic or the jeremiad forms of prophetic discourse. Though African Americans have depended heavily on the jeremiad, contextual restraints and rhetorical exigencies have not always allowed for jeremiadic appeal.

For instance, for many African Americans, the jeremiad at times posed a significant problem. Inherent in the jeremiad is that its proponents never question the foundational premise of its belief—or in prophetic terms, it never questions the *sacred.* As I understand the tenets of the jeremiad, rhetors using the jeremiad typically do not question their faith in America's promise and destiny. Historically, they never questioned their belief that they were the New Israel or chosen people or that America was indeed the Promised Land. Many African Americans, however, did not have confidence in or think that "the covenant" would work for them. Therefore, if African Americans adopted a prophetic persona to appeal to their audiences, they had to find other traditions or draw from other traditions (Johnson, "'To Make the World'" 23).

Christopher Hobson's *The Mount of Vision: African American Prophetic Tradition: 1800–1950* draws from the books in the Protestant Bible to argue that there are four traditions within African American prophecy. First is the Exodus-Deuteronomy tradition in which the prophet centers on a "key event in African Americans' own salvational history with God signifying both the end of slavery as a specific event and a pattern of saving acts in history" (38). Second is the Isaiah-Ezekiel tradition. Hobson argues that this tradition "emphasizes that the community can, with God's help, win restoration after suffering through a series of events in which its own efforts and God's instrumentality achieve reform in the United States' overall life" (39). The third tradition, the Jeremiah tradition, is similar to the jeremiad in that the prophet believes that the community has turned away from the covenant and needs to turn back. The fourth, the Daniel-Revelation tradition, is similar to the apocalyptic tradition in that the prophet believes that God is ushering in a "new day," "new kingdom," or "new way" (40–41).

While Hobson draws from biblical rhetoric to discover his types of prophetic rhetoric, I turn to the Black public address and oratorical tradition to discover mine. In my study of the African American rhetorical tradition—especially the career of Henry McNeal Turner—I identify at least four other types of prophetic rhetoric found primarily, but not exclusively, in the African American prophetic tradition. The first is *celebratory prophecy.* I define celebratory prophecy as a prophecy, typically grounded in a sacred covenant, that calls the people to celebrate an event that leads them to affirm the sacred (covenant). In other words, before the event, the prophet could not invoke the covenant because the audience that the prophet represents was not included in the covenant. Moreover, the prophet links the event to the will of God; thus, it becomes a sacred event worthy of celebration (Johnson, *Forgotten Prophet* 10).

The second type of prophecy used by African Americans is a *prophetic disputation* or *disputation prophecy*. Disputation occurs when the speaker offers a "quotation of the people's opinion" within the speech context and offers a refutation, "which corrects this opinion." Prophetic disputations function rhetorically by giving the speaker a chance not only to speak about the evils perpetrated by her opponents but also to do so in a way that creates a sense of empowerment, both for the speaker and for the community the speaker represents (Johnson, *Forgotten Prophet* 10).

In this way, prophetic disputations are similar to Gregg's ego-function of protest rhetoric because the prophet aims the rhetoric at the "protestors themselves," the ones who need affirmation of their personhood (74). While the prophet aims his rhetoric toward his opponents, the main thrust of his message appeals to his supporters. Prophetic disputations and, for that matter, prophetic rhetoric in general do not follow Gregg's view that the speaker needs self-affirmation and that the speaker is the primary audience of the message. What Gregg assumes is that the speaker needs "psychological refurbishing and affirmation" (74)—and perhaps in protest rhetoric, the speaker does. With prophetic rhetoric, the speaker needs no such affirmation. With prophetic rhetoric, before the speaker speaks, affirmation comes from the Divine. In other words, the speaker does not need approval or affirmation from anyone to speak. The prophet's ego is in check because the ego, the self—in fact, the whole person of the speaker—belongs to God (Johnson, "'To Make the World'" 23).

The third type of prophecy is *mission-oriented prophecy*. A mission-oriented prophecy is a constitutive rhetoric that calls a people to participate in a divine mission by reconstituting the people from their perceived identities. While constitutive rhetoric assumes that audiences are already a rhetorical effect and uses that identification to shape the message, a mission-oriented prophecy finds the constructed identities problematic and offers a new vision or identity for the people. Therefore, what the prophet does is to (re)constitute the people in an identity that would fit the divine call (Johnson, *Forgotten Prophet* 13).

The fourth type of prophecy used by African Americans is a type of prophetic discourse that I call *pessimistic prophecy* or the prophetic lament. Many Black orators who find racism too entrenched and covenant ideals unrealistic for Black Americans to attain become wailing and moaning prophets within what I call the lament tradition of prophecy. In this tradition, the prophet's primary function is to speak out on behalf of others and to chronicle their pain and suffering, as well as her or his own. By speaking, the prophet offers hope and encouragement to others by acknowledging their suffering and letting them know that they are not alone (Johnson, *Forgotten Prophet* 14).

Implications and Conclusion

I started this chapter by arguing for the inclusion of race in the study of religious communication broadly and in rhetoric and religion in particular. This is not to negate the good work done by scholars who study rhetoric and religion. Scholars of rhetoric and religion have done a lot to lessen the resistance in our field toward religion. However, what I am arguing is that along with the study of rhetoric and religion, we should also attend to race, and one way I suggest doing this is to examine the African American prophetic tradition.

An understanding of how race functions at the intersection of rhetoric and religion would be helpful in three primary ways. First, a study of race at the intersection of rhetoric and religion can expose some differences in how rhetoric is presented and performed. In my example using prophetic rhetoric, I attempted to demonstrate how scholars, in perpetuating the canon of prophetic rhetoric studies, sometimes missed a separate tradition of prophetic rhetoric. This is why scholars can publish books without including one rhetor of color or why someone can publish a survey of the field and leave out the most recent and relevant works of Black scholars who have published research on prophetic rhetoric. It is also why even when scholars examine speeches by Black figures they deem prophetic, they still use the European understanding of the jeremiad instead of seeing how race would lead the speaker to adopt a different type of appeal.

Second, a study of race at the intersection of rhetoric and religion would also highlight how religion (and theology) itself is already "raced." For example, there are a plethora of studies that examine white (conservative) evangelical support for Donald Trump. There are now some articles that explore the racial rhetoric used by Trump before and after he became president of the United States. What we have not done effectively is to merge the two. What I mean is this: as a field, we have not examined how race functions in the beliefs of white evangelicals, and since we have not done this, we do not connect Trump's racial rhetoric to his support from evangelicals. Many of us are surprised by white evangelical support of Trump because we had a belief about the morality, piety, and goodness of this religious group. However, a study of white evangelicalism with regard to race could demonstrate that not only have evangelicals been critical of the ways we understand race today, but more importantly, it is their religion (theology) that gives them license to support racist rhetoric and policies.

Finally, a study of race at the intersection of rhetoric and religion would answer Flores's call for all of us to take race more seriously in our rhetorical analyses. In the field of communication, several scholars have taken up that call and challenge. Many of them do not study religion, however. I argue that we who study rhetoric and religion can make a significant impact in our fields of study. We bring to the table an understanding of religion and its importance.

For instance, a study of Barack Obama's rhetoric is not complete without attending to his religious rhetoric and the counter–religious rhetoric against him. As others have demonstrated, Obama used religious rhetoric more than any of the modern-day presidents, yet many who examine his rhetoric and discourse do not see him as a religious orator. Imagine if we would embrace the fact that much of Obama's rhetorical theology comes from an understanding of Black Liberation Theology—a theology deeply rooted in an understanding of freedom, justice, equality, and race. That would mean we would have to reexamine our notions of what gets to be called religion.

A study of race at the intersection of rhetoric and religion would also force us to move away from white evangelical definitions of faith and to adopt other ways to see and experience faith and religion—and I, for one, would welcome that.

Entry Points for the Study of the African American Prophetic Tradition

When we begin teaching prophetic rhetoric and especially the African American prophetic tradition, working definitions are helpful. In my theorizing of prophetic rhetoric, I explicate a four-part rhetorical structure that one can use not only in determining if a text is an example of prophetic rhetoric but in taking an approach to rhetorical criticism (Johnson, "Prophetic Persona"). First, "speakers must ground prophetic discourse in what the speaker and the audience deem as sacred." Second, there must be an "element of consciousness-raising through a sharing or an announcement" of what I call the "real situation." In short, the prophet speaks the already known and bears witness to what the speaker believes to be the truth. Third, the speaker "charges, challenges, critiques, judges or issues warnings to the audience." Finally, the speaker offers hope and encouragement (Johnson, *Forgotten Prophet* 7–9).

Once we get a basic understanding of prophetic rhetoric, we then turn our attention to the African American prophetic tradition. Teachers must start from the position that unlike the prophetic rhetoric of the jeremiad, the African American prophetic tradition does not have its origins in freedom but instead in slavery, and it was shaped in segregationist America. Teachers must appreciate the dichotomous nature of the tradition. The African American prophetic tradition has expressed Black people's call for unity and cooperation, as well as their anger and frustrations. It has been both hopeful and pessimistic. It has celebrated the beauty and myth of American exceptionalism and its special place in the world, while at the same time damning it to Hell for not living up to the promises and ideals America espouses. It is a tradition that celebrates both the Creator or the Divine's hand in history—offering "hallelujahs" for deliverance from slavery and Jim and Jane Crow, while at the same time asking, "Where in the hell is God?" during tough and trying times. It is a tradition that has developed a theological outlook quite different at times from orthodoxy—one that finds God very close, but so far away (Johnson, "'To Make the World'" 22).

Once the definitions are set, we then can turn our attention to the scholarship of the African American prophetic tradition. Above, I have already mentioned some of the works, but I now would like to include others that help us better appreciate the genre. First, Willie J. Harrell Jr.'s *Origins of the African American Jeremiad: The Rhetorical Strategies of Social Protest and Activism, 1760–1861.* Expanding on the works of Wilson Jeremiah Moses and David Howard-Pitney, Harrell does a great job of expanding the jeremiad and placing it within the African American prophetic tradition.

Another book I would suggest is Richard T. Hughes's *Myths America Lives By: White Supremacy and the Stories That Give Us Meaning.* While not particularly centered on the African American prophetic tradition, the book does examine the "myths of America" and argues that it is the myth of white supremacy that informs all the other myths. To respond to these myths, Hughes argues that we must turn our attention to the Black rhetorical tradition and indeed the African American prophetic tradition.

In addition to these books, I suggest speech anthologies as well. Philip Foner and Robert Branham's still-relevant *Lift Every Voice: African American Oratory, 1787–1900* contains speeches and examples of the Black rhetorical tradition during the revolutionary, antebellum, and postbellum periods in America. Davis W. Houck and David E. Dixon's *Rhetoric, Religion, and the Civil Rights Movement, 1954–1965,* volumes 1 and 2 contain speeches of both Black and white activists during the civil rights period. It makes for a good source to compare and contrast the religious rhetoric used by Black and white activists during the time. The speeches in Shirley Wilson Logan's *With Pen and Voice: A Critical Anthology of Nineteenth-Century African-American Women* offers insight into how African American women used the prophetic tradition to get across their messages, and Martha Simmons and Frank A. Thomas's *Preaching with Sacred Fire: An Anthology of African American Sermons, 1750 to the Present* offers examples of how Black ministers and laypeople used the sermon as prophetic rhetoric.

Additional readings that teachers and students of the African American prophetic tradition may find useful are Robert E. Terrill's *Malcolm X: Inventing Radical Judgment*; Cornel West and Christa Buschendorf's *Black Prophetic*

Fire; Albert J. Raboteau's *American Prophets: Seven Religious Radicals and Their Struggle for Social and Political Justice*; and Christopher Z. Hobson's *James Baldwin and the Heavenly City: Prophecy, Apocalypse, and Doubt.*

There are articles that are worthy of mentioning as well that speak to the African American prophetic tradition. In "An Amostic Prophecy: Frederick Douglass' 'The Meaning of July Fourth for the Negro,'" Alan D. DeSantis places Douglass within the African American prophetic tradition, arguing that Douglass adopts the prophetic persona of the Old Testament prophet Amos, which allowed him to push against conventional notions of a typical Independence Day speech. In "Rhetoric of Doom and Redemption: Reverend Jermain Loguen's Jeremiadic Speech against the Fugitive Slave Law of 1850," Paul Minifee explores how Loguen uses both the American and African American jeremiad in a speech to white abolitionists about their duty to continue in their resistance to the sin of slavery, and David Holmes, in his essay "(Re-)Dressing the KKK: Fred Shuttlesworth's Precept Hermeneutic and the Rhetoric of African American Prophetic Patriotism," examines the prophetic rhetoric of the civil rights leader and primarily his use of apocalyptic rhetoric.

Elizabeth Vander Lei and Keith D. Miller, in "Martin Luther King, Jr.'s 'I Have a Dream' in Context: Ceremonial Protest and African American Jeremiad," merge both the ceremonial protest and the African American jeremiad to bolster our understanding of the African American rhetorical tradition, while Willie J. Harrell, in his essay "'The Reality of American Life Has Strayed from Its Myths': Barack Obama's *The Audacity of Hope* and the Discourse of the American Reclamation Jeremiad," examines the jeremiadic rhetoric in Obama's *The Audacity of Hope.*

Others are now beginning to build on the scholarship of the African American prophetic tradition, thereby making race a key component in their study of religious rhetoric. Established rhetorical scholars such as Monika Alston Miller ("Influence"), Theon Hill ("(Re)Articulating Difference"), David G. Holmes (*Where the Sacred*), Christopher A. House ("Crying"), along with up-and-coming scholars Steven Tramel Gaines ("No Half Savior"), Armondo Collins ("Disciple"), Dianna N. Watkins-Dickerson ("'You Are Somebody'"), and Earle J. Fisher (*Reverend Albert Cleage*), offer a glimpse of what the future holds.

WORKS CITED

Andrews, James R. Review of *The Prophetic Tradition and Radical Rhetoric in America*, by James Darsey. *Quarterly Journal of Speech*, vol. 84, no. 4, 1998, pp. 517–18.

Blum, Edward J. *W. E. B. Du Bois, American Prophet.* U of Pennsylvania P, 2007.

Browne, Steven H. Review of *The Prophetic Tradition and Radical Rhetoric in America*, by James Darsey. *Rhetoric & Public Affairs*, vol. 1, no. 3, 1998, pp. 458–62.

Carstarphen, Meta G., and Kathleen E. Welch. "Introduction: Looking in the Mirror." *Rhetoric, Race, and Resentment: Whiteness and the New Days of Rage*, special issue of *Rhetoric Review*, vol. 36, no. 4, 2017, pp. 255–58.

Chappell, David L. *A Stone of Hope: Prophetic Religion and the Death of Jim Crow*. U of North Carolina P, 2004.

Chebrolu, Rishi. "The Racial Lens of Dylann Roof: Racial Anxiety and White Nationalist Rhetoric on New Media." *Review of Communication*, vol. 20, no. 1, 2020, pp. 47–68.

Collins, Armondo R. "A Disciple of Malcolm X: Clarence 13X Smith's Embodied Black God Rhetoric." *Journal of African American Studies*, vol. 24, no. 3, 2020, pp. 337–56.

Countryman, Edward. "Countryman on Darsey, 'The Prophetic Tradition and Radical Rhetoric in America.'" *H-Pol/H-Net Reviews*, Michigan State U, Apr. 1998, www.h-net.org/reviews/showrev.php?id=1912.

Craig, Robert H. Review of *The Prophetic Tradition and Radical Rhetoric in America*, by James Darsey. *Journal of American History*, vol. 85, no. 2, 1998, pp. 634–35.

Crosby, Richard Benjamin. "'Which Is the Wisest Course?' Political Power and Prophetic Agency in Nineteenth-Century Mormon Rhetoric." *Journal of Communication & Religion*, vol. 34, no. 1, 2011, pp. 1–23.

Darsey, James. *The Prophetic Tradition and Radical Rhetoric in America*. New York UP, 1997.

DeSantis, Alan D., "An Amostic Prophecy: Frederick Douglass' 'The Meaning of July Fourth for the Negro.'" *Journal of Communication and Religion*, vol. 22, no. 1, 1999, pp. 65–92.

Fisher, Earle J. *The Reverend Albert Cleage Jr. and the Black Prophetic Tradition: A Reintroduction of the Black Messiah*. Lexington Books, 2021.

Flores, Lisa. "Between Abundance and Marginalization: The Imperative of Racial Rhetorical Criticism." *Review of Communication*, vol. 16, no. 1, 2016, pp. 4–24.

Foner, Philip S., and Robert James Branham. *Lift Every Voice: African American Oratory, 1787–1900*. U of Alabama P, 1998.

Gaines, Steven Tramel. "No Half Savior: Jarena Lee's Autobiography as Prophetic Rhetoric," *Carolinas Communication Annual*, vol. 33, 2017, pp. 62–76.

Glaude, Eddie S. *Exodus! Religion, Race, and Nation in Early Nineteenth-Century Black America*. U of Chicago P, 2000.

Gregg, Richard B. "The Ego-Function of the Rhetoric of Protest." *Philosophy & Rhetoric*, vol. 4, no. 2, 1971, pp. 71–91.

Harrell, Willie J., Jr. *Origins of the African American Jeremiad: The Rhetorical Strategies of Social Protest and Activism, 1760–1861.* McFarland and Company, 2011.

—. "'The Reality of American Life Has Strayed from Its Myths': Barack Obama's *The Audacity of Hope* and the Discourse of the American Reclamation Jeremiad." *Journal of Black Studies*, vol. 41, no. 1, 2010, pp. 164–83.

Haywood, Chanta M. *Prophesying Daughters: Black Women Preachers and the Word, 1823–1913.* U of Missouri P, 2003.

Hill, Theon E. "(Re)Articulating Difference: Constitutive Rhetoric, Christian Identity, and Discourses of Race as Biology." *Journal of Communication and Religion*, vol. 39, no. 1, 2016, pp. 26–45.

Hobson, Christopher Z. *James Baldwin and the Heavenly City: Prophecy, Apocalypse, and Doubt.* Michigan State UP, 2018.

—. *The Mount of Vision: African American Prophetic Tradition, 1800–1950.* Oxford UP, 2012.

Holmes, David. "(Re-)Dressing the KKK: Fred Shuttlesworth's Precept Hermeneutic and the Rhetoric of African American Prophetic Patriotism." *Journal of Black Studies*, vol. 42, no. 5, 2011, pp. 811–27.

—. *Where the Sacred and Secular Harmonize: Birmingham Mass Meeting Rhetoric and the Prophetic Legacy of the Civil Rights Movement.* Cascade Books, 2017.

Houck, Davis W., and David E. Dixon. *Rhetoric, Religion, and the Civil Rights Movement, 1954–1965.* Vol. 1., Baylor UP, 2006.

—. *Rhetoric, Religion, and the Civil Rights Movement, 1954–1965.* Vol. 2., Baylor UP, 2014.

Houdek, Matthew. "The Imperative of Race for Rhetorical Studies: Toward Divesting from Disciplinary and Institutionalized Whiteness." *Communication and Critical/Cultural Studies*, vol. 15, no. 4, 2018, pp. 292–99.

—. "Racial Sedimentation and the Common Sense of Racialized Violence: The Case of Black Church Burnings." *Quarterly Journal of Speech*, vol. 104, no. 3, 2018, pp. 279–306.

House, Christopher A. "Crying for Justice: The #BLACKLIVESMATTER Religious Rhetoric of Bishop T.D. Jakes." *Southern Communication Journal*, vol. 83, no. 1, 2018, pp. 13–27.

House, Christopher A., and Andre E. Johnson. Introduction. *Communication, Religion, and Race in America: 50 Years Later and Where Do We Go from Here?*, special issue of *Journal of Communication and Religion*, vol. 41, no. 1, 2018, pp. 5–7.

Howard-Pitney, David. *The African American Jeremiad: Appeals for Social Justice.* Temple Press, 2005.

Hughes, Richard. *Myths America Lives By: White Supremacy and the Stories That Give Us Meaning.* U of Illinois P, 2018.

Johnson, Andre E. *The Forgotten Prophet: Bishop Henry McNeal Turner and the African American Prophetic Tradition.* Lexington Books, 2012.

—. "The Prophetic Persona of James Cone and the Rhetorical Theology of Black Theology." *Black Theology: An International Journal*, vol. 8, no. 3, 2010, pp. 266–85.

—. "'To Make the World So Damn Uncomfortable': W.E.B. Du Bois and the African American Prophetic Tradition." *Carolinas Communication Annual*, vol. 32, 2016, pp. 16–29.

—. "Understanding the Rhetoric(s) of Race." *Journal of Contemporary Rhetoric*, vol. 5, nos. 3/4, 2015, pp. 64–66.

Johnson, Andre E., and Anthony J. Stone Jr., "'The Most Dangerous Negro in America': Rhetoric, Race, and the Prophetic Pessimism of Martin Luther King Jr." *Journal of Communication and Religion*, vol. 1, no. 21, 2018, pp. 8–22.

Kearl, Michelle Kelsey. "The Stolen Property of Whiteness: A Case Study in Critical Intersectional Rhetorics of Race and Disability." *Rhetoric Review*, vol. 37, no. 3, 2018, 300–313.

Kiewe, Amos. "Theodore Herzl's *The Jewish State*: Prophetic Rhetoric in the Service of Political Objectives." *Journal of Communication and Religion*, vol. 26, no. 2, 2003, pp. 208–39.

Logan, Shirley Wilson. *With Pen and Voice: A Critical Anthology of Nineteenth-Century African-American Women.* Southern Illinois UP, 1995.

Majocha, Kristen Lynn. "Prophetic Rhetoric: A Gap between the Field of Study and the Real World." *Journal of Communication and Religion*, vol. 39, no. 4, 2017, pp. 5–18.

Minifee, Paul. "Rhetoric of Doom and Redemption: Reverend Jermain Loguen's Jeremiadic Speech against the Fugitive Slave Law of 1850." *Advances in the History of Rhetoric*, vol. 16, no. 1, 2013, pp. 29–57.

Moses, William Jeremiah. *Black Messiahs and Uncle Toms: Social and Literary Manipulations of a Religious Myth.* Pennsylvania State UP, 1982.

Murphy, Mollie K., and Tina M. Harris. "White Innocence and Black Subservience: The Rhetoric of White Heroism in *The Help*." *Howard Journal of Communications*, vol. 29, no. 1, 2018, pp. 49–62.

Newman, Richard S. *Freedom's Prophet: Bishop Richard Allen, the AME Church, and the Black Founding Fathers.* New York UP, 2008.

Pittenger, Mark. Review of *The Prophetic Tradition and Radical Rhetoric in America*, by James Darsey. *American Historical Review*, vol. 104, no. 1, 1999, pp. 179–80.

Raboteau, Albert J. *American Prophets: Seven Religious Radicals and Their Struggle for Social and Political Justice.* Princeton UP, 2017.

Shulman, George. *American Prophecy: Race and Redemption in American Political Culture.* U of Minnesota P, 2008.

Simmons, Martha, and Frank A. Thomas. *Preaching with Sacred Fire: An Anthology of African American Sermons, 1750 to the Present.* W. W. Norton, 2010.
Souders, Michael. "The Prophetic Imagination and the Rhetoric of 'Freedom' in the Prosperity Gospel," *Journal of Communication and Religion*, vol. 37, no. 2, 2014, pp. 93–116.
Spencer, Leland. "Bishop Leontine Turpeau Current Kelly: Toward an Ironic Prophetic Rhetoric." *Western Journal of Communication*, vol. 80, no. 5, 2016, pp. 519–38.
Terrill, Robert E. *Malcolm X: Inventing Radical Judgment.* Michigan State UP, 2007.
—. "Protest, Prophecy, and Prudence in the Rhetoric of Malcolm X." *Rhetoric and Public Affairs*, vol. 4, no. 1, 2001, pp. 25–53.
Timmerman, David M. "Christian Pacifism and the Prophetic Voice: Dietrich Bonhoeffer's Peace Address." *Journal of Communication and Religion*, vol. 28, no. 2, 2005, pp. 153–71.
Vander Lei, Elizabeth, and Keith D. Miller. "Martin Luther King, Jr.'s 'I Have a Dream' in Context: Ceremonial Protest and African American Jeremiad." *College English*, vol. 62, no. 1, 1999, pp. 83–99.
Watkins-Dickerson, Dianna N. "'You Are Somebody': A Study of the Prophetic Rhetoric of Rev. Henry Logan Starks, DMin." *Journal of Communication and Religion*, vol. 43, no. 4, 2020, pp. 92–107.
West, Cornel, and Christa Buschendorf. *Black Prophetic Fire.* Beacon Press, 2014.
Woodyard, Kerith M. "Depatriarchalizing in Rhetorical Theory: Toward a Feminist Prophetic Tradition." *Ohio Communication Journal*, vol. 48, 2010, pp. 27–42.

Afterword

JONATHAN ALEXANDER

When I first started teaching writing over three decades ago, the common wisdom was that certain topics were best avoided—namely, abortion rights and capital punishment. While we might, as a field, be invested in helping students understand the protocols of civil discourse and debates, some arguments, especially those for which interlocutors might rely on religious belief or values, should not be engaged in the classroom, and we should discourage students from writing about them. On one hand, I think such injunctions served to protect the (mostly) liberal sensibilities of faculty, who didn't want to have to contend with what we took to be knee-jerk and reactionary positions about the preciousness of life for the unborn and the need to throw away other lives, often Black and poor. On the other hand, the rationale for avoiding abortion and capital punishment, particularly when arguments both con and pro rest on religious belief, suggested a rhetorical impasse, the inability to argue rationally (and perhaps even civilly) with those whose convictions were founded on belief systems that are, well, not rational. If we don't share a common set of values, based in empirical evidence, then we have no starting point from which to debate the rightness or wrongness of such hot-topic issues.

In retrospect, all of this seems wrongheaded. At worst, perhaps, the failure to figure out how to engage a plurality of belief systems, particularly when they diverge radically from a liberal academic perspective, has meant that we have forgone opportunities to explore why people believe the way they do, what animates their belief systems, what prompts investment in particular values that remain consequential, personally and politically, for believers and nonbelievers alike. As I write this afterword, in the aftermath of the inauguration of Joe Biden's presidency on the heels of the insurrection at the Capitol, I cannot help but think that many of the millions—tens of millions—who voted for Donald Trump did so out of religious conviction, believing that he was best equipped to defend their right to believe, and perhaps even to have their beliefs normalized in what they see as an increasingly (if not by now totally) secularized, even ungodly, public sphere. I can imagine fewer more pressing rhetorical tasks than to understand the continued circulation of beliefs and values that, from a liberal academic perspective, seem to stymie possibilities for building collective good will toward solving global problems of ecological crisis and prolonged economic and racial injustice.

But perhaps, again, I'm falling into the trap of my previous training. I see the rhetorical need, but I also immediately imagine barriers. I erect a binary. There are those who adhere to the still vaguely progressivist ideals of academic and liberal humanism, and then there are those who put their faith in things unseen, in beliefs and values grounded in (at worst, I think) dogmatic traditions that have served as justification for wars and genocides for centuries. As such, perhaps it's best not to tackle abortion as a subject in my writing class. More personally, how can I, a queer, unbelieving socialist, talk to people who espouse traditions that once put people like me to death—and who might still desire to do so?

The reality, though, is that the situation is far more complex than this simplistic binary describes. Fortunately, the editors and contributors to *Rhetoric and Religion in the Twenty-First Century: Pluralism in a Postsecular Age* recognize this and choose not to ignore but to confront the challenges of thinking about religion rhetorically. I commend them for not only tackling the intersections amongst rhetoric and religion but also for urging us in rhetorical studies not to shy away from the difficult work of understanding how "rhetoric and religion animate each other in profound ways." The editors are absolutely right: "religion continues to shape culture even in ostensibly secular situations." Recent events only confirm—and amplify—this claim. They also recognize that the challenge of thinking about religion rhetorically is not just creating dialogue between believers and nonbelievers but also grappling with the diversity of belief amongst believers. As they put it in the introduction, "The question for rhetorical studies is not simply how to recognize this diversity globally and in the United States but also how to encourage hospitable, just, and inclusive engagement with that diversity." The possibilities for divergence and disagreement, even conflict, only seem to multiply when considering differences across belief systems, but the work must still be undertaken.

Indeed, our editors and contributors turn this difficulty into a virtue. Embracing plurality, the editors set an ambitious task: they aim to "pursue the aspiration of pluralism through two interrelated means: interrogating extant rhetorics and inventing exigent rhetorics." They want to understand, genealogically, the development of diverse religious traditions so that we might all "take strides toward pluralism by recovering and theorizing rich rhetorical traditions that have thus far been invisible, misunderstood, or overlooked in the field of rhetorical studies." Their aim is one of rhetorical education, in creating opportunities for students to recognize "religion's functions and influence in our religiously diverse global context," thus collaterally "preparing communicators for thoughtful public participation" and "fostering writers and speakers who are equipped to engage with religious diversity in productive ways."

With such a goal, the editors and contributors place their faith in openness and its more ambitious practice, empathy. Essays in section one undertake the task of recognizing the diversity of belief already within religious traditions. Lisa King, in "To Do Things in a Good (Decolonial) Way: Putting Indigenous Rhetorics and Rhetorics of Religion in Conversation," reminds us of the overlaps and possibilities for productive conversation amongst Indigenous and non-Indigenous spiritual traditions. Lisa Zimmerelli's "Feminist Rhetorical Historiography and Religion" reconsiders how religion is a "primary generator of discourse" and must be considered when thinking through feminist standpoints. T J Geiger II, in "'Joy Anyway!' Narratives of Harm and Flourishing at the Intersections of Religious and LGBTQ+ Rhetorics," promotes the value of "rhetorical empathy," appealing to many religious traditions' regard for empathy as contradicting the stigmatization of queer people. And John C. Brereton and Cinthia Gannett's chapter, "'We Are Not Born for Ourselves Alone': Jesuit Rhetoric for the Twenty-First Century," aims to make visible the influence of Jesuit rhetorics on modern rhetorical scholarship and teaching.

The evidence is compelling. Reading these chapters prompted me to reflect on my own engagement with religious rhetorics—an engagement that has consciously been characterized during my adult life as more of a disavowal of the religious traditions from my youth that had castigated my queer desires. I cannot blame myself for such a disavowal; it likely helped me save my life. But my religious upbringing, first as a Catholic and then as a Southern Baptist, has profoundly shaped me, and for the better in some ways. I teach like a Southern Baptist preacher, and nearly everything I do as a pedagogue—theatrical modulation of voice; close reading and the grounding of my teaching in a text; the invitation to students to bear witness to what they are encountering and experiencing; a sense that what we do as literacy and rhetorical educators is lifesaving—I learned from Baptist preachers and pastors. What is more, I have been rethinking the story I tell in *Literacy, Sexuality, Pedagogy* about my childhood reading of C. S. Lewis's *Chronicles of Narnia*, a series that is often reduced to the level of starter-kit Christian propaganda for kids. In my book, I characterize the wardrobe through which Lewis's young protagonists enter Narnia as my first "closet," the pressure of religious belief at the time making my queerness unimaginable to me. But I was only telling part of the story. Lewis's flights of fancy fed my own imaginative abilities. And his allegory in *The Lion, the Witch, and the Wardrobe* taught me how texts can mean doubly, how multiple stories can be told at the same time. Whatever Lewis might think about my use of his text, he taught me that you can tell the story of a life many different ways, not just one way, and I needed to know that alternatives were possible. And in valorizing multiple stories, he also taught me one of the major lessons put forth by contributors to *Rhetoric and Religion in the Twenty-First Century*: religious rhetorics are everywhere, but they also (perhaps even despite themselves) embrace plurality. Dogma might try to convince us of the particularity of the truth it propounds, but the overriding truth is the sheer diversity of possible truths.

Having some foundational tenets set out in section one, the chapters in the second section of the book attempt to make the value of plurality not just a given but an exigence. Janice W. Fernheimer's chapter, "Creating Pathways for Ethical (Inter)Actions: New Directions for Jewish Rhetorics," mines different traditions to forward the importance of the "[r]elationship and preservation of difference through juxtaposition." Kurt Spellmeyer's "Buddhism and Rhetoric Unchained" seeks to multiply the opportunities for confusion, misunderstanding, disagreement, and misreading that lie at the heart of much Buddhist rejection of solid and stable ego—a rejection seen not as a cause for despair but for generative multiplicity and creativity. Rasha Diab's chapter, "Engaging with Arab(ic)-Islamic Religious Rhetorics: Why It Matters to Rhetorical Studies," presses on the crucial need to create opportunities for dialogue, particularly when traditions already share so much that they otherwise seek to deny. And, in "Race at the Intersection of Rhetoric and Religion," Andre E. Johnson argues, rightly, that we cannot address rhetorical and political issues of race without considering the complex and contradictory—and possibly innovative—ways in which religious discourses have shaped and continue to shape our individual and collective understanding of race.

These chapters get into the nitty gritty of how diversity of religious belief might contribute to conflict yet still also generate the need—the demand—for dialogue, for the reaching out for understanding and connection that animates most spiritual yearning. In her interlude, Patricia Roberts-Miller offers a comment that seems self-evident but is easily forgotten by some of us, including me: "It . . . seemed to me unreasonable that a person could be raised within a particular tradition and abandon it completely." She's absolutely right. As I reflected on my own life course as I read these chapters, I realized the extent to which it has been unreasonable for me to have been raised in particular traditions and then to abandon them completely. Except, of course, I haven't. If chapters in section one prompted me to realize how I had misread my own engagement with C. S. Lewis, then chapters in section two reminded me of my great late-life love of the work of Madeline L'Engle, the young-adult author who embraced plurality and spirituality, who refused dogma but held on to the fundamental desire in Christianity to embrace love—to love above all things. And Kurt Spellmeyer's engagement with Buddhism reminded me of my own reading in Buddhist philosophy and psychology in my thirties, my search in the work of Thich Nhat Hanh for a path of peace, and my discovery of how we all grapple with difficult emotions but how it is also our responsibility to nurture those emotions that keep us open and understanding of others, recognizing their own path, their own pain, their own possibility for love.

Reading L'Engle and Hanh started to heal me, reminding me that, even when religious traditions hurt me, there was still something good in them, something about the yearning for understanding and for connection, for an answer to the questions we pose about our meaningfulness to ourselves and to one another. We sometimes arrive at different answers, yes. But the contributors to this book embrace plurality as a way to approach any answer as always provisional, as an attempt. Hence the need for rhetoric, for an openness to ongoing dialogue. Such a rhetoric shifts our understanding of religious impulses from persuasion to desire, from dogmatic certainty to inquisitive openness, from the need to evangelize to the impulse to connect, however incomplete such connection might be.

Where does that leave me, both in the classroom and out of it? The editors of this volume suggest in their introduction that "the seeming collapse of the transcendent does not close the question of ultimate significance." Some hold too tenaciously to the belief that they have already found the transcendent, despite the fact that there is really no religious tradition that promises complete transcendence in this life. Still, the editors and contributors of this volume remind me that we are, all of us, looking for transcendence, even as we are faced with a world that denies us totalizing answers. Perhaps embracing that contradiction is the beginning of wisdom, personally, rhetorically, politically. I do not know yet how I will grapple in the classroom with the subjects of abortion and capital punishment—or climate crisis or racial injustice or economic precarity, or any subject to which one might propose an analysis including thoughts from a religious tradition. But *Rhetoric and Religion in the Twenty-First Century* convinces me I should try. And while the volume places a lot of faith in recognizing plurality as the necessary beginning of dialogue, that is at least a place to start. More importantly, the book has reminded me that I have never not been grappling with the legacies—and possibilities—of religious traditions in my own life. And for that, I am grateful.

WORKS CITED

Alexander, Jonathan. *Literacy, Sexuality, Pedagogy: Theory and Practice for Composition Studies*. Utah State UP, 2008.

Contributors

Jonathan Alexander is Chancellor's Professor of English and Informatics at the University of California, Irvine. He is the author, coauthor, or editor of twenty-two books, including the recent titles *Dear Queer Self: An Experiment in Memoir*; *The Routledge Handbook of Queer Rhetoric*, coedited with Jacqueline Rhodes; and *Stroke Book: The Diary of a Blindspot*.

Patricia Bizzell is Distinguished Professor of English Emerita at the College of the Holy Cross in Worcester, Massachusetts, where she taught first-year writing, rhetoric and public speaking, women's literature, and Jewish literature. She is currently working on a collection of essays examining the functions of fear and rage in public discourse. Women's rhetoric remains among the topics in her coedited collection *Nineteenth-Century American Activist Rhetorics*.

John C. Brereton is a professor emeritus of English at the University of Massachusetts Boston. He previously taught at the City University of New York, Columbia University, Wayne State University, Brandeis University, and Harvard University. Among his publications are *Traditions of Inquiry*; *A Plan for Writing*; *The Origins of Composition Studies in the American College, 1875–1925*; *The Norton Reader*; *Traditions of Eloquence* with Cinthia Gannett, and many essays on the history of rhetoric and composition.

Martin Camper is an associate professor of writing and the director of the Center for the Humanities at Loyola University Maryland, where he teaches writing, rhetoric, argument, and style. He is the author of *Arguing over Texts: The Rhetoric of Interpretation* along with several articles that have appeared in venues such as *Philosophy and Rhetoric*, the *Journal of Communication and Religion*, and *Argumentation and Advocacy*. His research has been recognized and supported by an award from the American Forensics Association and grants from the National Endowment for the Humanities and the International Society for the History of Rhetoric.

Beth Daniell retired in 2015 from Kennesaw State University after a career teaching rhetorical theory, research methods, and composition and directing composition programs. She wrote *A Communion of Friendship: Literacy, Spiritual Practice, and Women in Recovery*. She edited with Peter Mortensen *Women* *and Literacy: Local and Global Inquiries for a New Century* and with Elizabeth Vander Lei, Tom Amorose, and Anne Gere *Renovating Rhetoric in Christian Tradition*. She has also published many articles, reviews, and book chapters.

Michael-John DePalma is a professor and the director of professional writing and rhetoric at Baylor University. He is the author of *Sacred Rhetorical Education in 19th Century America: Austin Phelps at Andover Theological Seminary*. With Jeff Ringer, he edited *Mapping Christian Rhetorics: Connecting Conversations, Charting New Territories*, which was named 2015 Book of the Year by the Religious Communication Association. His work has appeared in *College Composition and Communication, College English, Rhetoric Review, Rhetoric Society Quarterly, Computers and Composition, Journal of the Assembly for Expanded Perspectives on Learning, Composition Forum, Journal of Second Language Writing*, and several edited collections.

Rasha Diab is an associate professor in the Department of Rhetoric and Writing and a faculty affiliate of the Departments of English and Middle Eastern Studies at the University of Texas at Austin. Her work centers on the rhetorics of peacemaking, Arab-Islamic rhetorics, and revisionist historiography. Her book *Shades of Sulh: The Rhetorics of Arab-Islamic Reconciliation* won the 2018 Conference on College Composition and Communication Outstanding Book Award. She is currently writing articles on peacemaking and pedagogy, al-Qalqaṣhandī's *maqāmah* and work on chancery writing, and a book tentatively titled *On Word Weaving and Peacemaking*.

Janice W. Fernheimer is the Zantker Charitable Foundation Professor of Jewish Studies; a professor of writing, rhetoric, and digital studies; and a faculty fellow of the James B. Beam Institute for Kentucky Spirits at the University of Kentucky, where she also directs the Jewish Studies Program. She is the author of *Stepping into Zion: Hatzaad Harishon, Black Jews, and the Remaking of Jewish Identity* and the coeditor with Michael Bernard-Donals of *Jewish Rhetorics: History, Theory, Practice*. She is the founder and past president of Klal Rhetorica, a scholarly organization of researchers working at the intersections of Jewish, English, rhetoric, and communication studies.

Cinthia Gannett is a professor emerita of English at Fairfield University. The author of *Gender and the Journal* and other essays on women's journal traditions, she has directed writing across the curriculum, writing centers, and writing programs at the University of New Hampshire, Loyola College of Maryland (now

Loyola University Maryland), and Fairfield. With John C. Brereton, she edited *Traditions of Eloquence: The Jesuits and Modern Rhetorical Studies* and helped found the International Society for the Study of Jesuit Rhetoric. Currently, she is coediting a collection on international writing studies and undertaking several archival projects in the history of composition/rhetoric.

T J Geiger II is an assistant professor of technical communication and rhetoric in the Department of English at Texas Tech University in Lubbock, Texas. He studies religious rhetorics and feminist rhetorics. He is the author of *Faithful Deliberation: Rhetorical Invention, Evangelicalism, and #MeToo Reckonings.* His publications also include articles in *College English*, *Composition Studies*, *Rhetoric Society Quarterly*, *Rhetoric Review*, and *Peitho*.

Andre E. Johnson is an associate professor of rhetoric and media studies at the University of Memphis. Grounded in an interdisciplinary understanding of scholarship, Johnson studies the intersection of rhetoric, race, and religion. He is the author of three national award–winning books: *The Forgotten Prophet: Bishop Henry McNeal Turner and the African American Prophetic Tradition*; *The Struggle over Black Lives Matter and All Lives Matter*, cowritten with Amanda Nell Edgar; and *No Future in This Country: The Prophetic Pessimism of Bishop Henry McNeal Turner.*

Lisa King is an associate professor of rhetoric, writing, and linguistics in the Department of English at the University of Tennessee, Knoxville. Her work is interdisciplinary and based on cultural rhetorics with an emphasis in contemporary Native American/Indigenous rhetorics. She is a coeditor of *Survivance, Sovereignty, and Story: Teaching American Indian Rhetorics* and the author of *Legible Sovereignties: Rhetoric, Representations, and Native American Museums.* Her current projects include a coedited collection with Andrea Riley Mukavetz titled *Decolonial Possibilities: Indigenously-Rooted Practices in Rhetoric and Writing* and an upcoming exhibition at McClung Museum tentatively titled *A Sense of Indigenous Place.*

Paul Lynch is an associate professor of English at Saint Louis University. He is the author of *After Pedagogy* and coeditor of *Thinking with Bruno Latour in Rhetoric and Composition.* His work has appeared in *College English*, *Contagion*, *Present Tense*, and *Rhetoric Society Quarterly*. His *Rhetoric Society Quarterly* article "On Care for Our Common Discourse: Pope Francis's Nonmodern Epideictic" won the 2018 Religious Communication Association's Article of the Year Award.

Beverly J. Moss is an associate professor of English at The Ohio State University, where she specializes in composition and literacy studies. Her scholarly and pedagogical interests include literacy in African American community spaces, composition theory and pedagogy, and writing center theory and practice. She is the author of *A Community Text Arises: A Literate Text and a Literacy Tradition in African-American Churches*, coauthor of *Everyone's an Author*, editor of *Literacy across Communities*, and coeditor of *Writing Groups Inside and Outside the Classroom* and *The Best of the Independent Journals in Rhetoric and Composition 2012*.

Laurent Pernot is a professor of Greek language and literature and the chair of the Department of Greek at the University of Strasbourg and a member of the Institut de France. He founded and directed the Center for the Analysis of the Religious Rhetorics of Antiquity at Strasbourg and served as the president of the International Society for the History of Rhetoric. His books include *Rhetoric in Antiquity*; *Epideictic Rhetoric*; *The Subtle Subtext: Hidden Meanings in Literature and Life*; and *Confluences de la philosophie et de la rhétorique grecques*.

Jeff Ringer is an associate professor of rhetoric, writing, and linguistics at the University of Tennessee, Knoxville. He is the author of *Vernacular Christian Rhetoric and Civil Discourse: The Religious Creativity of Evangelical Student Writers* and coeditor with Mike DePalma of *Mapping Christian Rhetorics*, which won the Religious Communication Association's Book of the Year Award for 2015. His scholarship has appeared in many of the field's top journals, and he is writing a book tentatively titled *The Many Emergences of Writing Transfer: A Genealogy*.

Patricia Roberts-Miller is a former professor of rhetoric and writing and former director of the University Writing Center at the University of Texas at Austin. Now retired, she devotes her time to writing, hosting workshops, recording podcasts, and visiting campuses and classrooms. She is the author of numerous books, including *Speaking of Race: How to Have Antiracist Conversations That Bring Us Together*; *Rhetoric and Demagoguery*; *Demagoguery and Democracy*; *Fanatical Schemes: Proslavery Rhetoric and the Tragedy of Consensus*; *Deliberate Conflict: Argument, Political Theory, and Composition Classes*; and *Voices in the Wilderness: Public Discourse and the Paradox of Puritan Rhetoric*.

Kurt Spellmeyer directed the Arts and Sciences Writing Program at Rutgers University–New Brunswick for thirty-five years. He has authored or edited four books, including *Arts of Living: Reinventing the Humanities for the Twenty-First*

Century and *Common Ground: Dialogue, Understanding, and the Teaching of Writing*. A Zen priest, he has served as sensei, or lead teacher, for the Cold Mountain Sangha in central New Jersey since 1994. He has written widely on Buddhism, most recently for *Tricycle Magazine*. He has also published *Buddha at the Apocalypse: Awakening from a Culture of Destruction*.

Elizabeth Vander Lei served as the director of first-year writing, department chair, and academic dean at Calvin University. One of the founding members of the Rhetoric and Religious Traditions Standing Group, Vander Lei coedited two collections on rhetoric and religious traditions: *Negotiating Religious Faith in the Writing Classroom*, with bonnie kyburz, and *Renovating Rhetoric in Christian Tradition*, with Tom Amorose, Beth Daniell, and Anne Gere.

Robert P. Yagelski is the Dorothy G. Griffin Professor of English Education at the University at Albany (SUNY). He is the founding director of the Program in Writing and Critical Inquiry, which he helped establish in 2013 and which he directed until 2022. He has authored or coedited three scholarly books, including *Writing as a Way of Being*, four college writing textbooks, and a children's book, and he has published numerous articles on writing and teaching in *College Composition and Communication*, *Research in the Teaching of English*, and *English Education*, among others.

Lisa Zimmerelli is an associate professor and the chair of writing at Loyola University Maryland. She has published essays on nineteenth-century American rhetoric, religious rhetoric, feminist historiography, and writing center tutor training and community engagement. Her awards for this scholarship include the 2013 *Rhetoric Society Quarterly* Charles Kneupper Award for best article.

Index